Essential Java for Scientists and Engineers

Essential Java
for
Scientists and Engineers

Brian D. Hahn

Department of Mathematics & Applied Mathematics
University of Cape Town
Rondebosch
South Africa

Katherine M. Malan

Department of Computer Science
University of Cape Town
Rondebosch
South Africa

OXFORD AMSTERDAM BOSTON LONDON NEW YORK PARIS
SAN DIEGO SAN FRANCISCO SINGAPORE SYDNEY TOKYO

Butterworth-Heinemann
An imprint of Elsevier Science
Linacre House, Jordan Hill, Oxford OX2 8DP
225 Wildwood Avenue, Woburn, MA 01801-2041

First published 2002

British Library Cataloguing in Publication Data
A catalogue record for this book is available from the British Library

Library of Congress Cataloguing in Publication Data
A catalogue record for this book is available from the Library of Congress

ISBN   978-0-7506-5991-8

For information on all Butterworth-Heinemann publications visit our website at www.bh.com

Typeset by Laserwords Private Limited, Chennai, India.

Transferred to Digital Printing 2011

FOR EVERY TITLE THAT WE PUBLISH, BUTTERWORTH-HEINEMANN
WILL PAY FOR BTCV TO PLANT AND CARE FOR A TREE.

Contents

Part III Some applications

Preface

This book serves as an introduction to the programming language Java. In addition it focuses on how Java, and object-oriented programming, can be used to solve science and engineering problems. As such, some of the examples necessarily involve aspects of first-year university mathematics, particularly in the final chapter. However, these examples are self-contained, and omitting them will not hinder your programming development.

Features

- The book is accessible to beginners, with no programming experience.

- We use a hands-on or 'dive-in' approach which gets you writing and running programs immediately.

- The fundamentals of Java programming are motivated throughout with many examples from a number of different scientific and engineering areas, as well as from business and everyday life. Beginners, as well as experienced programmers wishing to learn Java as an additional language, should therefore find plenty of interest in the book.

- It provides a good introduction to object-oriented programming. Solutions to problems throughout the book show how data and operations on that data can be modelled together in classes. In this way code is easy to maintain, extend and reuse.

- We have provided a pre-written package of code to help in such areas as

    - simple keyboard input and file input/output;
    - matrix manipulation;
    - scientific graphing.

Approach

- Our style is informal. New concepts are often motivated with a coded example before being generalized.

- Readers are frequently invited to try appropriate exercises at the end of each chapter as they advance through the chapter.

- Throughout the book, we use Java applications, rather than applets (although we do provide an example of an applet in Chapter 1).

- All the examples in this book have been compiled and interpreted using Sun Microsystems' Java 2 compiler (in particular version 1.3.1 of the Java Software Development Kit).

Resources

- Each chapter begins with a set of objectives and concludes with a summary and numerous exercises. These exercises have been gleaned from many years' experience of running hands-on programming courses and writing books for beginners and professionals alike, on problem solving in Basic, Fortran, Pascal, C, C++ and MATLAB.

- The appendices include a quick reference to Java syntax and solutions to selected exercises.

- The book's website, **www.bh.com/companions/essentialjava**, provides links to material such as:

  - code for the `essential` package, containing our pre-written classes;

  - Java source code of all completed code that appears in the text;

  - solutions to selected exercises in individual file format.

  Solutions to the remaining exercises are password-restricted, and are available only to lecturers who adopt the book for use in their courses. To obtain a password please e-mail jo.coleman@repp.co.uk with the following details: course title, number of students, your job title and work postal address.

Organization of the book

The book is organized into three parts:

1. **Essentials** (Chapters 1–6)
   This part covers what we believe to be the essentials of programming in Java: using pre-defined objects and methods, basic programming concepts and constructs (primitive data types, variables, expressions, loops and decisions), writing your own classes, debugging code, arrays.

2. **More advanced topics** (Chapters 7–10)
   Inheritance, building your own graphical user interfaces, exceptions, input and output.

3. **Some applications** (Chapters 11–13)
   Simulation, matrices (use of our `essential.Matrix` class in fields such as reachability, population dynamics, Markov processes, linear equations), numerical methods.

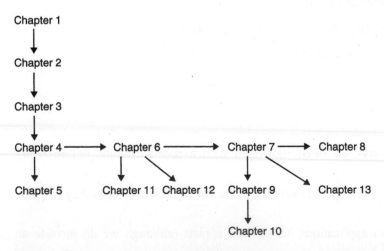

Figure 1 Dependency diagram showing relationships between the chapters

Dependencies between the chapters are shown in Figure 1. We strongly recommend that a course should cover at least the first seven chapters (including inheritance), even though all seven chapters are not strictly needed to proceed to some of the more advanced topics.

Acknowledgements

Our warm thanks to the following, who all contributed in some way to this book: Natalie Jones, Andy Shearman, Travis Milewski, Robb Anderson, Donald Cook, Mike Linck, Mike Rolfe and Kevin Colville.

We also wish to thank the University of Cape Town for study and research leave, and the University of Cape Town and the National Research Foundation for funding aspects of the project.

Finally, our thanks to our families for their love, understanding and encouragement during all the ups and downs of writing this book.

Brian D. Hahn
bdh@maths.uct.ac.za

Katherine M. Malan
kath@cs.uct.ac.za

January 2002

Part I
Essentials

1
Getting going

Objectives

By the end of this chapter, you should be able to do the following:

- set up your computer to be ready for programming in Java;
- compile and run a simple program which reads in from the keyboard and prints out to the screen;
- use the `Turtle` class and `Graph` class to draw graphics on the screen;
- write a simple Java program that can be run in a World Wide Web (WWW) browser (optional).

1.1 Introduction to programming

Computers have become an essential part of our everyday lives. Even if you don't use a computer for writing letters, browsing the Internet, or playing games, you are using computers every time you draw money from an ATM, use your cell phone, or phone automatic directory enquiries. A computer on its own has no intelligence. All that a computer can do is follow a detailed set of instructions, so it has to be programmed with these instructions for it to be useful. That's where the task of the programmer lies: in writing programs to make computers useful to people. Every bit of software, from your wordprocessor, to your web browser, was written by a programmer (or more likely, a team of programmers).

The set of instructions that a computer can understand is called *machine language*. In machine language, everything is encoded as binary numbers (1's and 0's). Not so long ago, programmers had to write programs in this machine language. Thankfully, we have now advanced to a stage where we can write programs in high-level languages, such as Java. It is the job of the *compiler* (just another program) to translate programs written in a programming language into machine code, so that it can be run on a computer. Some games programmers still choose to use low-level assembly language (very close to machine code), because the programs run faster.

Java as a programming language

Java has an interesting history. It was developed in 1991 by James Gosling of Sun Microsystems. Gosling was part of a secret team of 13 staff, called the 'Green Team'. The aim was not to develop a new language, but rather to develop digitally controlled consumer devices and computers. While developing a home-entertainment device controller (called *7), the team saw the need for a new processor-independent language. The first version was called 'Oak' (after the tree outside Gosling's window). Although *7 never took off, the language did and in 1995, Netscape announced that Java would be incorporated into Netscape Navigator. Since then, Java has gained enormous popularity as an Internet programming language. Although Java has become famous for its ability to do Internet programming, it is also a good general programming language. We chose to write a book on Java, because it is popular and a well-designed object-oriented language. One of the main features of Java (and part of the reason why it works so well on the Internet), is that it is platform independent. It achieves this by using something called the 'Java Virtual Machine' (JVM). As explained before, computers can only follow machine language instructions, so programs written in high-level languages have to be compiled into machine code for them to work. The problem is that each type of machine has its own machine language, so a program compiled for a MS Windows NT machine won't work on a Macintosh machine. What Java does is compile down to an intermediate code called *bytecode*. This bytecode is machine independent, but has to be *interpreted* by the JVM. This process of interpreting will be explained in Section 1.3.

1.2 Setting up your computer for programming in Java

There are two pieces of software which you will need before you can start programming:

- **An editor or an IDE (Integrated Development Environment).** An editor is a program which allows you to type in text and save it to a file. A text editor differs from a word processor in that it does not normally do formatting (such as different font sizes). Some text editors (such as Microsoft's Notepad) have no special features for programmers, while other editors have special features to support programmers. There are many shareware and freeware editors available from online software libraries (such as TUCOWS, which you can find at http://www.tucows.com). Look for an editor which has Java syntax colouring (also called *syntax highlighting*).

  IDE's, on the other hand, provide facilities for editing and compiling programs, as well as other support for programmers. The downside to using an IDE, is that you normally have to pay for it. A further factor to consider is that some Java IDE's provide features which complicate Java programming (such as the need to create projects), so in some cases it may even be easier to use a simple text editor, rather than an IDE. Sun has a list of recommended IDE's on their website (they are listed on the download page of Java 2). We have assumed in this book that you will be using a text editor rather than an IDE.

- **A Java compiler.** This is the software that will compile your program. We recommend that you use Sun Microsystems, Inc. Java Software Development Kit (SDK). This is the popular choice, mainly because it is freely available. In this book we have used version 1.3.1, but you are free to use a later version (instructions on how to download and install this are given below). Other Java 2 compatible compilers will also be fine.

Installing Java 2

The name 'Java 2' refers to all the releases of Sun's Java SDK starting with release 1.2 (and including releases 1.3.x). Versions before this were known as 'Java 1'. To set up Java 2 on your computer, do the following:

1. Using your favourite web browser, go to Sun's Java web site: http://www.java.sun.com
2. Follow the links from 'Products and APIs' to 'Java 2 Platform, Standard Edition' (the SDK). Select the relevant platform and follow the instructions. At the end of the installation, your directory structure should look something like the listing shown in Figure 1.1.
3. We recommend that you download the Java 2 Platform Standard Edition Documentation as well. As you learn to program, you will need to reference this documentation frequently and it will help to have it easily accessible.
4. You will need to change your PATH variable to include the folder which contains the `javac.exe` and `java.exe` files. You will find the details on how to do this in the `readme.html` file inside the jdk folder.

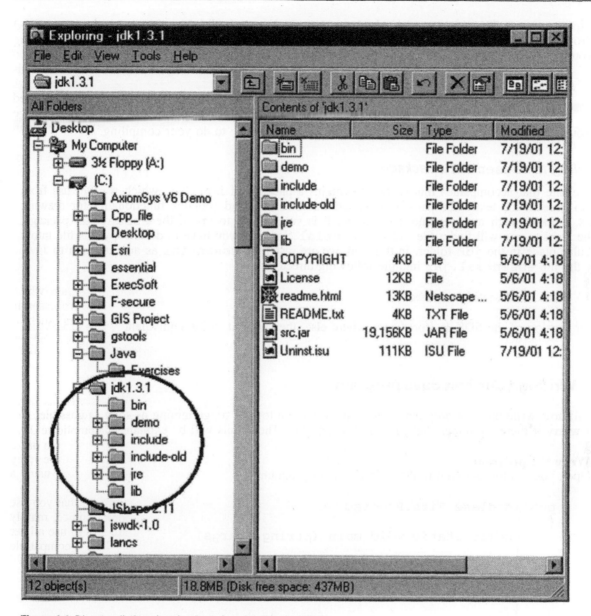

Figure 1.1 Directory listing showing how Java 2 will be installed

Jikes as an alternative compiler

You may find that the Java 2 compiler is slow on your computer at home. If you do find that it is very slow, you can try Jikes as an alternative faster compiler. Jikes is developed by IBM and is Open Source Software. It works with Sun's SDK, so you still need to install Java 2 as described above (you actually only need to install the runtime environment or JRE). Like Java 2, Jikes is free. You can download it from the following website:

```
http://oss.software.ibm.com/developerworks/opensource/jikes/
```

The zip file that you download contains a file called jikes.exe. The easiest way to set up Jikes is to do the following:

1. Change your PATH variable to include the folder which contains the file `jikes.exe`.
2. Provide a definition for JIKESPATH as follows (Note: this assumes that Java has been installed on your C: drive. If this is not the case, then change the folder accordingly):

```
set JIKESPATH=c:\jdk1.3.1\jre\lib\rt.jar;
                      c:\jdk1.3.1\jre\lib\ext\essential.jar
```

3. You can now use the command `jikes` in the place of `javac` to do your compiling.

Installing the `essential` package

The website that accompanies this textbook contains a package of Java code, which we will use from time to time in the text. This package is called `essential`, and contains functionality for drawing graphs, working with matrices and much more. It is very simple to install the `essential` package. On the website you will find a file called `essential.jar`. All you have to do is copy this file into a particular place in the `jdk` folder. In this way we are installing `essential` as an extension to Java. Copy the file `essential.jar` into the following directory:

```
c:\jdk1.3.1\jre\lib\ext
```

If your version of the SDK is stored somewhere else, then copy it to the equivalent `\jre\lib\ext` folder.

1.3 Writing your first Java program

We will now write our first program in Java. We want you to start programming as soon as possible, so don't worry if there are things that you don't understand. The details will be explained later.

1. **Write the program**
   Open your editor and type in the following Java program:

```java
public class FirstProgram
{
    public static void main (String[] args)
    {
        System.out.print("Hello, 2 + 3 = ");
        System.out.println(2 + 3);
        System.out.println("Good Bye");
    }
}
```

   Make sure you type it in *exactly* as it appears above. Java is case-sensitive, which means that it makes a difference if a letter is in uppercase or lowercase. In Java, `System` is not the same as `SYSTEM`, or even `system`.
2. **Save the program**
   Save the program in a file called `FirstProgram.java`. Once again, the case is significant, so make sure that the F and P are in uppercase and the rest are in lowercase.
3. **Compile the program**
   Open an MS-DOS Prompt window, change the directory to the directory where you saved your file and type in the following command:

```
javac FirstProgram.java
```

Figure 1.2 Results from running and compiling FirstProgram.java

After you push **Enter**, it should simply return to the prompt. If there are errors, you will have to go back to the editor and make sure you have copied down the code correctly. Remember that case is significant! Continue with steps 2 and 3 until you have no errors.

4. **Run the program**

Once your program has successfully compiled (with no errors), you can run the program by typing in the following command:

```
java FirstProgram
```

You should see the output shown in Figure 1.2.

What happens when a program is compiled?

When you compile `FirstProgram.java`, using the `javac` command, a file is created called `First-Program.class`. This `.class` file is in Java bytecode format (close to machine code). If you try to open this file with your text editor, you will either get an error, or it will display a few strange characters. When you run the program, using the `java` command, the `.class` file is interpreted by the Java Virtual Machine. If you want somebody else to run one of your programs, all you need to do is send them the `.class` file. As long as they have the Java Runtime Environment installed on their computer, they will be able to run your program, without needing to re-compile it for their machine.

Understanding FirstProgram

We will now explain how the program works. Figure 1.3 illustrates the parts of a simple Java program. The parts written in the grey area are what you will need every time you write a program. We call this the 'application template', because it is the basic structure within which we write simple programs. The only part of the grey area which will be different for different programs is the name of the program (also the name of the class). Each time you write a program, you must decide what to call your program. For example, here is the outline of a program called AnotherProgram:

```
public class AnotherProgram
{
    public static void main(String[] args)
    {
    }
}
```

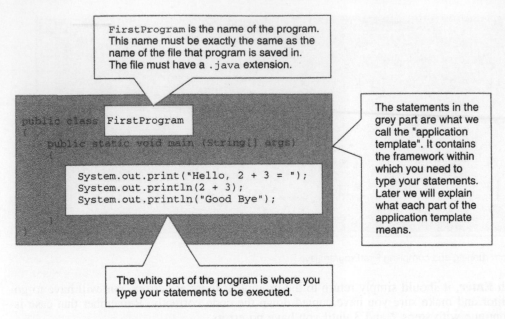

FirstProgram is the name of the program. This name must be exactly the same as the name of the file that program is saved in. The file must have a .java extension.

The statements in the grey part are what we call the "application template". It contains the framework within which you need to type your statements. Later we will explain what each part of the application template means.

The white part of the program is where you type your statements to be executed.

Figure 1.3 The parts of FirstProgram.java

This program will do nothing if it is run, because there are no statements between the middle curly braces. We call the curly braces *block markers*, because they mark the beginnings and endings of blocks of code. In the application template, the first curly brace and the last curly brace are block markers for the whole program, i.e. they denote the beginning and end of the program. The middle two braces are block markers for the portion of code called the *main method*. The purpose of the main method will be explained later.

Now try the following:

1. Make a copy of FirstProgram and save it as SecondProgram.java.
2. In SecondProgram.java, change the name of the program after the class statement to SecondProgram.
3. Save, compile and run SecondProgram.

You now have a copy of the program, which you can modify later.

Commands for printing to the screen

Now that you understand how to structure a simple program (even if you don't understand the detail), we will look at the statements inside the main method. Here are the statements inside our first program:

```
System.out.print("Hello, 2 + 3 = ");
System.out.println(2 + 3);
System.out.println("Good Bye");
```

First notice that each line terminates with a semi-colon. This indicates the end of a statement and is analogous to the full stop at the end of a sentence in the English language.

All three lines start with System.out, which refers to the screen of the computer. The command System.out.print is an instruction to the screen to print something out. The details of what should be printed are given inside the parentheses (round brackets).

In the case of the first statement, we are asking the screen to display a string . A string is simply a sequence of characters enclosed in double quotation marks. In the first line of our program, the string to

Table 1.1 Output illustrating the difference between print and println

Code	Output
System.out.println("hello"); System.out.println("there");	hello there
System.out.print("one "); System.out.print("two "); System.out.println("three "); System.out.print("four "); System.out.println("five ");	one two three four five

be printed is the sequence of characters, starting with the character 'H' and ending with an equals sign and a space. The result of the print statement is that the string is simply printed out exactly as it looks in between the quotes.

The second line is a little different. Firstly, it has a sum inside the parentheses, rather than a string, as in the first statement. What Java does in this case is to work out the answer to the sum (i.e. 5), before displaying it. If it had been inside quotes ("2 + 3"), then the answer would not have been worked out and would have been displayed simply as the character '2' followed by a space, the plus sign another space and the character '3'.

Secondly, it uses a command called println rather than print. The difference between println and print, is that println will display the details inside the parentheses and then output a new line (equivalent to pressing the enter key on the keyboard). The print command, on the other hand, stays on the same output line until more information is displayed. A few examples will illustrate this difference.

In Table 1.1 the left column gives examples of Java statements, while the right-hand column show what would be printed onto the screen when the statements are compiled and run as part of a Java program. Do you understand why the output will look like that?

Finally, the last statement simply displays the string "Good bye" before the program stops.

Now try to do Exercises 1.1 and 1.2 at the end of the chapter.

1.4 Input and output

We have looked at how to do output (printing things to the screen) using the print and println statements. In this section we will explain the difference between input and output and show how to get input from the keyboard using Java statements.

The important thing to realise when we talk about input and output in computing, is that it is in reference to the computer, not to ourselves. Output flows out of the computer and input flows into the computer. Examples of devices which display computer output are screens and printers. Input devices, on the other hand, include keyboards, mouse pointers and joysticks.

In Java, it is quite complicated to read in from the keyboard. To simplify things, we have created a class called Keyboard, which is part of the essential package (mentioned in Section 1.2). We will start by looking at a simple example which inputs the name of the person using the program:

```
import essential.*;

public class NameEcho
{
    public static void main (String[] args)
    {
        System.out.print("Enter your name: ");
        String name = Keyboard.readLine();
        System.out.println("Hello " + name + "!");
    }
}
```

Notice that the program starts with:

```
import essential.*;
```

This line is necessary when you are using any of the classes that are provided with this textbook. The name of the program (or class) is `NameEcho`, so to test it, you will need to save it in a file called `NameEcho.java`. Compile and run the program and see what happens.

Notice how the program pauses in order to get input from you, the user, via the keyboard. Type in your name at the prompt and see what happens.

How input from the keyboard works

In the second line of the program, the statement:

```
Keyboard.readLine();
```

reads in a line of text from the keyboard. When you push **Enter**, it will store the string in a variable called `name` (variables will be discussed in the next chapter). The last line of the program prints out the string "Hello", followed by the contents of the variable `name` (the string entered on the keyboard) and an exclamation mark. Notice that the '+' signs are not printed. When used between strings, a '+' sign concatenates the strings.

Now try Exercise 1.3.

Reading in numbers from the keyboard

In the example above, the `Keyboard` class was used with `readLine` to read in a string. If we want to read in a whole number, we need to use `readInt`, instead of `readLine`, as in the following example:

```
import essential.*;

public class Square
{
    public static void main (String[] args)
    {
        System.out.print("Enter a number: ");
        int num = Keyboard.readInt();
        System.out.println("The square is:" + (num*num));
    }
}
```

Notice in this program, the use of the `*` operator for performing multiplication . The statement:

```
int num = Keyboard.readInt();
```

suspends the program until a number is entered on the keyboard, followed by **Enter**. The number is then stored in the variable called `num` (which is of type `integer`). Try running this program to see how it responds to different input. What will happen if you type in a string instead of a number? What will happen if you type in a real number (such as 2.5)?

Now try to do Exercise 1.4.

Input without the `Keyboard` class (optional)

As mentioned before, the `Keyboard` class is there to simplify the process of reading input. For those who are interested, we have written an equivalent program to `Square`. Although it behaves the same as the previous program, this program is written without using the Keyboard class. We will not explain the details, since it is shown here purely for interest.

```java
import java.io.*;
public class Square2
{
    public static void main (String args []) throws IOException
    {
        BufferedReader in = new BufferedReader (
            new InputStreamReader(System.in));
        System.out.print("Enter a number: ");
        String s = in.readLine();
        int num = Integer.parseInt(s);
        System.out.println("The square is:" + (num*num));
    }
}
```

Notice that a package called java.io is imported (this is Java's standard package for performing input and output). The essential package is not needed, so is not imported.

Example: calculating compound interest

Let's look at a more complicated example using numbers to calculate compound interest:

```java
import essential.*;
public class CompoundInterest
{
    public static void main (String[] args)
    {
        System.out.print("Enter a balance: ");
        double balance = Keyboard.readDouble();
        System.out.print("Enter a rate: ");
        double rate = Keyboard.readDouble();
        balance = balance + (rate * balance);
        System.out.println("New balance = " + balance);
    }
}
```

This example uses real numbers rather than whole numbers. A real number in Java is called a double (or a float). These will be explained properly in Chapter 2. The user is asked to type in a balance and an interest rate (as a decimal fraction, e.g 15% should by typed as 0.15). The balance is then incremented by the interest rate and the new balance is printed out. Note the statement:

```java
balance = balance + (rate * balance);
```

The = sign performs *assignment* and has the effect of changing the variable on the *left*. This will be explained in more detail in Chapter 2. Compile and run the program to see how it works.

Now try Exercises 1.5 and 1.6.

1.5 Comments

A *comment* is a remark in a program which is meant to clarify something for the reader. It is ignored by the compiler. There are two ways to indicate comments in Java:

- Anything after a double slash (//) up to the next new line is interpreted as comment. This way of making a comment is suitable when the comment consists of a single line, or explains a single line of code. For example:

```
amt = amt+int*amt;   // increment the amount by the interest rate
```

- Comments may also be enclosed between the symbol pairs /* and */ . This form is suitable when we want to write a more extended comment, for example:

```
/*  This program models the growth of a rabbit colony over time.
 *  Assumptions:
 *      - start with male/female pair of baby rabbits.
 *      - it takes 2 months for a baby to become an adult.
 *      - adults produce a male/female pair of rabbits
 *         every month.
 */
```

Everything between /* and */ is ignored, so the extra stars are optional, but are a common way of emphasising that the text is a comment.

These forms of comments may not be 'nested', although they may be used to 'comment out' sections of code containing the // comment, e.g.

```
/*
// This is a comment
   ...
   ...
   ...
*/
```

1.6 Using objects

Throughout this book, you will be using Java code which has been written by other programmers. This code is organized into units called classes (this will be explained in more detail in Chapter 3). There are many classes which are provided as part of the core Java. You have already used one of these classes, namely the System class for printing out messages to the screen. As you progress through this book, you will use many more of these classes. In addition, we have provided a number of classes with this textbook. You have already come across the Keyboard class, and in this section we will show you how to use another two of these classes.

Using the Turtle class

The Turtle class can be used to draw shapes inside a window on the screen. The shapes that are drawn are based on commands given by you, the programmer, in Java. A turtle is represented as a triangle in the window. A turtle has a pen which can be either up or down.

- If the pen is up and the turtle walks, no line is drawn.
- If the pen is down and the turtle walks, a line is drawn (a turtle always starts with its pen down).

Here are some examples of commands that a turtle object understands:

- forward: walk forward a given number of steps;
- right: turn right by a given number of degrees;

- `left`: turn left by a given number of degrees;
- `home`: go back to the starting position;
- `warp`: move directly to a given point;

There can be many turtles drawing in the window at the same time. Compile and run the following program and see what happens (remember to call your file `TurtleDrawing.java`):

```
import essential.*;

public class TurtleDrawing
{
    public static void main (String[] args)
    {
        Turtle fred = new Turtle();  // create a Turtle called fred
        fred.forward(50);   // tell fred to move forward 50 paces
        fred.right(90);     // tell fred to turn right 90 degrees
        fred.forward(50);   // tell fred to move forward 50 paces
        fred.home();        // tell fred to go back to the origin
    }
}
```

Figure 1.4 shows what you should see on your screen. The turtle drawing area is a square of 200 by 200 units, with the origin in the middle. The top left of the window is the point $(-100, 100)$, whereas the bottom right corner is point $(100, -100)$. When you create a `Turtle` object, it always starts at the origin facing North. If you tell a turtle to go forward, it will walk in the direction in which it is facing.

We will now explain the program:

- First notice that the program starts off with the statement: `import essential.*;`. You have to put this statement in your program if you want to use any of the classes which are provided with the textbook (such as `Keyboard` or `Turtle`).
- The first statement inside `main` creates a `Turtle` object called `fred`. Before using the `Turtle` class, you have to construct (create) a `Turtle` object using the `new` keyword in this way. We will tell you more about constructors in Chapter 3.
- The second statement tells the object `fred` to move forward by 50 paces. Since `Turtle` objects start in the middle of the window and the distance to the edge is 100, this will mean that `fred` will move upwards, half way to the edge of the window, drawing a line as it moves forward.
- In the next 2 statements, `fred` turns right by 90° and goes forward another 50 paces. This results in a horizontal line of 50 units. After going forward, `fred` is facing East and is in the middle of the top right quadrant of the window.
- The last statement tells `fred` to go back home to the starting position, which is in the centre of the window and facing North. Since by default a turtle's pen is down, 3 lines are drawn for each movement of `fred`: two for the forward statements and one for the home statement.

Instructions that we give to `Turtle` objects (such as `forward`, `right` or home) are called *methods*. There are many more methods which you can use with the `Turtle` class. For a list of these methods, you need to know how to get help on the `essential` package.

Help on the `essential` *package*

All the classes inside the `essential` package are documented in help files which you can browse. On our website you will find a link to **essential API**. Click on this link and you will see a list of **All Classes** in the left-hand frame. Click on the **Turtle** link. This will bring up a description of the `Turtle` class in the right-hand frame. In the table called **Method Summary**, you will see a list of methods which you can use with a `Turtle` object. Notice that the methods `forward`, `home` and `right` are listed. Some

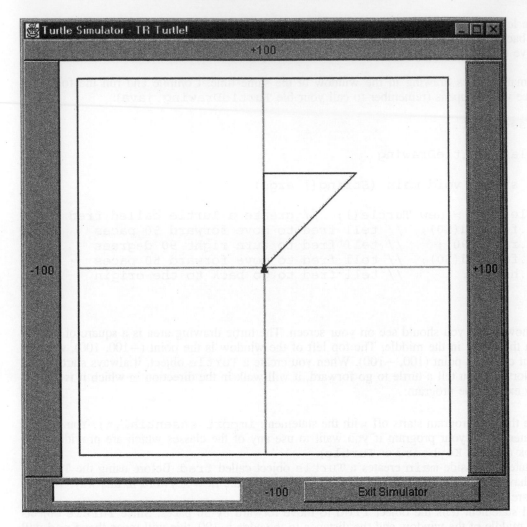

Figure 1.4 Output from running `TurtleDrawing.java`

of the methods which you can easily try out are: `left`, `penUp`, `penDown`, `setAngle` and `warp`. You will learn more about methods in Chapter 3.

Now try to do Exercises 1.7 to 1.10

Using the `Graph` class

We will now introduce a further class of the `essential` package, namely the `Graph` class. This class can be used for drawing graphs based on a number of points. Run the following program and see what happens:

```
import essential.*;

public class TestGraph
{
    public static void main (String[] args)
    {
        Graph g = new Graph();  // create a Graph object called g
        g.addPoint(-2,-4);
```

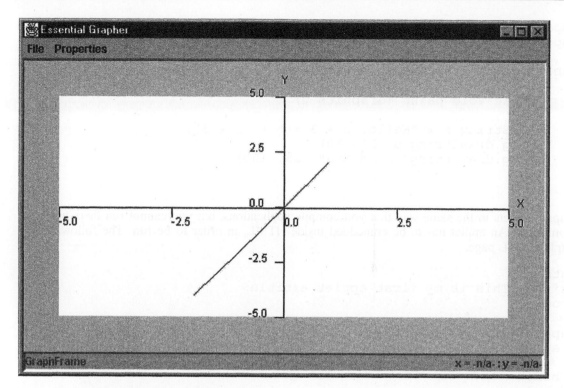

Figure 1.5 Output from running `TestGraph.java`

```
        g.addPoint(0,0);
        g.addPoint(1,2);
    }
}
```

The output that you should get is shown in Figure 1.5.

When you create a `Graph` object, using the keyword `new`, a window is created for displaying the graph. We call this window *Essential Grapher*. By default, the axes are set to the ranges −5 to 5 for both the X and the Y axes. You can change these ranges by using the `setAxes` method. Try adding this statement to the `TestGraph` program, compile and run it and see what happens:

```
        g.setAxes(0,10,0,6);
```

You can also set some of the properties of the Essential Grapher window using the menu, under **Properties**. Try changing some of the properties using the menu and see what happens. Notice also that as you move the mouse pointer over the Essential Grapher window, the X and Y values are displayed at the bottom right.

Now try to do Exercises 1.11 and 1.12.

1.7 Java on the WWW (optional)

Every Java program is either an *application* or an *applet*. The programs we have been writing until now have been applications. Applets are very similar to applications, except that they run in a web browser. Applets are therefore Java programs that run on the WWW. In this book, we will be working with applications, rather than applets. However, since we know that many of you will be curious to see how Java works on the web, in this section we will show you a simple example of an applet. The program below is an applet equivalent to the application `FirstProgram` that we wrote in Section 1.3.

```
import java.applet.*;
import java.awt.*;

public class FirstApplet extends Applet
{
    public void paint (Graphics g)
    {
        String s = "Hello, 2 + 3 = " + (2 + 3);
        g.drawString(s, 25, 50);
        g.drawString("Good Bye", 25, 100);
    }
}
```

You compile applets in the same way that you compile applications, but you cannot run them using the java command. An applet has to be embedded inside HTML, in order to be run. The following is a very simple HTML page.

```
<html>
<title> This is my first applet </title>
<body>

<applet code = FirstApplet.class width=200 height=200>
</applet>

</body>
</html>
```

Notice the chunk in the middle, which is a reference to FirstApplet (the .class file). To run this applet, you have to save this as a file with an .html extension and then open it with your browser. There is a Java application called *Applet Viewer* that enables you to run applets without using a web browser. You can run the Applet Viewer from the command line using the appletviewer command followed by the html file that you wish to view. For example, to run the HTML file above (assuming it is saved as FirstApplet.html), type the following command:

```
appletviewer FirstApplet.html
```

This command will create and display a small window with the applet running inside.

Summary

- The set of instructions that a computer can understand is called *machine language*.
- A compiler is a program that translates programs written in a high-level language (such as Java) to machine code.
- Java achieves platform independence by compiling down to *bytecode*, which is interpreted by the Java Virtual Machine.
- You can compile a Java program using the javac command and run a program using the java command.
- A Java program must be saved in a file with a .java extension. The name of the file must be the same name as the class.
- Block markers (curly braces) mark the beginning and end of a block of code.
- Commands for printing to the screen include System.out.print and System.out.println.
- Every statement in Java is terminated by a semi-colon.

- A string is a sequence of characters enclosed in double quotation marks.
- Input from the keyboard can be made using the Keyboard class, which comes with the essential package.
- When you use classes from the essential package, you have to import it using the command import essential.*;
- Comments in a program are meant to assist the human reader and are ignored by the compiler.
- In Java, comments either follow a double slash(//), or are enclosed in the pair of symbols * and *\.
- The Turtle class is part of the essential package and can be used to draw shapes inside a window.
- The Graph class is also part of the essential package and can be used for drawing graphs of points.
- Applets are Java programs that run on the web.

Exercises

1.1 Write a Java program which will print out the following:

```
Stars:
*****
The End
```

1.2 What would be printed onto the screen if the following Java statements were run?

```
System.out.println("Here is some output:");
System.out.println("4 + 5");
System.out.print(4 + 5);
System.out.print(" = ");
System.out.println(9);
```

1.3 Write a program that asks the user to enter their surname. After that it should ask the user for their first name. It should then print out the person's first name followed by a space and their surname.

1.4 Write a program that asks the user to enter a whole number and then prints out the number doubled.

1.5 Write a program that asks the user to enter two whole numbers. Your program should then print out the value of the two numbers multiplied. For example, if the user enters 40 and 10, your program should print out 400.

1.6 Change your program from the previous exercise to work with real numbers.

1.7 What will be the result from running the following program? Draw the resulting diagram with a pencil and paper before running the code.

```
import essential.*;

public class TurtleEx1
{
   public static void main (String[] args)
```

```
    {
      Turtle sid = new Turtle();   // create a Turtle called sid
      sid.backward(50);
      sid.right(90);
      sid.forward(50);
      sid.penUp();
      sid.home();
    }
  }
```

1.8   What will be the result from running the following program?

```
import essential.*;

public class TurtleEx2
{
  public static void main (String[] args)
  {
    Turtle sam = new Turtle();   // create a Turtle called sam
    sam.left(45);
    sam.forward(50);
    sam.left(90);
    sam.forward(50);
    sam.left(90);
    sam.forward(100);
    sam.left(90);
    sam.forward(100);
    sam.left(90);
    sam.forward(50);
    sam.left(90);
    sam.forward(50);
  }
}
```

1.9   What will be the result from running the following program?

```
import essential.*;

public class TurtleEx3
{
  public static void main (String[] args)
  {
    Turtle t = new Turtle();   // create a Turtle called t
    t.penUp();
    t.forward(100);
    t.right(135);
    t.penDown();
    t.warp(100,0);
    t.warp(0,-100);
    t.warp(-100,0);
    t.warp(0,100);
  }
}
```

1.10 Write a program, using the `Turtle` class, to draw a square with sides of length 100, with the centre of the square positioned at the origin of the window.

1.11 Write a program that uses Essential Grapher to draw a graph of the following points:

```
(0   , 0  )
(0.5, 3  )
(1   , 4  )
(2   , 4.5)
(5   , 4.8)
```

In your program, change the axes to suitable values.

1.12 Write a program that uses Essential Grapher to draw a graph of the following equation:

```
y = 2x - 3;
```

Hint: calculate two points which are fairly far away from each other and add these as points to the graph.

2
Java programming basics

Objectives

By the end of this chapter you should be able to write short Java programs which:

- evaluate a variety of formulae;
- make repetitive calculations;
- make simple decisions.

You presumably bought this book because you want to learn how to write your own programs in Java. In this chapter we will look in detail at how to write short Java programs to solve simple problems involving basic arithmetic operations, repetition and decisions. There are two essential requirements for successfully mastering the art of programming:

1. The exact rules for coding instructions must be learnt;
2. A logical plan for solving the problem must be designed.

This chapter is devoted mainly to the first requirement: learning some basic coding rules. Once you are comfortable with these, we can gradually go on to more substantial problems, and how to solve them using Java's object-oriented machinery.

All Java constructs introduced in the text are summarized in Appendix C.

2.1 Compound interest again

In Chapter 1 you ran a program to compute compound interest. The following variation on that program (which you should also run) highlights some basic concepts which we will discuss below.

```
public class CompInt
{
    public static void main(String[ ] args)
    {
        double balance, interest, rate;
        balance = 1000;
```

```
rate = 0.09;
interest = rate * balance;
balance = balance + interest;
System.out.println( "New balance: " + balance );
    }
}
```

We saw in Chapter 1 that when you compile a Java program with the `javac` command the result is a bytecode file with the extension `.class`. You subsequently run (execute) the bytecode with the `java` command. During compilation, space in the computer's *random access memory* (RAM) is allocated for any numbers (data) which will be generated by the program. This part of the memory may be thought of as a bank of boxes, or *memory locations*, each of which can hold only one number at a time (at the moment). These memory locations are referred to by symbolic names in the program. So, for example, the statement

```
balance = 1000
```

allocates (when it is executed) the number 1000 to the memory location named `balance`. Since the contents of `balance` may be changed during the program it is called a *variable*.

The statements between the inner *block markers* { ... } in our program `CompInt` are interpreted as follows during the compilation process:

1. Create memory locations for storing three variables of type `double`
2. Put the number 1000 into memory location `balance`
3. Put the number 0.09 into memory location `rate`
4. Multiply the contents of `rate` by the contents of `balance` and put the answer in `interest`
5. Add the contents of `balance` to the contents of `interest` and put the answer in `balance`
6. Print (display) a message followed by the contents of `balance`

Note that these instructions are *not carried out* during compilation. All that happens is that they are translated into bytecode.

When you run (execute) the program, these translated statements are carried out *in order from the top down*. Figure 2.1 shows how the memory locations change as each statement is executed. Understanding the order in which program statements are carried out is very important, particularly if you are used to spreadsheeting, which is entirely different. Spreadsheet formulae can be calculated in any particular order; or rather, you don't usually need to be concerned about the order in which cell formulae are calculated. However, this is most emphatically not the case when you program in a language like Java. You have to get the statements into the correct order so that when they are executed in that sequence they will carry out the required tasks correctly.

After execution of our translated statements, in the order shown, the memory locations used will have the following values (see Figure 2.1):

```
balance  : 1090
interest : 90
rate     : 0.09
```

Note that the original content of `balance` is lost.

It is worth lingering over the statement

```
balance = balance + interest;
```

since it is an example of a very common programming device to *update* (increment) a variable (`balance`). Java evaluates the expression on the right-hand side of the equals sign, and places the answer in the variable on the left-hand side (even if the variable appears on both sides). In this way the old value of `balance` is replaced by its new value.

Statement	Memory after statement is executed		
`double balance, interest, rate;`	balance		
	interest		
	rate		
`balance = 1000;`	balance	1000	
	interest		
	rate		
`rate = 0.09;`	balance	1000	
	interest		
	rate	0.09	
`interest = rate * balance;`	balance	1000	
	interest	90	
	rate	0.09	
`balance = balance + interest;`	balance	1090	
	interest	90	
	rate	0.09	

Figure 2.1 How the memory locations (variables) in `CompInt` change as each statement is executed.

The remaining statements in the program are also very important:

`public class CompInt`

is a *class declaration*. Everything inside the block markers that follow is part of the class declaration—remember to close all opening block markers! We will discuss classes in detail in Chapter 3.

The name of the file in which the program is saved must be the same as the name of its `public` class, i.e. the class `CompInt` must be saved in `CompInt.java`.

`public static void main(String[ ] args)`

is technically a *method* of the `CompInt` class.

Methods *do* things. For the moment just think of `main` as doing whatever needs to be done, i.e. whatever follows in the block markers { ... }.

A `static` method is associated with its class, rather than with an instance of the class— this distinction will be explained in Chapter 3.

All the variables in a program must be declared with a *data type*. This is done here by `double`, which means they are all double-precision floating point numbers with or without fractional parts.

Incidentally, if you are fussy about how many decimal places appear in the output, using the `Math.round` method is probably the easiest way of specifying two decimal places, for example:

```
System.out.println( Math.round(balance*100)/100.0 );
```

It works as follows. First, `balance` is multiplied by 100, then the product is rounded to the nearest integer, and finally the result is divided by 100—leaving two decimal places.

Now try Exercise 2.1 at the end of the chapter.

Before we can write any more complete programs there are some further basic concepts which need to be introduced.

2.2   Primitive data types

Java has a number of *primitive data types*, of which `int` and `double` are two examples. The different data types and their properties are summarized in Table 2.1. We will come across most of them in due course.

Bits and bytes

Before we go any further we need to look briefly at how information is represented in a computer. A *bit* is the basic unit of information in a computer. It is something which has only two possible states, usually described as "on" and "off". The *binary digits* 0 and 1 can be used to represent these two states mathematically (hence the term *digital* computer). The word "bit" in a contraction of "*bi*nary digi*t*".

Numbers in a computer's memory must therefore be represented in *binary code*, where each bit in a sequence stands for a successively higher power of 2. The binary codes for the decimal numbers 0 to 15, for example, are shown in Table 2.2.

A *byte* is eight bits long. Since each bit in a byte can be in two possible states, this gives 2^8, i.e. 256, different combinations.

Table 2.1 Primitive data types in Java

Type	Size (bits)	Range
boolean	1	true or false
char	16	Unicode 0 (\u0000) to Unicode $2^{16} - 1$ (\uFFFF)
byte	8	-127 to $+127$
short	16	$-32\,768$ to $+32\,767$
int	32	$-2\,147\,483\,648$ to $+2\,147\,483\,647$
long	64	$-9\,223\,372\,036\,854\,775\,808$ to $+9\,223\,372\,036\,854\,775\,807$
float	32	$\pm 3.40282347E+38$ to $\pm 1.40239846E-45$
double	64	$\pm 1.79769313486231570e+308$ to $\pm 4.94065645841246544e-324$
void	–	–

Table 2.2 Binary and hexadecimal codes

Decimal	Binary	Hexadecimal	Decimal	Binary	Hexadecimal
0	0000	0	8	1000	8
1	0001	1	9	1001	9
2	0010	2	10	1010	A
3	0011	3	11	1011	B
4	0100	4	12	1100	C
5	0101	5	13	1101	D
6	0110	6	14	1110	E
7	0111	7	15	1111	F

Hexadecimal code (see Table 2.2) is often used because it is more economical than binary. Each hexadecimal digit stands for an integer power of 16. E.g.

$$2A = 2 \times 16^1 + 10 \times 16^0 = 32 + 10 = 42$$

One byte can be represented by two hex digits.

Octal code is less common than hexadecimal: each digit represents a power of 8.

Computer memory size (and disk capacity) is measured in bytes, so 64K for example means slightly more than 64 000 bytes (since 1K actually means 1024). Computers are sometimes referred to as 16- or 32-bit machines. This describes the length of the units of information handled by their microprocessors (chips). The longer these units, the faster the computer.

Numeric constants

A *numeric constant* is just a number used in a program. For example, in the statement

```
int num = 400;
```

num is a variable and 400 is a numeric constant.

An *integer numeric constant* has no decimal places and may be written with or without a plus or minus sign.

A *floating point numeric constant* may be written in two ways. It may be written as a signed or unsigned string of digits with a decimal point, e.g.

```
0.09    37.    37.0    .0    0.    -.123456
```

It may also be written in *scientific notation* with an integer exponent. In this form a decimal point is not necessary. For example:

```
2.0e2          (200.0)
2e2            (200.0)
4.12e+2        (412.0)
-7.321e-4      (-0.0007321)
```

double *is default*

A floating point constant is of type double by default. It can be *coerced* into type float if necessary with the suffix f (or F). The following statement, for example, generates a compiler error which usually confounds beginners:

```
float rate = 0.09;
```

The error occurs because 0.09 is double type by default and Java won't let you assign a double type to a float type, because it won't fit (although it allows the reverse, which is called *upcasting*). The remedy is to write

```
float rate = 0.09f;
```

Now try Exercises 2.2 and 2.3.

2.3 Names

Identifiers

An *identifier* is the symbolic name used to represent items in a Java program, e.g. `rate`, `println`. An identifier must

- start with a letter, underscore character (_) or dollar symbol;
- consist of only the above characters and digits.

An identifier may be of any length.
Examples:

```
r2d2        // valid
pay_day     // valid
pay-day     // invalid
pay day     // invalid
2a          // invalid
_2a         // valid
name$       // valid
```

Java has special keywords, which are reserved and may not be used as identifiers. They are the obvious ones, like `double`, `class`, `int`, `void`, and also some less obvious ones like `super` and `finally`. See Appendix A for a complete list of Java keywords.

Case sensitivity

It may come as a surprise to you, if you are not familiar with Java, that identifiers are *case sensitive*, e.g. `rate` and `Rate` are different variables.

You need to bear in mind that case sensitivity extends to class and file names. For example, the program in Section 2.1 must be saved in the file `CompInt.java`, because the class name is `CompInt` (and not `Compint` or `compint`).

Many programmers write identifiers representing variables in lowercase except for the first letter of the second and subsequent words. This style is known as *camel caps*, the uppercase letters representing (with a little imagination) a camel's humps, e.g. `camelCaps`, `milleniumBug`, `endOfTheMonth`.

Variables

A variable is the name given by a program to a storage location. It is helpful to distinguish between two types of variables in Java:

- a primitive data variable, i.e. the name given to a storage location which will hold a primitive data type, such as `balance`, `interest` and `rate` in `CompInt`;
- an object *handle*, i.e. the name of an object, such as `tred` (the `Turtle` object in Chapter 1). Objects are discussed in detail in Chapter 3.

If you use a variable in a program without initializing it, the compiler generates an error.

Every variable declared should be described in a comment. This makes for good programming style.

Beware: if an integer type (i.e. `byte`, `short`, `int`, `long`) is increased above its maximum value in a calculation its value "wraps around" to the minimum and starts again. For example, the code

```
int n, m;
n = Integer.MAX_VALUE;   // largest integer
m = n+1;
System.out.println( m );
```

results in the output

        -2147483648

Try Exercise 2.4.

2.4 Vertical motion under gravity

We will now show you a Java program that uses a well-known physics formula.

If a stone is thrown vertically upward with an initial speed u, its vertical displacement s after a time t has elapsed is given by the formula $s = ut - gt^2/2$, where g is the acceleration due to gravity. Air resistance has been ignored. We would like to compute the value of s, given u and t. Note that we are not concerned here with how to derive the formula, but how to compute its value. The logical preparation of this program is as follows:

1. Assign values of g, u and t
2. Compute the value of s according to the formula
3. Output the value of s

Drawing up a plan like this may seem trivial and a waste of time. Yet you would be surprised how many beginners, preferring to dive straight into Java, try to program step 2 before step 1. It is well worth developing the mental discipline of planning your program first. Type your plan into your text editor in the form of comments in the main body of the program. Then add the Java statements corresponding to each comment below the comment.

The program is as follows:

```
public class Vertical
{
    public static void main(String[ ] args)
    {

        //1. Assign values of g, u and t
        double g = 9.8;  // acceleration due to gravity
        double s;  // vertical displacement
        double t;  // time
        double u;  // launch velocity

        t = 6;
        u = 60;

        //2. Compute the value of s according to the formula
        s = u*t - g/2*t*t;

        //3. Output the value of s
        System.out.println( "s: " + s + " metres" );
    }
}
```

New concepts raised in this program are discussed in the following sections.

2.5   Operators, expressions and assignments

Many of the programs that you will be writing will include mathematical expressions, such as

```
u*t - g/2*t*t
```

These expressions are evaluated by means of *operators* when a program runs. Java has a number of different kinds of operators for evaluating expressions, e.g. arithmetic, increment, decrement, relational, logical, etc. We are going to look at the first three kinds in this section.

Arithmetic operators

- There are five arithmetic operators: + (addition), - (subtraction), * (multiplication), / (division), and \% (modulus). An operator with two *operands* is called a *binary* operator. When it has only one operand it is called *unary*. Addition and subtraction can be unary or binary. Here are some examples of expressions involving these operators:

```
a + b / c
-a        // unary minus
b / (2 * a)
```

- When both operands in a division are of an integer type, the fractional part is truncated (chopped off).
- The modulus operation returns the integer remainder after division of its integer operands. The sign of the remainder is the product of the signs of the operands. For example:

```
10 / 3   // evaluates to 3 (fractional part is truncated)
10 % 3   // evaluates to 1 (remainder when 10 is divided by 3)
-10 % 3 //   evaluates to -1
```

- Java performs real arithmetic in double precision, so coercion to float may be necessary, as described in Section 2.2. For example,

```
float x = 1.68/2;
```

generates a compiler error, which can be corrected as follows:

```
float x = 1.68f/2;
```

- There is no exponentiation (raise to the power) operator. However, a^b, for example, may be computed with a method in the Math class: Math.pow(a, b). To compute $\sqrt{n}$ use Math.sqrt(n).

Precedence

The usual *precedence* rules of arithmetic are followed: * and / have a higher precedence than + and -. If you are in doubt you can always use parentheses, which have an even higher precedence. Thus a + b * c is evaluated by default as a + (b * c).

Where arithmetic operators in an expression have the same precedence the operations are carried out from left to right. So a / b * c is evaluated as (a / b) * c, and *not* as a / (b * c).

Try Exercises 2.5 to 2.8.

The precedence levels of all Java operators discussed in this book are shown in Appendix B.

Increment and decrement operators

If you are not familiar with Java (or C, to which Java is related) you will find the increment (++) and decrement (--) operators intriguing. They provide a shorthand way of increasing or decreasing their operands by 1. E.g.

```
c++;        // increase c by 1
++c;        // increase c by 1
x--;        // decrease x by 1
--x;        // decrease x by 1
```

So, for example, `c++` is the same as the slightly more long-winded `c = c + 1`. (Did you realise that this is where C++ gets its name: one more than C?)

When these operators appear in assignments (i.e. *variable = expression*) their position is crucial, since the expression on the right may be incremented or decremented before or after its value is assigned to the variable on the left. And so we have *post*-incrementing/decrementing, e.g.

```
a = x++;    // set a to x, then increment x
b = x--;    // set b to x, then decrement x
```

and *pre*-incrementing/decrementing, e.g.

```
a = ++x;    // increment x, then set a to new value of x
b = --x;    // decrement x, then set b to new value of x
```

The *pre* means the increment or decrement occurs *before* the assignment is made.

Note that it does not make sense to have `x++` on the left-hand side of an assignment, so it is not allowed.

The pre-increment and pre-decrement operators both have higher precedence than the arithmetic operators. So the code

```
int x = 1;
int y;
y = x + ++x;
```

sets x to 2 and y to 4. x is first incremented to 2, and then added to its new value to give 4.

Old-time C programmers delighted in writing concise yet obscure code like this. The practice stems from the days when computer memory was limited, and when execution time was critical; sometimes the obscure code runs a little faster.

However, with the multi-megabytes of RAM and Pentium power available today you simply can't use those excuses any more. Why not say what you mean, and replace the last statement above with:

```
++x;
y = x + x;      // no ambiguity now!
```

Post-incrementing or decrementing is a little more subtle. The code

```
int x = 1;
int y;
y = x + x++;
```

sets y to 2. You can think of the post-incrementing being done in a temporary register, and only being applied to its operand after the expression is evaluated. Once again, it is better to write clearly what you mean, i.e.

```
y = x + x;
x = x + 1;
```

Assignments and assignment operators

Simple assignments

The simple assignment operator is the equal sign (=). We have already seen a few examples of its use. The most common form of a simple assignment is

var = *expr*;

The expression *expr* on the right is evaluated and its value assigned to the variable var on the left, e.g.

```
x = a + Math.sqrt( b ) + Math.cos( c );
n = n + 1;          // increase the value of n by 1 (or n++)
```

Note the *direction* of the assignment: from the right-hand side of the equals sign to the left. It is a common programming error to get the assignment the wrong way around, as in

```
n + 1 = n;    // wrong way!  wrong way!  wrong way!
```

Java expects a single variable on the left-hand side and will object if it finds anything else.

More examples

The formulae

$$F = \frac{GME}{r^2},$$

$$c = \frac{\sqrt{a^2 + b^2}}{2a},$$

$$A = P\left(1 + \frac{r}{100}\right)^n$$

may be translated into the following simple assignments:

```
f = G * m * e / (r * r);
c = Math.sqrt( a * a + b * b ) / (2 * a);
a = p * Math.pow( 1 + r/100, n );
```

Try Exercises 2.9 to 2.10

Assignment operators

A statement like

```
sum = sum + x;
```

occurs so frequently in Java that it may be written more concisely as

```
sum += x;
```

The double symbol += is called an *assignment operator*. (The plus operator must be on the left of the equals operator, otherwise it would be the unary addition operator.)

There are more assignment operators, such as -=, *=, /= and %=. Each assignment operator reduces the expression

var = *var op expr* ;

to the shorter form

> *var op= expr;*

Their precedence level in the general scheme of things is shown in Appendix B.

Cast operators

When an integer, for example, is divided by another integer, the decimal part of the result is lost (truncated) even if it is assigned to a `float` or `double` variable. However, the use of a *cast operator* can fix this. For example,

```
x = (float) 10 / 3;
```

assigns the value of 3.333333 (instead of 3) to x by using the `(float)` cast operator. Note that the integer 10 is cast to a `float` before the division takes place.

Cast operators are available for any data type, and are formed by placing parentheses around the data type name.

Try Exercises 2.11 to 2.20.

2.6   Repeating with `for`

So far we have seen how to get data into a Java program, how to temporarily store it in variables, how to evaluate simple expressions, and how to output the results. In this section we look at a new and powerful feature: repetition. We start by showing you some examples, which you should run. We will then explain in detail how the `for` loop works.

As a very simple introductory example run the following code:

```
for (int i = 1; i <= 10; i++)
{
    System.out.print( i + "   " );
}
```

You should get this output:

```
1   2   3   4   5   6   7   8   9   10
```

Can you see what's going on? Change the `print` statement to `println` and see what happens.

Turtle spirals

In Chapter 1 we introduced you briefly to our `Turtle` class. We would like to use the turtle to draw more interesting figures, for example, a spiral. To draw a spiral, the turtle has to move forward a certain amount, change direction slightly, move forward slightly more, change direction again, move forward slightly more, and so on. If we create a turtle called `terry`, and variable `step`,

```
Turtle terry = new Turtle();
double step = 10;
```

then the group of three statements

```
terry.forward(step);
terry.right(30);
step += 5;
```

carry out the basic movement of taking a step, changing direction, and increasing the step. We simply have to repeat these three statements to draw our spiral. Here's the obvious way to do it:

```java
import essential.*;

public class MyTurt
{
    public static void main(String[] args)
    {
        Turtle terry = new Turtle();
        double step = 10;

        terry.forward(step);
        terry.right(30);
        step += 5;

        terry.forward(step);
        terry.right(30);
        step += 5;

        terry.forward(step);
        terry.right(30);
        step += 5;

        terry.forward(step);
        terry.right(30);
        step += 5;
    }
}
```

This program produces the rather crude attempt at a spiral in Figure 2.2. Clearly we could use cut-and-paste to paste in as many copies of the three statements as we need. But that would be very tedious; our program would become very long. What we want is a construction which repeats the three statements for us. Java has such a device, called a `for` loop. The following program produces exactly the same result as `MyTurt`, by repeating the group of three statements four times:

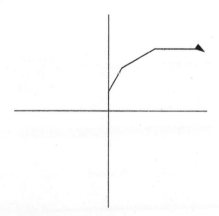

Figure 2.2 A crude spiral

```
import essential.*;

public class SmartTurtle
{
    public static void main(String[] args)
    {
        Turtle terry = new Turtle();
        double step = 10;

        for (int i = 1; i <= 4; i++)
        {
            terry.forward(step);
            terry.right(30);
            step += 5;
        }
    }
}
```

In fact, the for loop is so powerful, we might as well use it to draw the much better looking Spiral of Archimedes in Figure 2.3 (the steps and angles have been made smaller to get a neater spiral):

```
import essential.*;

public class ArchSpiral
{
    public static void main(String[] args)
    {
        Turtle terry = new Turtle();
        double step = 0.5;
        double increment = 0.03;
        double degree = 5;
```

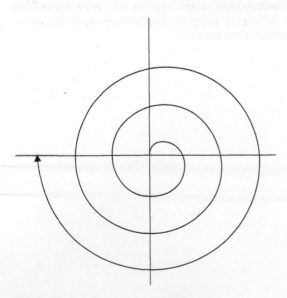

Figure 2.3 The Spiral of Archimedes

```
        int numSpirals = 3;
        int numLoops = (int)(360/degree) * numSpirals;

        for (int i = 1; i <= numLoops; i++)
        {
            terry.forward(step);
            step += increment;
            terry.right(degree);
        }

    }
}
```

The variable numLoops is used here as a counter. It evaluates to 216, which is the number of times the basic group of three statements is repeated!

Growing an investment

The following program computes the value of an initial investment of $1000 over a period of 10 years where interest of 12 per cent is compounded annually. Run it and see if you can follow how it works.

```
public class Invest
{
    public static void main( String args[ ] )
    {
        double bal = 1000;      // initial balance
        double rate = 0.12;     // interest rate

        for (int year = 1; year <= 10; year++)
        {
            bal = bal + rate*bal;
            System.out.println( year + "   " +
                           Math.round( 100*bal )/100. );
        }
    }
}
```

Output:

```
 1  1120.0
 2  1254.4
 3  1404.93
 4  1573.52
 5  1762.34
 6  1973.82
 7  2210.68
 8  2475.96
 9  2773.08
10  3105.85
```

In this example, the for construct is used to repeat the two statements

```
        bal = bal + rate*bal;
        System.out.println( year + "   " + ... );
```

10 times. Such a structure where the number of repetitions is determined by the user in advance (i.e. 10), is sometimes called *determinate repetition*.

The for *statement*

The for loop is one of the most powerful constructs in programming. Its most common form is

```
for (int i = j; i <= k; i++)
{
    statements
}
```

Note:

- In this case i (the loop *counter*, or *index*) is any integer variable, and j and k may be constants, variables or expressions.
  It is recommended that the counter i be declared int in the for header as above. The effect of this is that i is defined only in the scope of the block markers following the for header. This device prevents i from conflicting with a variable of the same name outside the for loop.
- *statements* are executed repeatedly.
- The values of j and k determine how many repeats are made.
- i starts with the value j, and is incremented *at the end* of each loop.
- Looping stops once i exceeds the value of k, and execution proceeds in the normal way with the next statement after the for.
- i will have the value $k + 1$ after completion of the loop.

More generally, for has the syntax

```
for (initialization; condition; increment)
{
    statements
}
```

where *initialization* creates and initializes the loop counter, looping continues while *condition* is true, and *increment* defines how the loop counter is incremented. All three are expressions.

The important thing to note here is that if a *group* of statements is to be repeated by a for loop the statements must be enclosed in *block markers* {...}. Statements thus enclosed are treated syntactically as a single statement.

It is also important to understand at what stage during the execution of the loop the three phases *initialization*, *condition* and *increment* occur. Consider the following example,

```
for (int i = 1; i <= 3; i++)
{
    System.out.println( i*2 );
}
```

which has the output

```
2
4
6
```

Here is a blow-by-blow account of how the for executes:

1. The counter i is created and initialized to the value 1. This phase (*initialization*) occurs *once only*.
2. *condition* is tested: 1 <= 3 is **true**.
3. Since *condition* is true, *statements* are executed: the value of i*2 (2) is printed.
4. *increment* occurs: the value of i increases to 2.

5. *condition* is tested: 2 <= 3 is **true**.
6. Since *condition* is true, *statements* are executed: the value of i*2 (4) is printed.
7. *increment* occurs: the value of i increases to 3.
8. *condition* is tested: 3 <= 3 is **true**.
9. Since *condition* is true, *statements* are executed: the value of i*2 (6) is printed.
10. *increment* occurs: the value of i increases to 4.
11. *condition* is tested. 4 <= 3 is **false**.
12. The loop terminates and control passes to the statement following the for block markers.

A very common error is to end the for clause with a semi-colon:

```
for (year = 1; year <= 10; year++); { ... }
```

Can you explain what happens if you do this in the Invest program? The semi-colon *terminates the statement to be executed*: in this case nothing—except incrementing year. So basically nothing is repeated 10 times, after which the two statements in the block markers are executed exactly *once*.
Try Exercises 2.21 to 2.22.

Alternative ways of counting with for

In our examples of for thus far we have started counting at 1, which is a fairly natural thing to do, e.g.

```
for (int i = 1; i <= 10; i++)
```

Many programmers prefer to start counting at 0 (it depends on how you were brought up), in which case *condition* has to be changed subtly in order to secure the correct number of repeats:

```
for (int i = 0; i < 10; i++)
```

Either way is acceptable; it just depends on whether you prefer counting from 0 or 1. For example, you could rewrite the for in Invest as

```
for (int year = 0; year < 10; year++)
```

However, year must then be replaced by (year+1) in the println statement to reflect the correct year in the output. (Why would year++ be wrong here?)
In this book we will generally start counting at 1 in for loops, except in the case of array subscripts, which invariably start at 0 (see Chapter 6).

Square rooting with Newton

The square root x of any positive number a may be found using only the arithmetic operations of addition, subtraction and division, with *Newton's method*. This is a neat iterative (repetitive) procedure that refines an initial guess.
The structure plan of the algorithm to find the square root, and the program with sample output for $a = 2$ is as follows:

1. Input a
2. Initialize x to 1 (the initial guess
3. Repeat 6 times (say)
     Replace x by $(x + a/x)/2$
     Print x

```
import essential.*;
```

```java
public class MySqrt
{
// square-rooting with Newton
    public static void main(String args[])
    {
        double a;          // number to be square-rooted
        double x = 1;      // guess at sqrt(a)

        System.out.print( "Enter number to be square-rooted: " );
        a = Keyboard.readDouble();

        for (int i = 1; i <= 6; i++)
        {
            x = (x + a/x)/2;
            System.out.println( x );
        }
        System.out.println( "Java's sqrt: " + Math.sqrt(a) );
    }
}
```

Output:

```
Enter number to be square-rooted: 2
1.5
1.4166666666666665
1.4142156862745097
1.4142135623746899
1.414213562373095
1.414213562373095
Java's sqrt: 1.4142135623730951
```

The value of x converges to a limit, which is $\sqrt{a}$. Note that it is virtually identical to the value returned by Java's `Math.sqrt`. Most computers and calculators use a similar method internally to compute square roots and other standard mathematical functions.

Factorials!

Run the following program to generate a list of n and $n!$ (spoken as 'n factorial', or 'n shriek') where

$$n! = 1 \times 2 \times 3 \times \ldots \times (n-1) \times n.$$

```java
int n;
long fact = 1;
System.out.print( "Enter n: " );
n = Keyboard.readInt();
System.out.println( n );

for (int k = 1; k <= n; k++)
{
    fact = k * fact;
    System.out.println( k + "!= " + fact );
}
```

• Change the above program so that only the final answer is printed out, and not all the intermediate values. For example, if 20 is entered for the value of n, the only output should be

```
20!= 2432902008176640000
```

- Can you figure out what's happening when you try to compute $n!$ for $n > 20$?

Limit of a sequence

`for` loops are ideal for computing successive members of a sequence (as in Newton's method above). The following example also highlights a problem that sometimes occurs when computing a limit. Consider the sequence

$$x_n = \frac{a^n}{n!}, \quad n = 1, 2, 3, \dots$$

where a is any constant, and $n!$ is the factorial function defined above. The question is: what is the limit of this sequence as n gets indefinitely large? Let's take the case $a = 10$. If we try to compute x_n directly we could get into trouble, because $n!$ gets large very rapidly as n increases, and numerical *overflow* could occur. However, the situation is neatly transformed if we spot that x_n is related to x_{n-1} as follows:

$$x_n = \frac{ax_{n-1}}{n}.$$

There are no numerical problems now. The following program computes x_n for $a = 10$, and increasing values of n. Run it.

```
int k = 30;        // number of terms
double a = 10;
double x = 1;

for (int n = 1; n <= k; n++)
{
    x = a * x / n;
    System.out.println( n + "   " + x );
}
```

Try Exercises 2.23 to 2.25.

Reading data from a text file

Another common use of the `for` statement is in reading data from files. Suppose you want to compute the average of some data you have been collecting. As an example, use your text editor to create the following text (ASCII) file, and save it under the name `nums.txt`:

```
10 3.1 7.2 4.5 9.9 6.0 7.9 3.7 9.2 6.5 3.9
```

The first value (10) is the number of data values to be read; it is followed by your 10 data values. The following program reads them and prints their average:

```
import essential.*;

public class ReadNums
{
    public static void main(String args[])
    {

        double n, x, sum, avg;
```

```
        sum = 0;
        FileIO f1 = new FileIO( "nums.txt", FileIO.READING );
        n = f1.readDouble();

        for (for i = 1; i <= n; i++)
        {
            x = f1.readDouble( );
            sum += x;
        }

        avg = sum / n;
        System.out.println( "Mean: " + avg );
    }
}
```

Note:

- File I/O (input/output) is a bit cumbersome in Java, so once again we have provided you with an easy-to-use class in the essential package called FileIO. The statement

  ```
  FileIO f1 = new FileIO( "nums.txt", FileIO.READING );
  ```

  creates a FileIO object f1 which you can think of as a pipe (input stream) connecting your program to the file nums.txt. The READING field specifies that the file is opened for reading only, so that the data can't be accidentally overwritten.
- The readDouble method reads the next data value from the file.
- For the data in this example, the mean is 6.19.
- A more realistic situation is where you don't know the exact number of data values (or couldn't be bothered to count them!). We will see in Chapter 4 how to read an unknown amount of data from a file.

Try Exercise 2.26.

2.7 Deciding with if

The for loop enables us to write some fairly impressive programs, but when we extend our programming repertoire to include the ability to make decisions the sky's the limit. Run the following short program (you can change the output it makes if you like). Note that there is no output if you enter an age of 20 or more.

```
import essential.*;

public class Age
{
    public static void main(String[] args)
    {

        int age;
        System.out.print( "How old are you? " );
        age = Keyboard.readInt();
        System.out.println( age );
```

```
            if (age < 20)
                System.out.println( "Enjoy your teens while you can!" );
        }
    }
```

Now extend the `if` statement to look as follows

```
    if (age < 20)
        System.out.println( "Enjoy your teens while you can!" );
    else
        System.out.println( "Getting on a bit aren't we?" );
```

and check that the output is different depending on whether the age entered is less than 20, or 20 and above.

Here's another one to try—run it a few times:

```
    public class SpinCoin
    {
        public static void main(String[ ] args)
        {
            double x;
            x = Math.random();
            if (x < 0.5)
                System.out.println( "Heads" );
            else
                System.out.println( "Tails" );
        }
    }
```

Sometimes you get `Heads`, sometimes `Tails`. The program doesn't change, but the output does!

The `random` method of the Java `Math` class generates a random number x such that $0 \le x < 1$. Roughly half the time x will be less than 0.5. We can therefore *simulate* spinning a coin by printing `Heads` or `Tails` depending on whether the random number is less than 0.5 or not. Try Exercise 2.27.

Here's another example. If you open a savings account at the Random Bank you get an initial (random) free gift of up to $10000. After a year interest is compounded at 12 per cent if your balance is $5000 or more, or at 9 per cent if it is less than $5000:

```
    public class RandBank
    {
        public static void main(String[] args)
        {
            double bal, finBal, rate;
            bal = 10000*Math.random();

            if (bal < 5000)
                rate = 0.09;
            else
                rate = 0.12;

            finBal = bal + rate * bal;
            bal = Math.round(100*bal)/100.0;
            finBal = Math.round(100*finBal)/100.0;

            System.out.println( "Initial balance: " + bal );
            System.out.println( "Rate: " + rate );
```

```
            System.out.println( "Final balance: " + finBal );
      }
}
```

The `if-else` statement

The simplest form of the `if` statement is

```
if (condition)
    statement1 ;
else
    statement2 ;
```

- The `else` clause is optional.
- If *condition* is true, *statement1* is executed; otherwise, if the `else` clause is present, *statement2* is executed.
- Both *statement1* and *statement2* may be groups of statements enclosed in block markers.
- The *condition* is a *boolean* or *logical* expression. The six *relational operators* `==` , `!=` , `<` , `<=` , `>` and `>=` (see Table 2.3) are used to construct logical expressions.

The `if-else-if` statement

The Random Bank now decides to go one better. It offers a random opening balance of up to $15000. Interest of 9 per cent still applies to balances of less than $5000, but balances of over $10000 earn 15 per cent. Interest of 12 per cent applies to balances of $5000 or more but less than $10000.

Replace the `bal` assignment statement and the `if-else` structure in the `RandBank` program with the following:

```
bal = 15000*Math.random();

if (bal < 5000)
     rate = 0.09;
else if (bal < 10000)
     rate = 0.12;
else
     rate = 0.15;
```

Run the new program a few times to verify that the correct interest rates are selected.
   Try Exercise 2.28.

The `if-else-if` ladder

The following layout is recommended for the general `if-else-if` statement:

Table 2.3 Relational operators

Operator	Meaning
<	less than
<=	less than or equal
==	equal
!=	not equal
>	greater than
>=	greater than or equal

```
if (condition1 )
    statement1 ;
else if (condition2 )
    statement2 ;
else if (condition3 )
    statement3 ;
...
...
else
    statement ;
```

This is called the if-else-if *ladder*. Java evaluates the conditions from the top down. When it finds a true condition, it executes the associated statement, and bypasses the rest of the ladder. If none of the conditions are true, it executes the last statement (if there is an else clause).

You need to arrange the logic carefully so that not more than one of the conditions is true.

for *and* if: *counting passes*

You can put an if statement inside a for loop. A lecturer has got tired of marking scripts. Use the following code to write a program for her which generates 1000 random marks in the range 0–99.99 and calculates the pass rate (percentage of students who obtain 50 or more):

```
double mark;        // random mark 0-99.99
double pass = 0;    // number passing
double fail = 0;    // number failing

for (int i = 1; i <= 1000; i++)
{
    mark = 100*Math.random();

    if (mark < 50)
        fail = fail + 1;
    else
        pass = pass + 1;
}
```

Rolling dice

When a fair dice is rolled, the number uppermost is equally likely to be any integer from 1 to 6. So if Math.random() is a random number in the range [0, 1), 6*Math.random() will be in the range [0, 6), and 6*Math.random()+1 will be in the range [1, 7), i.e. between 1 and 6.9999. Discarding the decimal part of this expression with Math.floor() gives an integer in the required range. The next program does the following:

- Generates (and prints) numberOfThrows random integers in the range 1 to 6.
- Counts the number of 'sixes' thrown.
- Estimates (and prints) the probability of throwing a six by dividing the number of sixes thrown by numberOfThrows. Using random numbers like this to mimic a real situation based on chance is called *simulation* (see Chapter 12).

```
import essential.*;
public class Prob6
{
```

```
public static void main(String[ ] args)
{
    int numberOnDice;
    int numberOfThrows;
    int numberOfSixes = 0;
    double probOfSix;

    System.out.print( "How many rolls: " );
    numberOfThrows = Keyboard.readInt();

    for (int i = 1; i <= numberOfThrows; i++)
    {
        numberOnDice = (int) Math.floor(6*Math.random())+1;
        if (numberOnDice == 6)
            numberOfSixes++;
        System.out.print( numberOnDice + " " );
    }

    System.out.println("\n");
    probOfSix = numberOfSixes/ ((double) numberOfThrows);
    System.out.println( probOfSix );
}
}
```

Sample output for 100 throws:

```
1 1 5 5 6 2 5 1 5 1 2 3 1 4 1 2 4 3 4 5 4 6 3 4 4 5 5 5 3 5 2 4 6 1 5 1 4
6 5 3 6 2 3 2 4 3 6 1 2 4 2 3 2 1 6 3 2 2 2 3 4 5 2 3 5 1 2 6 6 3 2 5 3 2
4 1 2 5 2 4 5 1 6 1 3 6 4 2 6 4 3 3 3 6 1 4 2 5 3 6

0.14
```

(you can check that there are 14 sixes if you like!)
Note:

- Although Math.floor returns a 'mathematical integer', it is technically of double type. A type-cast is therefore necessary to coerce it to int type.
- Conversely, when probOfSix is calculated one of the integers on the right must be coerced to double to avoid truncation of the decimal part of the result.
- Each time you run the program you will get slightly different results, which is what you would expect if you rolled a real dice.
- Repeat with some larger values of numberOfThrows. The larger it is, the closer the proportion of sixes gets to the theoretical expected value of 0.1667, i.e. 1/6.
- Can you see why it would be incorrect to use Math.round instead of Math.floor?
  The problem is that Math.round rounds in both directions, whereas Math.floor always rounds down.

Try Exercises 2.29 to 2.33.

Logical operators

Logical expressions can be combined with each other using *logical operators*.
As an example, consider the quadratic equation,

$$ax^2 + bx + c = 0,$$

which has equal real roots, given by $-b/(2a)$, provided that $b^2 - 4ac = 0$ *and a $\neq$ 0*. This translates to the following Java statements:

```
if ((b*b - 4*a*c) == 0 && (a != 0))
    x = -b/(2*a);
```

Note the double equal sign in the test for equality, and also that the compound logical expression must be enclosed in parentheses. The && operator is called the *logical AND*.

More logical operators are shown in Table 2.4, in order of precedence. As usual, parentheses may be used to change the order of precedence. Table 2.5 shows the effects of these operators on the logical expressions *expr1* and *expr2*.

Here is another example:

```
(finalMark >= 60) && (finalMark < 70)      // 2- grade
```

It is a good idea to use parentheses to make the logic clearer, even if they are syntactically unnecessary.

Boolean variables

Java has a primitive data type called *boolean*. Variables of this type can take on the values true or false. You can assign a constant or a logical expression to a boolean variable, e.g.

```
boolean d = true;
...
d = b*b < 4*a*c;
```

You can print the value of a boolean variable (or indeed a boolean expression). For example,

```
System.out.println( 2*2 == 4 );
```

results in the output

```
true
```

Try Exercises 2.34 and 2.35.

Table 2.4 Logical operators

Operator	Precedence	Meaning
!	1	NOT (logical negation)
^	2	exclusive OR
&&	3	AND
||	4	inclusive OR

Table 2.5 Truth table for logical operators (T = true; F = false)

expr1	expr2	!expr1	(expr1 && expr2)	(expr1 || expr2)	(expr1 ^ expr2)
F	F	T	F	F	F
F	T	T	F	T	T
T	F	F	F	T	T
T	T	F	T	T	F

Nested `if`s

In general, `else` belongs to the most recent `if` that does not already have an `else` associated with it. This is sometimes called the *dangling else problem*. You can always use block markers to avoid this, but be careful. The next example illustrates the importance of correctly placed block markers.

Consider once again programming the solution of the familiar quadratic equation, $ax^2 + bx + c = 0$. It is necessary to check whether $a = 0$, to prevent a division by zero:

```
disc = b * b - 4 * a * c;
if (a != 0)
    if (disc < 0)
        System.out.println( "Complex roots" );
    else
    {
        x1 = (-b + sqrt( disc )) / (2 * a);
        x2 = (-b - sqrt( disc )) / (2 * a);
    }
```

Inserting an extra pair of block markers as shown below (`// inserted`), however, makes a division by zero certain if $a = 0$. This error, which we obviously want to avoid, occurs because the `else` is now forced to belong to the first `if`, instead of the second one by default (in spite of the suggestive tabulation):

```
disc = b * b - 4 * a * c;
if (a != 0)
{                           // inserted
    if (disc < 0)
        System.out.println( "Complex roots" );
}                           //  inserted
else
{
    x1 = (-b + sqrt( disc )) / (2 * a);
    x2 = (-b - sqrt( disc )) / (2 * a);
}
```

The `switch` *statement*

An `if-else-if` ladder can become rather unwieldy if you want to test for a number of specific values. An example would be a simple menu selection program. In such cases the `switch-case` statement is more appropriate. Here's an example:

```
int choice;
System.out.println( "Enter your choice (any integer)" );
choice = Keyboard.readInt();
switch (choice)
{
    case 1:
        System.out.println( "Do this" );
        break;
    case 2:
    case 3:
        System.out.println( "Do that" );
        break;
```

```
            default:
                System.out.println( "Do the other" );
    }
```

Note:

- If the user enters 1, the string "Do this" is printed.
  If the user enters 2 or 3, "Do that" is printed.
  If any other integer is entered, "Do the other" is printed.
- The selection must be based on an integer or character (see below) value (choice in this example).
- A break statement is needed in each case to pass control out of the entire switch statement if that case is selected. If break is omitted the subsequent cases are executed.
- There may be more than one case value for a given action.
- The case values do not have to be in any particular order.

2.8 Characters

A variable of the primitive data type char holds a single character. Literal character values (character *constants*) are written between single quote marks:

```
    char c = 'a';
```

Characters are represented in Java by the *Unicode* character set, which is a set of integer values. For example, the (small) letters of the alphabet are represented by the actual integer values 97, 98, ..., 122. A Java character constant is in fact the integer value in the Unicode set representing that character. For example, 'a' represents the integer value of the character a (97).

Try Exercises 2.36 and 2.37.

Escape sequences

A backslash (\) followed by a special character is called an *escape sequence*. Escape sequences can be used to format output to a certain extent.

Common escape sequences are listed in Table 2.6. Escape sequences can be used as individual characters in single quotes, or as characters in a string. For example, the code

```
    System.out.println( "\t1st\t2nd\n" + '\t' + 1 + '\t' + 2 );
```

produces the output

```
    1st 2nd
    1   2
```

Table 2.6 Common escape sequences

Escape sequence	Meaning
\n	move the cursor to the beginning of the next line
\t	move the cursor to the next tab stop
\r	move the cursor to the beginning of the current line without advancing to the next line
\\	print a backslash character
\'	print a single-quote character
\"	print a double-quote character

2.9 Math methods

The standard Java Math class contains a number of methods which are useful in scientific and engineering calculations, such as abs, cos, exp, floor, log, sqrt, etc. These are all used with the class name, e.g. Math.sqrt(2).

Consult the Java documentation for the complete list (see Chapter 3: **Using the Java API**).

Try Exercises 2.38 to 2.40.

2.10 Programming style

Programs that are written any old how, while they may do what is required, can be difficult to follow when read a few months later, in order to correct or update them (and programs that are worth writing will need to be maintained in this way).

Some programmers delight in writing terse and obscure code; there is at least one annual competition for the most incomprehensible C program. A large body of responsible programmers, however, believe it is extremely important to develop the art of writing programs which are well laid out, with all the logic clearly described. Serious programmers therefore pay a fair amount of attention to what is called *programming style*, in order to make their programs clearer and more readable both to themselves, and to other potential users. You may find this irritating, if you are starting to program for the first time, because you will naturally be impatient to get on with the job. But a little extra attention to your program layout will pay enormous dividends in the long run, especially when it comes to debugging (finding and fixing errors).

Some hints on how to improve your programming style are given below.

- You should make liberal use of comments, both at the beginning of a program, to describe briefly what it does and any special methods that may have been used, and also throughout the coding to introduce different logical sections.
- The meaning of each variable should be described briefly in a comment when it is initialized.
- Blank lines should be freely used to separate sections of coding (e.g. before and after loop structures).
- Coding inside structures (e.g. fors and ifs) should be indented (tabulated) a few columns to make them stand out.
- Blanks should be used in expressions to make them more readable, e.g. on either side of operators and equal signs.
  However, blanks may be omitted in places in complicated expressions, where this may make the logic clearer.

Summary

- Identifiers are the symbolic names given to items in a Java program. They are case sensitive. They must start with a letter, an underscore or a dollar.
- A variable is a chunk of memory which has a symbolic name and whose value may be changed.
- All variables must be declared with a type.
  Java has a number of primitive data types, including int and double.
- An expression is a means of evaluating a formula using constants, operators, variables and methods.
- There are a number of different kinds of operators for evaluating expressions, which operate according to rules of precedence.
- The arithmetic operators are +, -, *, / and % (modulus). When an integer is divided by another integer the fractional part of the quotient is truncated. The relational operators <, <=, >, >=, ==

(equals), and != (not equal) compare two operands. The logical operators && (AND), || (OR), and ! (negation) operate on true/false operands.

- The increment ++ and decrement -- operators increase and decrease their operands by 1. The operators may come before (pre) or after (post) their operands.
- There are ten assignment operators: +=, -=, *=, /=, %=, >>=, <<=, &=, |=, and ^=.
- Parentheses may always be used to override the precedence rules.
- Variables may be coerced into a different type by typecasting.
- A for loop repeats a block of statements.
- A group of statements may be enclosed in {block markers}. The group is then treated as a single statement.
- Data may be input from a disk file with the FileIO class of the essential package.
- if-else enables a program to decide between alternatives.
- A boolean variable is true or false.
- The switch statement enables you to make selections based on the value of an integer or character variable.
- Single character constants are enclosed in single quotes.
- Simple principles of programming style should be used to make programs clear and readable.

Exercises

2.1 (a) Run the program CompInt in Section 2.1 as it stands.
   (b) Change the second statement to

```
balance = 2000;
```

   and make sure that you understand what happens when you run the program again.
   (c) Leave out the line

```
balance = balance + interest;
```

   and re-run the program. Can you explain what happens?
   (d) Try to rewrite the program so that the original content of balance is *not* lost. Change the println statement to output the original balance followed by the new balance.

2.2 Convert the following numbers to scientific notation:

$$1.234 \times 10^5, \quad -8.765 \times 10^{-4}, \quad 10^{-15}, \quad -10^{12}.$$

2.3 Decide which of the following constants are not acceptable in Java, and state why not:

(a) 9,87   (b) .0   (c) 25.82   (d) -356231
(e) 3.57*E2   (f) 3.57E2.1   (g) 3.57E+2   (h) 3,57E-2

2.4 State, giving reasons, which of the following are invalid Java identifiers:

(a) a2   (b) a.2   (c) 2a   (d) 'a'one
(e) aone   (f) _x_1   (g) miXedUp   (h) pay day
(i) U.S.S.R.   (j) Pay_Day   (k) min*2   (l) native

2.5 Evaluate the following expressions yourself before checking the answers in a Java program:

```
1 + 2 * 3
2 / 2 * 3
4 / 2 * 2
1+4 / 4
1 + 4 % 2
Math.pow(2*2, 3)
5 % 3 % 2
2 * (1 + 2)/3
1/2e-1
```

2.6 Write some Java statements to evaluate the following expressions and print the answers.

(a) $\dfrac{1}{2 \times 3}$

(b) $2^{2 \times 3}$

(c) $1.5 \times 10^{-4} + 2.5 \times 10^{-2}$

(d) $\sqrt{2}$

(e) $\dfrac{3+4}{5+6}$

(f) the sum of 5 and 3 divided by their product

(g) 2^{3^2}

(h) the square of 2π

(i) $2\pi^2$

(j) $\dfrac{1}{\sqrt{2\pi}}$

(k) $\dfrac{1}{2\sqrt{\pi}}$

(l) the cube root of the product of 2.3 and 4.5

(m) $\dfrac{1 - \frac{2}{3+2}}{1 + \frac{2}{3-2}}$

(n) $1000 \left(1 + \frac{0.15}{12}\right)^{60}$

(o) $(0.0000123 + 5.678 \times 10^{-3}) \times 0.4567 \times 10^{-4}$ (use scientific notation, e.g. 1.23e-5 ...; do *not* use Math.pow)

2.7 Evaluate the following expressions, given that float a = 2, float b = 3, float c = 5, and int i = 2, int j = 3.

```
a * b + c
a * (b + c)
b / c * a
b / (c * a)
a / i / j
```

```
i / j / a
17 / 5
4 / 3 / 4
4 / (3 / 4)
17 % (4 % 3)
```

2.8 Translate the following expressions into Java:

(a) $p + \frac{w}{u}$ (b) $p + \frac{w}{u+v}$ (c) $\frac{p+\frac{w}{u+v}}{p+\frac{w}{u-v}}$ (d) $x^{1/2}$

(e) y^{y+z} (f) x^{y^z} (g) $(x^y)^z$ (h) $x - \frac{x^3}{3!} + \frac{x^5}{5!}$

2.9 Water freezes at 32° and boils at 212° on the Fahrenheit scale. If C and F are Celsius and Fahrenheit temperatures, the formula

$$F = \frac{9C}{5} + 32$$

converts from Celsius to Fahrenheit.
Write a program to convert a temperature of 37° C (normal human temperature) to Fahrenheit (98.6°).

2.10 Engineers often have to convert from one unit of measurement to another; this can be tricky sometimes. You need to think through the process carefully.
For example, convert 5 acres to hectares, given that an acre is 4840 square yards, a yard is 36 inches, an inch is 2.54 cm, and a hectare is 10 000 m². The best approach is to develop a formula to convert x acres to hectares. You can do this as follows.

one square yard = $(36 \times 2.54)^2$ cm²
so one acre   = $4840 \times (36 \times 2.54)^2$ cm²
                  = 0.4047×10^8 cm²
                  = 0.4047 hectares
so x acres   = $0.4047x$ hectares

Once you've got the formula (but not until you've got the formula!), Java can do the rest:

```
x = 5;                   // acres
h = 0.4047 * x;          // hectares
System.out.println( h );
```

Develop formulae for the following conversions, and use some Java statements to find the answers.

(a) Convert 22 yards (an imperial cricket pitch) to metres.
(b) One pound (weight) = 454 grams. Convert 75 kilograms to pounds.
(c) One day in 2001 rates of exchange were: one pound sterling = 12.87 SA rand, and one SA rand = 0.107 US dollars. Convert 100 US dollars to pounds sterling.
(d) Convert 49 metres/second (terminal velocity for a falling person-shaped object) to km/hour.
(e) One atmosphere pressure = 14.7 pounds per square inch (psi) = 101.325 kilo Pascals (kPa). Convert 40 psi to kPa.
(f) One calorie = 4.184 joules. Convert 6.25 kilojoules to calories.

2.11 Translate the following into Java statements:

    (a)   Add 1 to the value of i and store the result in i.
    (b)   Cube i, add j to this, and store the result in i.
    (c)   Divide the sum of a and b by the product of c and d, and store the result in x.

2.12 What's wrong with the following Java statements?

    (a)   `n + 1 = n;`
    (b)   `Fahrenheit temp = 9*C/5 + 32;`
    (c)   `2 = x;`

2.13 Write a program to calculate x, where

$$x = \frac{-b + \sqrt{b^2 - 4ac}}{2a}$$

and $a = 2$, $b = -10$, $c = 12$ (Answer 3.0)

2.14 The steady-state current I flowing in a circuit that contains a resistance $R = 5$, capacitance $C = 10$, and inductance $L = 4$ in series is given by

$$I = \frac{E}{\sqrt{R^2 + \left(2\pi\omega L - \frac{1}{2\pi\omega C}\right)^2}}$$

where $E = 2$ and $\omega = 2$ are the input voltage and angular frequency respectively. Compute the value of I. (Answer: 0.0396)

2.15 There are eight pints in a gallon, and 1.76 pints in a litre. The volume of a tank is given as 2 gallons and 4 pints. Write a program which inputs this volume in gallons and pints and converts it to litres. (Answer: 11.36 litres)

2.16 Write a program to calculate petrol consumption. It should assign the distance travelled (in kilometres) and the amount of petrol used (in litres) and compute the consumption in km/litre as well as in the more usual form of litres per 100 km. Write some helpful headings, so that your output looks something like this:

Distance	Litres used	km/L	L/100km
528	46.23	11.42	8.76

2.17 Write some statements in Java which will *exchange* the contents of two variables a and b, using only one additional variable t.

2.18 Try Exercise 2.17 *without* using any additional variables!

2.19 A mortgage bond (loan) of amount L is obtained to buy a house. The interest rate r is 15 per cent (0.15) p.a. The fixed monthly payment P which will pay off the bond exactly over N years is given by the formula

$$P = \frac{rL\left(1 + \frac{r}{12}\right)^{12N}}{12\left[\left(1 + \frac{r}{12}\right)^{12N} - 1\right]}.$$

    (a)   Write a program to compute and print P if $N = 20$ years, and the bond is for $50 000. You should get $658,39.

(b) It's interesting to see how the payment P changes with the period N over which you pay the loan. Run the program for different values of N (use `Keyboard.readInt`). See if you can find a value of N for which the payment is less than $625.

(c) Now go back to having N fixed at 20 years, and examine the effect of different interest rates. You should see that raising the interest rate by 1 per cent (0.01) increases the monthly payment by about $37.

2.20 It's useful to be able to work out how the period of a bond repayment changes if you increase or decrease your monthly payment P. The formula for the number of years N to repay the loan is given by

$$N = \frac{\ln\left(\frac{P}{P - \frac{rL}{12}}\right)}{12\ln\left(1 + \frac{r}{12}\right)}.$$

(a) Write a new program to compute this formula. Use `Math.log` for the natural logarithm ln. How long will it take to pay off the loan of $50000 at $800 a month if the interest remains at 15 per cent? (Answer: 10.2 years—nearly twice as fast as when paying $658 a month!)

(b) Use your program to find out by trial-and-error the smallest monthly payment that can be made to pay the loan off—this side of eternity. **Hint:** recall that it is not possible to find the logarithm of a negative number, so P must not be less than $rL/12$.

2.21 What are the values of x and a after the following statements have been executed?

```
a = 0;
i = 1;
x = 0;
a = a + i;
x = x + i / a;
a = a + i;
x = x + i / a;
a = a + i;
x = x + i / a;
a = a + i;
x = x + i / a;
```

2.22 Rewrite the statements in Exercise 2.21 more economically by using a `for` loop.

2.23 Work out by hand the output of the following program for n = 4:

```
int n;
double s = 0;
System.out.print( "Number of terms? " );
n = Keyboard.readInt();

for (int k = 1; k <= n; k++)
{
    s = s + 1.0 / (k*k);
}

System.out.println( Math.sqrt(6*s) );
```

If you run this program for larger and larger values of n you will find that the output approaches a well-known limit. Can you figure out what it is?

2.24 Suppose you deposit $50 per month in a bank account every month for a year. Every month, after the deposit has been made, interest at the rate of 1 per cent is added to the balance, e.g. after one month, the balance is $50.50, and after two months it is $101.51.
Write a program to compute and print the balance each month for a year. Arrange the output to look something like this:

```
MONTH             MONTH-END BALANCE

  1                    50.50
  2                   101.51
  3                   153.02
 ...
 12                   640.47
```

2.25 If you invest $1000 for one year at an interest rate of 12 per cent, the return is $1120 at the end of the year. But if interest is compounded at the rate of 1 per cent *monthly* (i.e. 1/12 of the annual rate), you get slightly more interest because it is compounded. Write a program which uses a for loop to compute the balance after a year of compounding interest in this way. The answer should be $1126.83. Evaluate the formula for this result separately as a check: 1000×1.01^{12}.

2.26 Ten students in a class write a test. The marks are out of 10. All the marks are entered in a text file marks.txt. Write a program to compute and display the average mark. Try it on the following marks:

```
    5   8   0   10   3   8   5   7   9   4    (Answer: 5.9)
```

2.27 Change the program SpinCoin in Section 2.7 so that Heads is twice as likely as Tails in the long run.

2.28 Change the program RandBank in Section 2.7 to generate random balances of up to $20000 and introduce a fourth interest of 20 percent for balances between $15000 and $20000.

2.29 Work through the following program by hand. Draw up a table of the values of i, j and m to show how their values change while the program executes. Check your answers by running the program.

```
int m;
int i = 1;

for (int j = 3; j <= 5; j++)
{
    i++;
    if (i == 3)
    {
        i += 2;
        m = i + j;
    }
}
```

2.30 The electricity accounts of residents in a very small town are calculated as follows:
  • if 500 units or less are used the cost is 2 cents per unit;
  • if more than 500, but not more than 1000 units are used, the cost is $10 for the first 500 units, and then 5 cents for every unit in excess of 500;

- if more than 1000 units are used, the cost is $35 for the first 1000 units plus 10 cents for every unit in excess of 1000;
- in addition, a basic service fee of $5 is charged, no matter how much electricity is used.

Write a program which reads any five consumptions from a text file, and uses a `for` loop to calculate and display the total charge for each one. For example, if the data in the file is 200 500 700 1000 1500, the answers will be $9, $15, $25, $40, $90.

2.31 Income tax is usually calculated on the basis of the following sort of table:

Taxable income	Tax payable
$10000 or less	10 per cent of taxable income
between $10000 and $20000	$1000 + 20 per cent of amount by which taxable income exceeds $10000
between $20000 and $40000	$3000 + 30 per cent of amount by which taxable income exceeds $20000
more than $40000	$9000 + 50 per cent of amount by which taxable income exceeds $40000

For example, the tax payable on a taxable income (i.e. after deductions) of $30 000 is $3000 + 30% of ($30 000 − $20 000), i.e. $6000.

Write a program which reads the following list of taxable incomes (dollars) from a text file and displays them with the tax payable in each case: 5000, 10 000, 15 000, 22 000, 30 000, 38 000 and 50 000.

2.32 A plumber opens a savings account with $100 000 at the beginning of January. He then makes a deposit of $1000 at the end of each month for the next 12 months (starting at the end of January). Interest is calculated and added to his account at the end of each month (before the $1000 deposit is made). The monthly interest rate depends on the amount A in his account at the time when interest is calculated, in the following way:

$$
\begin{aligned}
A &\le 110000: \quad 1 \text{ per cent} \\
110000 < A &\le 125000: \quad 1.5 \text{ per cent} \\
A &> 125000: \quad 2 \text{ per cent}
\end{aligned}
$$

Write a program which displays, for each of the 12 months, under suitable headings, the situation at the end of the month as follows: the number of the month, the interest rate, the amount of interest and the new balance. (Answer: values in the last row of output should be 12, 0.02, 2534.58, 130263.78).

2.33 Section 2.6 has a program for computing the members of the sequence

$$
x_n = \frac{a^n}{n!}.
$$

The program displays every member x_n computed. Adjust it to display only every 10th value of x_n.

Hint: the expression `n%10` (where n is `int`) will be zero only when n is an exact multiple of 10. Use this in an `if` statement to display every tenth value of x_n.

2.34 Determine whether the following logical expressions are true or false and check your answers by printing them:

```
3 > 2
2 > 3
-4 <= -3
```

```
1 < 1
2 != 2 || 3 == 3
```

2.35 Write a program to input values for a, b and c and to print the values of the two logical expressions

```
(a != 0) || (b != 0) || (c != 0)
```

and

```
!((a == 0) && (b == 0) && (c == 0))
```

These two expressions are logically equivalent, and are false only when $a = b = c = 0$. Verify this assertion by running your program with different values of a, b and c.

2.36 (a)   See if you can use a `for` loop to print all the letters of the alphabet.
Hint: use the skeleton
```
for (char c = 'a'; ... )
    ...
```
(b)   Now print the alphabet backwards.

2.37 It's quite fun to generate random (small) letters to see what is the longest real word in any language that occurs in a sample of such letters. See if you can write some code to generate, say, 20 lines each of 60 random letters.
Hints:

- You will need to transform `Math.random` with something like

```
n + (Math.random() * m)
```

where n and m are integers chosen cunningly to make the result fall in the range 97 ... 122.
- You will also have to use the cast operator `(char)` to cast the result as a `char` for printing.

2.38 Translate the following formulae into Java expressions:

(a) $\ln(x + x^2 + a^2)$
(b) $[e^{3t} + t^2 \sin(4t)] \cos^2(3t)$
(c) $4 \tan^{-1}(1)$ (inverse tangent)
(d) $\sec^2(x) + \cot(y)$
(e) $\cot^{-1}(x/a)$

2.39 There are 39.37 inches in a metre, 12 inches in a foot, and three feet in a yard. Write a program to input a length in metres (which may have a decimal part) and convert it to yards, feet and inches. (Check: 3.51 metres converts to 3 yds 2 ft 6.19 in.)

2.40 To convert the variable `mins` minutes into hours and minutes you would use `Math.floor(mins/60)` to find the whole number of hours, and `mins%60` to find the number of minutes left over. Write a program which inputs a number of minutes and converts it to hours and minutes.
Now write a program to convert seconds into hours, minutes and seconds. Try out your program on 10000 seconds, which should convert to 2 hours 46 minutes and 40 seconds.

3

Solving a problem in Java

Objectives

By the end of this chapter, you should be able to do the following:

- understand the role of the class provider, class user and end user;
- use classes, by creating objects and calling methods;
- understand how primitives and objects are stored in memory and be able to trace a program;
- write a simple class to be used by others;
- decide when it is appropriate to use `static` methods in classes;
- find help in the Java API.

3.1 Introduction

Up till now you have been writing all your code in a main method. As programs become more complicated, this will become unwieldy. We need a better way of structuring our code, and a good way is to use an *object-oriented* approach. There are a number of reasons for structuring our code better:

- When problems become more complicated, it is easier to tackle the problem by breaking it up into bite-sized chunks and solving it in parts, rather than trying to solve the whole problem all at once.
- Code that is structured logically is easier to read and understand, not only for ourselves, but for other programmers as well.

In particular, when we structure our code in an object-oriented way, there are further benefits:

- Thinking in objects (rather than processes) is often a more natural way of thinking of a problem. We recognize that if you have learnt to program in a procedural language, thinking in objects may seem unnatural at first. We hope that, as you work through this book, you will come to see the benefits of solving a problem using an object-oriented approach.
- The data and the processes (methods) that operate on that data are grouped together into a logical unit called an object (we say that an object *encapsulates* both the data and the methods of an object). Such an object is a well-contained unit, which can very easily be re-used as a component, by other programmers, without them needing to know the details of how it was implemented.
- We can use inheritance. This is a powerful concept which will be explained in Section 2.

3.2 The class provider, class user and end user

While you write programs, you will be acting in different roles (see Table 3.1). Up till now, you have acted in the role of the class user and end user. This chapter will show you how to also play the role of the class provider.

For example, a programmer called Andy wrote the Graph class. While Andy was writing the Graph class, he was acting in the role of the class provider. In Section 1.6, we wrote a program which used the Graph class. At that point, we were acting in the role of the class user. When we ran the program and viewed the output (the graph window), we were acting in the role of the end user. In this way, as a programmer we will be switching roles (imagine it as putting on different hats) as we are writing programs.

3.3 What are objects and classes?

When we declare a variable, we must specify the type. For example:

```
int x;        // the variable x is of type integer
Turtle fred;  // the variable fred is of type Turtle
```

A type is either a primitive data type (such as int, char, or float), or a class (such as Turtle, or Graph). Notice that primitive data types start with a lowercase letter, whereas classes start with an uppercase letter. When we declare a variable of a class, we call it an *object*. In the examples above, fred is an object, whereas x is a primitive data variable (x is not an object). Objects differ from primitive variables in two main ways:

1. Whereas a primitive data variable only contains data, an object contains both data and methods (i.e. it can *do* things). In the examples above, fred can *do* things: go forward or turn right, etc, unlike the primitive variable x which does not have methods.
2. Objects are stored in memory in a different way to primitive variables.

These concepts will be explained further in the next few sections.

Table 3.1 Different roles played by programmers when writing programs

Class Provider 	The class provider is the programmer who writes classes to be used by other programmers. Sometimes you will need to put on your class provider hat, and write generic code which can be used by other programmers (including yourself).
Class User 	The class user is also a programmer. When you are performing the role of a class user, you will be using classes written by class providers. Sometimes you will first play the role of the class provider, then play the role of the class user in order to test that your class works, as it should.
End User	The end user is not a programmer, but rather somebody who is using the final program. The role of the end user is to interact with the program through the user interface. The end user therefore does not see the source code of the program, but only the final product. We draw the end user hat as a crown to emphasise the importance of the end user. All programmers should concentrate on writing programs which meet the end user's needs. Sometimes you will need to put on an end user hat to test your program from an end user's perspective.

Looking at the Turtle *class in more depth*

In the previous two chapters, we used classes which were written by other programmers. We did not need to see the Java source code of these classes to know how to use them. All we needed to know was which methods we could use. This list of methods is called the *interface* to the class. Take the Turtle class for example: we were able to use this class without seeing the Java source code. The inner workings of the class are hidden — we only need to know what methods are available to use the class (see Figure 3.1).

We will now look at the inner workings of the Turtle class. A single Turtle object is made up of the following variables (see Figure 3.2):

- The xCoordinate and yCoordinate store the current position of the Turtle object in the display window. Both values start off as 0 (the origin of the window). These values change as the turtle moves.
- The angle stores the current direction in which the turtle is facing. This value also starts off as 0, and changes in response to the right and left methods. (The angle variable also changes in response to the home method.)

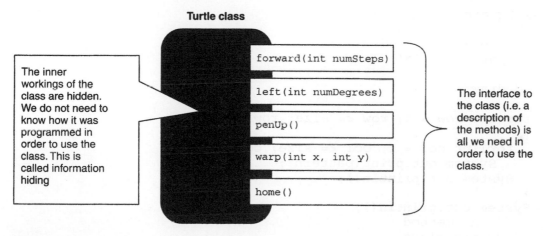

Figure 3.1 The Turtle class as a black box, showing some of the methods. As a class user, we only need to know the interface to use the class

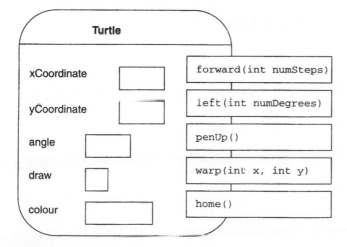

Figure 3.2 The data members of the Turtle class

- The draw variable is a boolean and stores whether the Turtle object should draw as it moves or not. This value starts off as true, and changes to false in response to the penUp method.
- The last variable is the colour variable which stores the colour in which the Turtle object draws.

In this way, the Turtle class contains both variables (called *data members*) and actions which affect these variables (called *methods*). The variables stored inside a class are called by many different names. We will usually refer to them as *data members*, but they are also known as *data attributes* or *fields*.

3.4 Writing and using a simple class

We will now show you a simple example of a class and step you through the process of compiling and using a class. Note: we are not talking about a class which contains the main method (as we have been writing until now). Here we are writing a class which can be used by a main method in a different class.

1. Type the following Java code into a file called Square.java:

```
class Square
{
  int size = 2;
  char pattern = '*';

  void draw()
  {
    for(int row = 1; row <= size; row++)
    {
      for(int col = 1; col <= size; col++)
        System.out.print(pattern);
      System.out.println();
    }
    System.out.println();
  } // draw method
} // Square class
```

2. Compile this file, but do not run it. (If you try to run it, it will generate an error, since there is no main method).
3. Type the following code into a file called UseSquare.java:

```
public class UseSquare
{
  public static void main (String[] args)
  {
    Square s1 = new Square();
    s1.draw();
    s1.size = 5;
    s1.draw();
    s1.pattern = '&';
    s1.draw();
  } // main method
} // UseSquare class
```

4. Compile and run the UseSquare class. You should see output as shown in Figure 3.3.

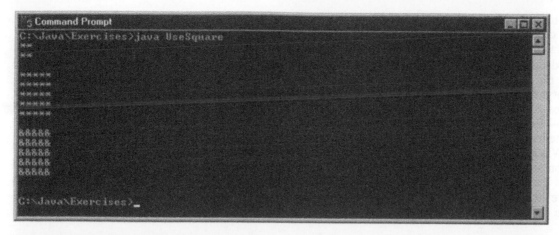

Figure 3.3 Output from running UseSquare.java

We will now explain the details of what we have done. The Square class defines a *template* for Square objects. What this means is that it is a description of what objects will look like and how they will behave. The first two lines of code are:

```
int size = 2;
char pattern = '*';
```

This is how we define the data members of a class. By declaring these attributes, we are defining a new type called Square, which is a structure containing two primitive data variables: an integer and a character.

The class is more than a just a structure, however, since it also contains a method, which draws a square. The appearance of the square will depend on the current values of the size and pattern data members.

In the main method of UseSquare, the first statement creates a Square object called s1. At this point s1 is made up of both size(which has a value of 2) and pattern (which has a value of '*'). The second statement calls the draw method (in object-oriented terminology, we say it *invokes* the method). This effectively results in a jump to the first line of the draw method, which is a for loop (methods will be discussed in more detail in Section 3.7). Once all the statements in the draw method have been executed, the program jumps back to the main method and executes the next statement, which is:

```
s1.size = 5;
```

This statement changes the value of the size variable of the object. When the draw method is called for a second time, the size variable is 5, so it draws a bigger square shape. In the same way, the pattern attribute is changed and the draw method is called for a third time to draw a square of ampersands.

Now do Exercises 3.1 to 3.4 at the end of the chapter.

3.5 How memory works

It is important to understand how memory works, because primitive data variables and objects behave differently, depending on the way they are stored.

What is memory?

Memory is part of the hardware of your computer and is used for storing data. There are two main stores of data inside your computer: *memory* and *disk storage*.

Disk storage is the hard drive of your computer: a circular disk which spins around when you switch on your computer. The important thing about disk storage, is that it is *persistent*, which means that anything that you save onto your disk is still there when you turn off your computer. Files are stored on your hard drive. The size of hard drives is currently measured in gigabytes (approximately 10^9 bytes) for most PC's.

Memory, on the other hand, is usually measured in megabytes. When somebody asks you "How many megs does your computer have?", they are referring to the capacity of the memory (more correctly known as RAM—Random Access Memory). Memory is temporary storage. It disappears when your computer is switched off. Have you ever had the experience of working on your computer when the electricity failed? When the power came back on, did you find that you had lost some of the work you were doing? When you are using a program, like a word processor, your document is being stored in memory. When you push the save button, it is written to disk and so is safe from a power cut. Luckily, many programs now have regular automatic backup facilities. You can think of memory as a large table of boxes which can store data (a bit like a spreadsheet) where each box has an address for referencing its position.

How objects and primitives are stored in memory

When we declare a primitive data variable, a small amount of memory is set aside for that variable. The amount of memory which is set aside is dependent on the type of the variable. Only a single bit is needed to store a `boolean` variable (1 represents `true` and 0 represents `false`), whereas 32 bits are needed to store an `int`. When an object is created, memory is allocated for all data members in the class. For example, when a `Square` object is created, memory is allocated for both an integer (for the `size` attribute) and a character (for the `pattern` attribute). Consider the following program:

```
public class Memory
{
    public static void main(String[] args)
    {
        int x = 25;
        Square s1 = new Square();
        s1.size = 5;
        Square s2;
        s2 = new Square();
        s2.pattern = '$';
    }
}
```

A graphical representation of how the memory is allocated and the values change is shown in Figure 3.4.

In the first statement, a primitive data variable is declared and initialized. In the second statement, a `Square` object is created. The variable `s1` is a reference to the whole object (not just a single value). We call such a reference a *handle*. To access the `size` attribute of the object, we have to precede it with the handle name and a dot.

In the fourth statement, `s2` is declared, but not created. This means that the handle has been created, but there is no object in memory yet. If at this point, we try to access the `size` or `pattern` attribute of `s2`, an error will be generated, because the data members do not exist yet. In the next statement, the object is created with the `new` keyword and the `size` and `pattern` data members take on the default values specified in the class. After the object has been created properly, the data members can be accessed (as in the last statement), and the value of the `pattern` attribute is changed.

The `null` keyword

When we declare a handle to an object and we have not yet created the object, the handle does not reference or point to any object. Such a reference is known as a *null reference*. You can use the keyword `null` to refer to the value inside a null reference. For example:

Statement	Memory after statement is executed
`x = 25;`	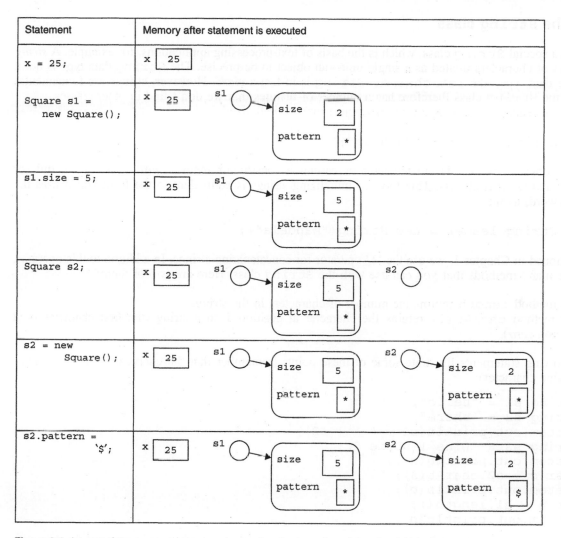
`Square s1 = new Square();`	
`s1.size = 5;`	
`Square s2;`	
`s2 = new Square();`	
`s2.pattern = '$';`	

Figure 3.4 A trace of the program `Memory.java`, showing how the values of variables change in memory

```
Turtle t;
...
if (t == null)
  System.out.println("t is null");
clse
  t.forward(50);
```

You can also explicitly assign a handle to `null`, for example:

```
String s = "hello";
...
s = null;
```

Now do Exercise 3.5.

3.6 The String class

Java has a special String class, which is the basis of text-processing applications, for example. A *string* is a series of characters treated as a single unit—an object to be precise. The String data type is not a primitive data type, like int, char, etc. String is in fact a *class*. However, strings are fundamental to Java; the String class therefore has a number of features that we don't find in other classes.

One such feature is the way a String object may be initialized:

```
String leader = "Mandela";
```

Here the object leader is created *without* calling a constructor method with new, as we did for Turtle and Graph objects. This form of initializing strings is equivalent to the form which uses the new keyword, as in:

```
String leader = new String("Mandela");
```

As mentioned in Chapter 1, we use the '+' operator for concatenating strings. In addition to this operator, there are many methods that you can use with the String class. Here are two of them:

- The method length returns the number of characters in the string.
- The method charAt(i) returns the character at position i in a string (the first character is at position *zero*).

The following statements illustrate some of these points (remember that the character '\n' represents the newline character):

```
String s1 = "hello";
String s2 = "there";
System.out.println(s1 + ' ' + s2);
String s3 = "Line 1\nLine 2";
System.out.println(s3);
char c = s2.charAt(3);
System.out.println(c);
int n = s1.length();
System.out.println(n);
```

A representation of the state of the variables in memory at the end of these statements is shown in Figure 3.5, and the output from these statements is:

```
hello there
Line 1
Line 2
r
5
```

Do you understand why?

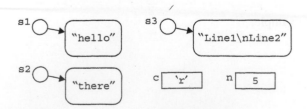

Figure 3.5 The state of the variables in memory

Equality testing of strings

In Section 2.7 you learnt about the `==` operator, for testing whether two primitives have the same value. What do you expect the output to be of the following statements?

```
int x1 = 5;
int x2 = 5;
String s1 = new String("cat");
String s2 = new String("cat");
System.out.println(x1 == x2);
System.out.println(s1 == s2);
```

Although the output of the first `println` is `true`, the result of the second `println` is `false`. The reason for this is that when you say: `s1 == s2`, you are comparing the values of the *handles*, not the insides of the objects. Handles are almost like primitives, except that they contain references to objects rather than the usual primitive values. Although we draw handles as arrows pointing to objects, they are really just integers, which are the addresses of objects. So, when we compare the handle `s1` to the handle `s2`, we are comparing the values of the addresses stored inside them, not the actual strings. Even though the two strings are the same, they are two different objects with different addresses. The handles are therefore not equal.

If you want to test for equality of strings, you have to use the `equals` method found in the `String` class. To get the correct answer (`true`) above, we would have to change the statement to:

```
System.out.println(s1.equals(s2));
```

Note that `equals` is case-sensitive, so the statement:

```
"hello".equals("Hello");
```

would evaluate to `false`. To compare two strings ignoring case, use the `equalsIgnoreCase` method. Now do Exercises 3.6 to 3.8.

3.7 Understanding methods

In this section we will explain the terminology of methods as you have been using them until now. In the next section we will show you how to write methods.

A method is a block of Java statements inside a class, which has a name and performs an action (or actions). We can identify methods by the parentheses (round brackets) which appear after the method name, for example:

```
b.setTitle("Amazon");        // setTitle is a method
```

From the class user's perspective, a method of a class can be described in terms of:

1. The name of the method.
2. The data in: this is the external data (if any) required by the method to do its job.
3. The data out: this is the answer (if any) produced by the method.
4. The side effect: this is anything that the method does which results in some kind of change. Examples of side effects are: any screen output, or changes in the state of the object caused by the method.

The examples in Table 3.2 illustrate these four properties (there are other properties, such as `static`, which will be described later).

Method arguments

When we refer to the individual elements of the 'data in', we call them *arguments*. In Table 3.2, some methods have no arguments. This means that the method can do its job without needing any data from

Table 3.2 Examples of method calls and their properties (t and g refer to existing `Turtle` and `Graph` objects respectively).

Example statements	Method name	Data in	Data out	Side effect
`double x = Math.sqrt(7)`	`sqrt`	7 (the number to be squared)	2.6457 ... (a double, the square root of the data in)	None
`t.forward(50)`	`forward`	50	None	The state of t changes and consequently the output on the screen changes
`t.penUp()`	`penUp`	None	None	The state of t changes
`int y = Keyboard.readInt()`	`readInt`	None	An int (whatever the user types in)	Keystrokes are read in from the keyboard
`System.out.print(5)`	`print`	The number 5	None	5 is printed on the screen
`double r = Math.random()`	`random`	None	A random number between 0 and 1	None
`t.warp(50,50)`	`warp`	50 and 50 (indicating new location for t)	None	The state of t changes and the output on the screen changes
`g.addPoint(5,-4)`	`addPoint`	5 and -4 (coordinates of point to be added to g)	None	The state of g changes to include an additional point

the class user. One example is the `Turtle penUp()` method: the `Turtle` object itself can change its `draw` attribute to `false`. The `forward` method, on the other hand, takes one argument and the `warp` method takes two arguments. Both these latter methods are not able to do the job, unless you supply them with the required arguments.

Return types

The 'data out' of a method is called the *return value*. This value has a type associated with it. For example, the `Math.sqrt` method has a return type of `double`. In contrast, the `Keyboard.readInt()` method has an `int` return type. When a method has no return type, we say its type is `void`, meaning 'nothing'.

Signature of a method

Every method has what is called a *signature*. The signature is a way of identifying a method. Since it is common to have multiple methods with the same name in a single class, the name alone is not sufficient for identifying a method. The signature of a method is therefore a combination of the name and the number and type of arguments. A class may not declare two methods with the same signature, or a compile-time error occurs. When two methods (with different signatures) in a class have the same name, we call it *overloading* (we will see examples of this in Section 3.8). In Chapter 7, we use a different concept called *overriding*, where two methods in related classes have the *same* signatures.

Constructors

Constructors are special methods that have the purpose of *creating* objects and *initializing* the data members. Constructors always have the same name as the class. Calls to constructors are preceded by the new keyword. The following statements are examples of calls to constructors:

```
Turtle t = new Turtle();
Graph g = new Graph();
String s = new String("hello");
```

Classes can have multiple constructors. When there are no arguments in a constructor, we call it the *default constructor*. When there are arguments in a constructor, we call it a *parameterized constructor*.

The Turtle class has a parameterized constructor which you can use instead of the default constructor. This constructor takes one argument: the colour that the Turtle object should use when drawing. The Java colours are defined in the package java.awt, so to use this constructor, you have to import the package. Here is a sample program that uses both the default and parameterized constructors of the Turtle class (note the American spelling of colour).

```
/* This program draws 4 spirals in different colours */
import essential.*;
import java.awt.*;   // for using Java colours

public class Spirals
{
  public static void main(String[] args)
  {
    Turtle black = new Turtle();
    Turtle blue = new Turtle(Color.blue);
    Turtle red = new Turtle(Color.red);
    Turtle green = new Turtle(Color.green);

    black.right(45); //turn away from centre by 45 degrees
    blue.right(135);
    red.right(225);
    green.right(315);

    // draw spirals
    for(int i = 1; i <= 48; i++)
    {
      black.forward(6-i/8);
      blue.forward(6-i/8);
      red.forward(6-i/8);
      green.forward(6-i/8);
      black.left(10);
      blue.left(10);
      red.left(10);
      green.left(10);
    }
  }
}
```

Now do Exercise 3.9.

More on the import *statement*

A *package* is a group of classes in the same directory. For example, say your friend Jack gave you a package, called jack of classes that he wrote. Figure 3.6 shows the directory structure of his classes.

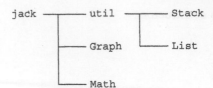

Figure 3.6 Directory structure of Jack's classes

There are four classes:

- `Graph` and `Math` are stored in directory `jack`.
- `Stack` and `List` are stored in directory `jack\util`.

In your program, you could import individual classes or whole directories of classes, as the following examples show:

- `import jack.*;`   `// imports only Graph and Math`
- `import jack.Graph;`   `// imports only Graph`
- `import jack.util.*;`   `// imports only Stack and List`
- `import jack.util.List;`   `// imports only List`

Note the use of the dot operator to refer to subdirectories. Also note the *wildcard* `'*'`, which matches all classes in a given directory, but *not* any classes in subdirectories.

Packages are usually zipped into `.jar` files (see Section 3.16), so the original directory structure is hidden inside the file.

3.8 Example: simulating a rabbit colony

We would like to write a program which models how a rabbit colony grows over time. We start with a single male-female pair of baby rabbits. It takes two months for a baby to become an adult. At the beginning of the month in which the pair reaches adulthood, they produce a pair of male-female baby rabbits. They continue producing a single male-female pair of babies every month after that.

Data members of `RabbitColony`

Putting on the class provider hat, we start by deciding what data members are needed to describe a rabbit colony. We will need three variables: one variable for storing the number of pairs of baby rabbits, one for storing the number of pairs of rabbits that are 1 month old, and a third variable for storing the number of pairs of adult rabbits. The beginning of our class would therefore look something like this:

```
class RabbitColony
{
   int babies = 1; /* number of pairs of baby rabbits
                                   (starting with 1) */
   int young = 0;  /* number of pairs of 1-month old rabbits */
   int adults = 0; /* number of pairs of adult rabbits */
}
```

Methods of `RabbitColony`

We next decide what methods we need in our class, i.e. what would the class user want to do with a rabbit colony? We decided on the following methods:

- a method which grows the colony for 1 month,
- a method which grows the colony for any number of months, and
- a method which returns the total number of rabbits in the colony.

This is the outline of the class with empty methods:

```
class RabbitColony
{
    int babies = 1; /* number of pairs of baby rabbits
                                         (starting with 1) */
    int young = 0;  /* number of pairs of 1-month old rabbits */
    int adults = 0; /* number of pairs of adult rabbits */

    // grow the rabbit colony by one month:
    void grow()
    {
    }

    // grow the rabbit colony by n months:
    void grow(int n)
    {
    }

    // calculate the total number of rabbits and return the value
    int getNumRabbits()
    {
    }
}
```

The first grow method takes no arguments and returns nothing. It will simply change the state of the object (i.e. increase the variables in the class). The second grow method takes an integer as an argument (the number of months to grow the colony). It also returns nothing, since it just updates the variables. The getNumRabbits takes no arguments, but returns an integer.

Using the RabbitColony class

Before we write the code inside the methods, we will take off the *class provider* hat and put on the *class user* hat to see how this class could be used. This is an approach often used by programmers: to imagine how your class will be used before you have finished writing it. It helps to ensure that the methods you have chosen make sense. Here is a sample program that uses the RabbitColony class:

```
public class UseRabbitColony
{
    public static void main(String[] args)
    {
        RabbitColony rc = new RabbitColony();
        rc.grow(6);         // grow rabbit colony for 6 months
        int num = rc.getNumRabbits();
        System.out.println("Number of rabbits after 6 months = " + num);
    }
}
```

We will run this later, when we have finished writing the class. Note that we have used the default constructor for creating the RabbitColony object. Although we have to provide code for all methods in the class, the default constructor is an exception, since it is automatically defined if we do not write our own constructor. In Section 3.10, we will write our own constructor.

Now that we have a better idea of how the class can be used, we can go ahead and write the methods.

Defining the `grow()` method

In the grow method, we have to simulate how the number of babies, young and adults increase in one month. We have to convert the following facts into Java code:

- all the current young rabbits become adults;
- all the current babies become young;
- all the adult pairs (including the new ones) each produce a single baby pair.

Here is the Java code corresponding to the statements above:

```
// grow the rabbit colony by one month:
void grow()
{
    adults += young;   // all the young become adults
    young = babies;    // all the current babies become young
    babies = adults;   // all adult pairs produce a baby pair
}
```

Note that the *order* of these statements is significant. Can you see why? Do Exercise 3.10.

Defining the `grow(int n)` method

The parameterized `grow` method must grow the colony for any number of months. The first thing to notice is the variable n. In the argument list of the method definition we have to indicate the type of the argument (in this case an `int`). We also have to specify a name for the argument, so that we can refer to it inside the method. We have chosen to call it n, but could have chosen any other suitable name. In the `main` method, where we used the `RabbitColony` class, we grew the colony for 6 months (`rc.grow(6)`), but we could have used any number as an argument. We call the number 6 an *actual parameter*. In the method definition, we call the variable n a *formal parameter*.

Inside the method, all we do is call the `grow()` method n times. Here is the code:

```
// grow the rabbit colony for n months
void grow(int n)
{
    for(int i=1; i<=n; i++)
        grow();
}
```

Notice that we don't need to precede the method call with the object name in this case, because we are inside the class.

Defining the `getNumRabbits()` method

The `getNumRabbits` method must calculate the total number of rabbits and return the answer. Here is the code:

```
// calculate the total number of rabbits and return the value
int getNumRabbits()
{
    int num = 2*(babies + young + adults);
    return num;
}
```

The first statement calculates the total number of rabbits, by adding the pairs and then multiplying by two. This is stored in a variable called num. The Java keyword for producing an answer from a method is `return`. In this way the method returns the value stored inside num.

Tracing `UseRabbitColony`

We will now explain how `UseRabbitColony` works, by tracing through the program. The first statement is:

```
RabbitColony rc = new RabbitColony();
```

It creates the object in memory with the default values, as illustrated in Figure 3.7.
The second statement is:

```
rc.grow(6);
```

It results in a jump to the second `grow` method. Note: Java knows to use the second `grow` method and not the first one, because we have given it an argument. In the method, n will take on the value of 6 (only for the duration of this method call). The body of the loop will therefore execute 6 times. Each time, the program jumps to the other `grow` method to execute the three statements there. Table 3.3 shows how the variables change on each loop iteration. See if you can work them out for yourself.
The third statement of the program is:

```
int numR = rc.getNumRabbits();
```

Java will first evaluate the right hand side. To do so, it has to jump to the `getNumRabbits` method. At this stage, `babies` contains 5, `young` contains 3 and `adults` contains 5. These values are totalled and multiplied by 2 to produce an answer of 26, which is returned to the calling statement and stored in numR. Finally, this value is printed out.
Now do Exercises 3.11 to 3.13.

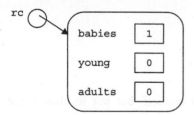

Figure 3.7 A `RabbitColony` object with default values

Table 3.3 Variable trace of
`rc.grow(6)`

i	babies	young	adults
1	0	1	0
2	1	0	1
3	1	1	1
4	2	1	2
5	3	2	3
6	5	3	5

3.9 Access modifiers

One of the features of object-oriented programming is that the data inside an object can be hidden from the class user. The only way the class user can then access or change the attributes of an object is through the methods. For example, in the Turtle class, you cannot change the xCoordinate and yCoordinate directly, but only through the methods: forward, backward, warp and home. One of the reasons for this is that it can prevent you, the class user, from setting the variables to senseless values. For example, in the following statements, the Turtle object would go out of the drawing area:

```
Turtle t = new Turtle();
t.right(45);
t.forward(500);
```

If you executed these statements, you would notice that the turtle would not move (although it would turn right). In this way, the methods of the Turtle object can control the way the class user changes the variables. If you were able to change the xCoordinate and yCoordinate directly, then this could not have been prevented.

The public and private keywords

When we are defining classes, we need some way of indicating which elements of the class should be hidden from direct access by the class user, and which elements can be accessed freely by the class user. The keyword private, when written in front of either a data member declaration or a method definition, indicates that the element should be hidden from the class user. The keyword public, on the other hand, indicates that the element can be accessed directly by the class user.

In the Turtle class for example, the xCoordinate is declared as private, whereas the forward method is declared as public. The class looks something like this:

```
public class Turtle
{
    ...
    private double xCoordinate;
    ...
    public void forward(double distance)
    {
        ...
    }
    ...
}
```

It is possible, therefore, with a Turtle object t, to call the forward method, but not to change the xCoordinate value directly:

```
t.forward(100);      // OK
t.xCoordinate = 50;  // WRONG!
```

In our RabbitColony class, the data members should be declared as private and the methods as public. This is because we would not want the class user to change the number of rabbits directly, since we are simulating the growth in a particular way.

Other access modifiers

There are two other access modifiers, namely, and protected and, if left unspecified, package. Table 3.4 lists the four access modifiers in decreasing levels of strictness. Table 3.4 refers to a *package*, which is basically a group of classes which have been declared as being in the same package (see Section 3.16, where we show you how to write your own package). If your class is not specified as

Table 3.4 Access modifier keywords with associated visibility

`private`	only visible within the class itself
`package`	visible within the class itself and other classes in the same package
`protected`	visible within the class itself, other classes in the same package and subclasses outside the package
`public`	visible from anywhere

being in a particular package (as is the case with all classes that we have written until now), it ends up in the *default* package, which is a package that has no name. The keyword `package` is never actually typed as an access modifier, it is merely a level of access defined when no access modifier is specified. Subclasses have to do with inheritance and will be discussed in Chapter 7.

3.10   Example: simulating the growth of trees

We want to write a program which simulates the growth of trees. The aim is to model the growth of different trees over time. We would like to see how tall a tree grows, given a particular growth rate. As before, our approach to solving this problem will be the following:

1. Decide on data members.
2. Decide on methods.
3. Write a `main` method to test how the class can be used.
4. Write the methods.
5. Test the class by running the `main` method.

Data members for the `Tree` class

For each `Tree` object, we will need to store the height of the tree, as well as the growth rate. We will conform to standard measurement units and store the height in metres and the growth rate in cm/year. Here is the beginning of our class:

```
public class Tree
{
    /* This class simulates the growth of a tree,
     * given an initial height and a growth rate.
     */
    private float height; // height of tree in metres
    private float rate;    // growth rate in cm/year
```

Notice that we have specified our data members as `private`, because we do not want the class user to change these values directly.

Methods of the `Tree` class

Our `Tree` class should be able to simulate growing, so we should have a method for doing this. As with the `RabbitColony` class, we will define two `grow` methods, one for growing a tree for one year and the other for growing the tree for any number of years. The class user will need to find out how tall a tree is after growing for a number of years, so we need to provide a method for returning the height. We will call this method `getHeight`. It is standard practice in Java for methods that return values of data members, to be named starting with the word `get`. In contrast, methods that change the values of data members directly, are named starting with the word `set`. These `get` and `set` methods are known as *mutator* methods.

The class user needs some way of setting the initial height and growth rate of a tree. This could be done with `set` methods, but since the values will only be set once (when a `Tree` object is created), we will rather let the class user set the values through a constructor. Constructors differ from other methods in various ways. Since constructors have the same name as the class, they start with a capital letter (assuming that you have conformed to the Java convention of naming your class starting with a capital letter). Another difference is that return types are not specified for constructors.

We will therefore be writing four methods:

- `public Tree(float h, float r)` // parameterized constructor // for setting the height and growth rate
- `public void grow()`
- `public void grow(int n)`
- `public float getHeight()`

After writing a `main` method, we will provide the code inside these methods.

A `main` *method to test the class*

To test our class, we want to write a program that creates three different trees. All three trees start at the same height (0.1 m), but have different growth rates. We grow all trees for 30 years and then print out their heights. Here is a sample program:

```java
public class UseTree
{
  public static void main(String args[])
  {
    Tree normalTree = new Tree(0.1f, 15f);
    Tree desertTree = new Tree(0.1f, 6f);
    Tree jungleTree = new Tree(0.1f, 25f);
    normalTree.grow(30);
    desertTree.grow(30);
    jungleTree.grow(30);

    System.out.println("Normal Tree after 30 years: "
                  + normalTree.getHeight() + "m");
    System.out.println("Desert Tree after 30 years: "
                  + desertTree.getHeight() + "m");
    System.out.println("Jungle Tree after 30 years: "
                  + jungleTree.getHeight() + "m");
  }
}
```

Writing the methods

We start by writing the code for the constructor. All that this constructor needs to do is set the `height` and `rate` data members to the values supplied by the class user. Here is the code:

```java
/* Parameterized constructor for setting height
 * and growth rate
 */
public Tree(float h, float r)
{
  height = h;
  rate = r;
}
```

Try to write the code for the remaining methods on your own, before looking at the rest of the class below:

```
/* grow() method simulates the tree growing
 * by one year
 */
public void grow()
{
  float add = rate/100;  // convert rate to metres per year
  height += add;         // then increment height
}

/* grow(int n) method simulates the tree
 * growing for n years
 */
public void grow(int n)
{
  for(int i=1; i<=n; i++) grow();
}

/* getHeight() method returns the current
 * height of the tree
 */
public float getHeight() {
  return height;
}
```

After writing the methods, you should always return to the main method, and run it to ensure that the class works as it should.

Now do Exercise 3.14.

When to define a default constructor

Java programmers are sometimes unsure of when it is necessary or not to define a default constructor in a class. In the RabbitColony class we defined no constructors and yet we were able to create RabbitColony objects using calls to the default constructor. When no constructors are defined in a class, Java defines its own default constructor for that class. However, when a parameterized constructor is defined in a class, the default constructor is no longer automatically defined by Java. In our Tree example, we consciously did not define a default constructor, because we need the class user to specify the height and growth rate when a Tree object is created. Because we defined a parameterized constructor and not a default constructor, the following statement will generate an error:

```
Tree t = new Tree();
```

We could, however decide to allow the class user to create objects in this way. We will then have to define a default constructor, so that the above statement no longer generates an error.

You might find that there are situations where you will have to define an *empty* default constructor, to prevent compiler errors. In the RabbitColony class, for example, you might decide to provide a parameterized constructor to initialize the data members (babies, young and adults) to any values. Calls to the default constructor will then no longer work, so you will have to define a default constructor. This default constructor, however, will have nothing to do, because all the data members are initialized where they are declared, so it will be empty:

```
public RabbitColony()
{
}
```

Now do Exercises 3.15 to 3.16.

The this *keyword*

There may be times when you need some way of referring to the *current object* from inside the class. The keyword for doing this is `this`. One of the places where `this` is useful is when you are setting data members in a parameterised constructor, such as in the `Tree` example:

```
/* Parameterized constructor for setting height
   and growth rate */
public Tree(float height, float rate)
{
   this.height = height;
   this.rate = rate;
}
```

Notice that instead of using h and r as formal parameters, we have used the full variable names `height` and `rate`. Inside the method, `this.height` refers to the data member `height`, whereas `height` refers to the actual parameter sent to the method. In the same way, `this.rate` refers to the data member and `rate` refers to the actual parameter.

3.11 Scope

The *scope* of a variable is the region of code within which the variable can be referred to by its name. Scope is distinct from *visibility*. Visibility (set with an access modifier) refers to whether a data member can be used from *outside* the class by other classes. Scope, on the other hand, refers to any variable (not just data members) and where it can be used within a class. Figure 3.8 shows a sample class `TestScope` containing variables with different scope:

• Data member `num` has the entire class as its scope.

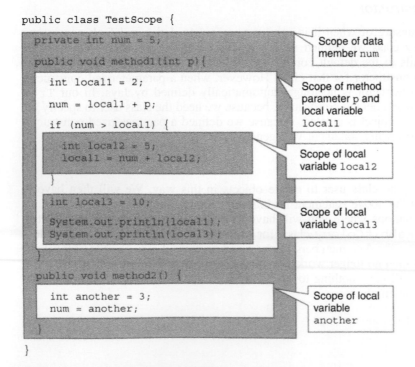

Figure 3.8 Sample program indicating the scope of different variables

- Local variables are variables that are declared within a block of code, such as a method or a `for` loop. The scope of a local variable extends from its declaration to the end of the code block in which it was declared. Examples in `TestScope` are `local1`, `local2`, `local3` and `another`.
- The scope of a method parameter is the entire method for which it is a parameter, as in the case of parameter `p`.

If a variable is referenced outside its scope, an error will be generated. For example, the following code will generate an error:

```
int num = Keyboard.readInt();
if(num > 10)
{
   int value = num;
}
System.out.println(value);   // error: value not defined
```

You can have more than one variable with the same name in the same class, as the following example illustrates:

```
public class Hidden
{
  private int num = 5;
  public void method1()
  {
    int num = 10;
    System.out.println(num);
  }
  public void method2()
  {
    System.out.println(num);
  }
}
```

If `method1` is called, the output will be `10`, whereas if `method2` is called, the output will be `5`. When you use a variable, Java looks for the declaration in the smallest enclosing block (e.g. when using `num` in `method1`, Java first looks inside `method1` for a declaration of num). If no declaration is found, Java looks in the next enclosing block (in the case of `method2`, the next enclosing block will be the class).

Now try Exercise 3.17.

3.12 More on object handles

In this section, we look at two aspects of object handles that you should be aware of. The first is that if you pass an object to a method, the method can change the values inside the object (this is not the case with primitive variables). The second aspect is that equality testing for the values inside objects cannot be achieved using the equals operator (`'=='`).

Passing objects to methods

We first look at the detail of what happens when we pass primitive values to methods. Look at the following two classes (stored in separate files):

```
public class Dog
{
  private int age, dogAge;
```

```
   public void setAge(int a)
   {
      age = a;
      a = a * 7;      // convert to dog years
      dogAge = a;
   }
}

public class TestDog {
   public static void main(String[] args)
   {
      Dog spot = new Dog();
      int yrs = 2;
      System.out.println("Value of yrs before calling setAge: " + yrs);
      spot.setAge(yrs);
      System.out.println("Value of yrs after calling setAge: " + yrs);
   }
}
```

The output of this program is:

```
Value of yrs before calling setAge: 2
Value of yrs after calling setAge: 2
```

Figure 3.9 shows how the values in memory change as the program progresses. The first two statements allocate space for a Dog object, called spot, and an int variable, called yrs. When the setAge method is called, the *value* inside yrs is *copied* to a separate temporary store called a (the method parameter). The value inside a is then copied into spot.age. The value inside a is then changed to 14 and this is copied into spot.dogAge. At the end of method setAge, the temporary variable a is discarded.

The important thing to notice here is the following: *although the value of* a *has changed, this has had no impact on the value of* yrs. In other words: the method setAge has not changed the value of the actual parameter yrs, even though the formal parameter a changed. We call this way of passing variables to methods, *call-by-value*, since the value is sent to the method, rather than the actual variable. In Java, primitives are always passed call-by-value to methods.

In contrast, objects in Java are passed *call-by-reference*. This means that a method can change the values inside an object passed to it as a parameter. The following example will illustrate this (to run the program, save all three classes in separate files):

```
public class Person
{
   private String firstname;
   private String surname;
   public Person(String f, String s)
   {
      firstname = f;
      surname = s;
   }
   public void setSurname(String s) { surname = s;}
   public String getSurname() { return surname;}
   public String toString()
   {
      return firstname + " " + surname;
   }
}
```

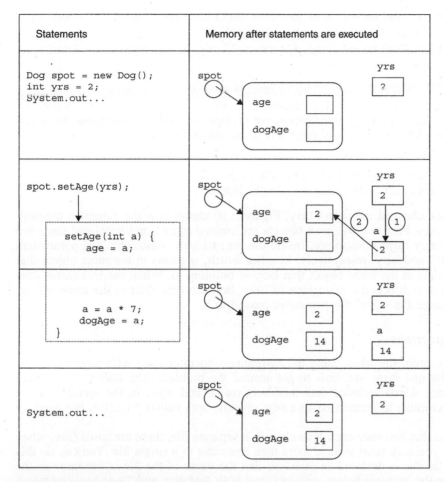

Figure 3.9 Call-by-value parameter passing

```java
public class Marriage
{
  private Person wife, husband;
  public Marriage(Person w, Person h)
  {
    // husband takes on the wifes surname (just to be different):
    h.setSurname(w.getSurname());
    husband = h;
    wife = w;
  }
} // end of class Marriage

public class TestMarriage
{
  public static void main(String args[])
  {
    Person girl = new Person("Jill","Hope");
    Person boy = new Person("Jack","Hill");
```

```
      System.out.println("Value of boy before calling Marriage: " + boy);
      Marriage couple = new Marriage(girl, boy);
      System.out.println("Value of boy after calling Marriage: " + boy);
   }
}
```

The program creates two `Person` objects and then creates a `Marriage` object consisting of the two `Person` objects. Note that in the `Marriage` constructor, we change the husband's surname to be the same as the wife's surname (we have purposefully done this to be unconventional!).

The output of the program is:

```
Value of boy before calling Marriage: Jack Hill
Value of boy after calling Marriage: Jack Hope
```

This shows that the method has changed the object boy. Figure 3.10 shows how the values in memory change as the program progresses. First two `Person` objects are created (`girl` and `boy`) and these are passed as parameters to the `Marriage` constructor. Inside the `Marriage` constructor, the parameters w and h act as *aliases* to `girl` and `boy`, respectively. In other words, w points to the same object that `girl` is pointing to and h points to the same object that `boy` is pointing to. When the `surname` data member of h is changed, this also affects the `surname` of `boy`, because they refer to the *same* object. In this way, a method can change the value of a parameter passed to it.

Object handles and assignment

Many Java programmers have problems when using the assignment operator ('=') with object handles. In this section we explain why and show you how to get around the problem. The following program defines a class called `Person`, which includes data members `name` and `age`. In the second part of the `main` method, we are attempting to create two `Person` objects, both called `"jack"`, but aged 25 and 50.

Although it is recommended that you save each Java class in a separate file, there are cases (say, when classes are very small) where you may want to save more than one class in a single file. You can do this as long as only *one class* in the file is declared as `public` and the name of the file is the same as the name of the `public` class. In the example below, you can save both `Person` and `TestAssignment` in a file called `TestAssignment.java`.

```
class Person
{
  public String name;
  public int age;

  public Person(String s, int a)
  {
    name = s;
    age = a;
  }
}

public class TestAssignment
{
  public static void main(String[] args)
  {
    int x1 = 5;
    int x2;
    x2 = x1;
    x2 = 6;
```

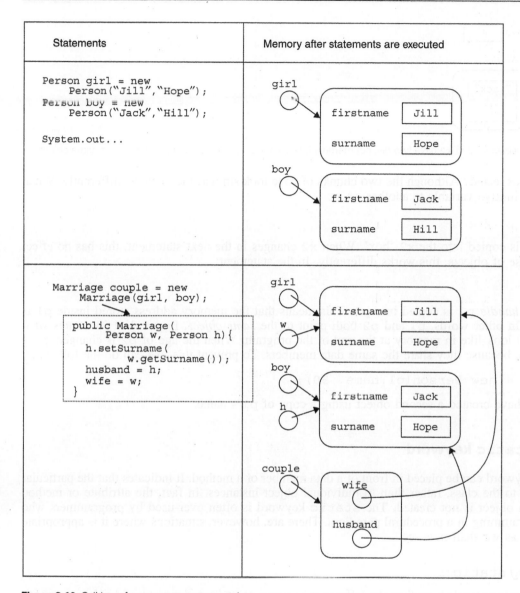

Figure 3.10 Call-by-reference parameter passing

```
    System.out.println(x1);

    Person p1 = new Person("jack", 25);
    Person p2;
    p2 = p1;
    p2.age = 50;
    System.out.println(p1.age);
    }
}
```

The output of this program is:

```
5
50
```

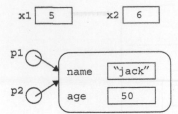

Figure 3.11 The variables x1 and x2 have two distinct memory locations, but handles p1 and p2 point at the same object

Is that what you expected? Although the two chunks of code look similar, they behave differently. When we assign one primitive variable to another, as in:

```
x2 = x1;
```

the *value* of x1 is copied into the x2 'box'. When x2 changes in the next statement, this has no effect on x2. In the case of objects, this works differently. In the statement:

```
p2 = p1;
```

the value of the *handle* p1 is copied into p2. This means that the memory address stored inside p1 is copied into p2. In other words, p1 and p2 both point to the *same object*. Figure 3.11 illustrates what the variables will look like in memory at the end of the program. When the age of p2 is changed, p1's age also changes, because they share the same data members. To prevent this, we can do the following:

```
Person p2 = new Person(p1.name, 50);
```

In this way, we have created a second object using a copy of p1's name.

3.13 The static keyword

The static keyword can be placed in front of a data member or a method. It indicates that the particular element belongs to the class, rather than to individual object instances. In fact, the attribute or method exists even if an object is not created. The static keyword is often over-used by programmers who are used to programming in a procedural paradigm. There are, however, situations where it is appropriate to use static, as we shall now see.

Understanding static

We will use a simple example to explain the difference between static and non-static data members. What would you expect to be the output of the following program? Draw the objects in memory and trace the statements to work it out. If you want to run the program, you can save both classes in the same file, but remember that you must call it StaticTest.java and not Num.java.

```
class Num
{
    int num = 47;
}

public class StaticTest
{
    public static void main(String args[])
    {
        Num n1 = new Num();
        Num n2 = new Num();
```

```
        System.out.println("n1.num: " + n1.num);
        System.out.println("n2.num: " + n2.num);
        n1.num++;
        System.out.println("n1.num: " + n1.num);
        System.out.println("n2.num: " + n2.num);
    }
}
```

The output would be:

```
    n1.num: 47
    n2.num: 47
    n1.num: 48
    n2.num: 47
```

If you now insert the keyword `static` before `int num = 47` in `Num.java`, would you expect the output to change? The output does in fact change to the following:

```
    n1.num: 47
    n2.num: 47
    n1.num: 48
    n2.num: 48
```

By inserting `static`, the variable `num` now belongs to the class `Num` and is no longer an element of the objects `n1` and `n2`. When `n1.num` is updated, it means that `n2.num` is also updated, since they refer to the *same variable*. We call such `static` variables, *class variables*.

Constants

Constants are data members which are not variables, since they do not change or vary between objects. Constants are both `static` and `final`. The keyword `final` indicates that the element cannot change its value, once it has been assigned. If you try to re-assign a `final` data member, the compiler will generate an error. Constants are useful when you have a value which you use repeatedly, but which will not change in the program. By declaring a constant, you give the value a name, which is often a more convenient way of referring to the value.

An example of a constant in Java, is `Math.PI`. Notice that the data member `PI` is referenced by the class name `Math` and not through an object handle. This indicates that `PI` is `static`. It is also `final`, which means that you will not be able to re-assign `PI` to some other value. The following are examples of constant definitions:

```
    static final double RATE = 11.34;
    static final int NUM_MONTHS = 12;
    static final String COUNTRY = "South Africa";
```

Static methods

Sometimes it is appropriate to write a class, which does not contain any variable data members, but only methods and constants. In this case it does not make sense to create objects of the class, because all objects will be the same. Such methods, which do not use any attribute variables, are called `static` methods. If a `static` method needs any data to do its job, the class user must send the data to the method (via the argument list).

Examples of `static` methods can be found in the `Math` class. This class is a 'home' for many mathematical functions. All methods inside the `Math` class are `static` and the only data defined in the class are constants (such as `PI`). To use these methods, the class user does not have to create a `Math` object, but can simply call the methods using the class name. Here are some examples of calls to methods of the `Math` class (you can assume that `x` and `y` already have values):

```
double num = Math.sin(45);
float maximum = Math.max(x,y);
```

Further examples of `static` methods can be found in the `Keyboard` class, for example:

```
Keyboard.readInt()
```

Since it does not make sense to have multiple objects of type `Keyboard`, these methods were defined as `static`.

It is not incorrect to create an object of either the `Keyboard` or `Math` classes before using the methods. It would simply be unnecessary, since all objects would be the same. For example:

```
Keyboard kb = new Keyboard();
String s = kb.readLine();
Math mathObj = new Math();
double num = mathObj.sin(45);
```

In contrast to this, in the case of non-`static` methods, an object has to be created before the method can be used. Take the `Turtle` class for example: say we wanted to call the `forward` method. We could only do this after creating a `Turtle` object (which has an associated position, direction, colour and pen status). The `forward` method works with three pieces of data: the `distance` to go forward (which is sent to the method via the argument list), the `xCoordinate` and `yCoordinate` (which are both object data attributes). Calling the `forward` method will change the `xCoordinate` or `yCoordinate` of the given `Turtle` object, given the distance to be moved. It does not make sense (and so Java does not allow it) to call the `forward` method directly with the `Turtle` class, because it is not clear which object this should affect:

```
Turtle.forward(50); // WRONG!
```

We will now create a useful class called `Convert`, which contains `static` methods for doing conversions between different measuring units. We will start by adding two methods for converting from Celsius to Fahrenheit and vice versa. Here is the class:

```
public class Convert
{

  // convert a value c from Celsius to Fahrenheit
  public static double celsToFahr(double c)
  {
    return 9*c/5 + 32;
  }


  // convert a value f from Fahrenheit to Celsius
  public static double fahrToCels(double f)
  {
    return ((f - 32)*5)/9;
  }
}
```

Here is a sample main method which uses the methods in this class:

```
public static void main(String[] args){
  System.out.println("100 Fahrenheit = " + Convert.fahrToCels(100)
                                          + " Celsius");
  System.out.println("37 Celsius = " + Convert.celsToFahr(37)
                                      + " Fahrenheit");
}
```

Now do Exercises 3.18 to 3.20.

The `main` *method revisited*

We are now ready to look at the `main` method in a bit more detail. The `main` method always starts with the following keywords:

```
public static void
```

Given what we have learnt, we should understand that:

- `public` means that the method can be called from outside the class. It is actually called by the Java interpreter.
- `static` means that it belongs to the class, so can be executed whether or not an object exists of that class.
- `void` means that the method does not return an answer.

Because `main` is a static method, it does not really matter where we put it. Suppose we have written a class called `Person`, which we want to test. We can create a separate class called `TestPerson` which contains a `main` method and uses the class, but there is a second option. We could also write the `main` method *inside* the `Person` class, for example:

```
class Person
{
  private String name;
  private int age;

  public Person(String s, int a)
  {
    name = s;
    age = a;
  }

  public void print()
  {
    System.out.println(name + " is " + age + " years old");
  }

  public static void main(String[] args)
  {
    Person p = new Person("Sue", 18);
    p.print();
  }
}
```

A `static` method is placed inside a class, purely as a 'home'. `static` methods do not have access to any non-`static` data members or methods, even in the same class (unless it is through an object handle). This is because a `static` method is part of the class, not of the individual objects.

There are advantages to placing a `main` method inside the class you are testing. Firstly, the tester code is stored in the same file as the class being tested and so can easily be reused as a test if the class changes. Secondly, this approach results in fewer files.

3.14 Naming conventions

There are certain conventions for the naming of classes, methods, variables and constants in Java. We recommend that you conform to these conventions, otherwise your code will look *odd* to other programmers.

1. Names of classes should start with an uppercase letter, and continue with lowercase characters. Each logical word inside the name should start with an uppercase as well. Underscores are not used. Examples: Tree, RabbitColony, TurtleDrawing.
2. Method names and variables should start with a lowercase letter and continue in the same way as class names. Examples: x, desertTree, grow, getNumRabbits.
3. Constants should be written entirely in uppercase, with underscores between logical words. Examples: MAX_SIZE, PI.

3.15 Using the Java API

The Java API (Application Programmer's Interface) contains descriptions of all the classes which are part of standard Java. If you have installed the Java 2 documentation, you will see a docs folder in the jdk1.3.1 folder. To browse the API, click on index.html in the docs folder. If you have not installed the documentation, you can find it online at:

    http://java.sun.com/j2se/1.3/docs/api/

When you open the documentation, you should see a window with three frames. The top left frame shows a list of packages, the bottom left frame shows a list of all classes and the right-hand frame describes each package. We will look at the String class as an example.

In the list of classes, scroll down until you see **'String'** and click on it. Look through the description (don't worry if you don't understand all of it) and scroll down to **'Constructor Summary'**. Notice how many constructors there are for creating String objects. Scroll down to the **'Method Summary'** table. You should recognize some of these methods. The return type for each method is shown on the left and the parameters are specified in parentheses. If you click on any of the methods, you will jump down to a more detailed description of the method. In this way, you can browse the API to find out what methods are in a given class and how each method can be used.

Now do Exercises 3.21 to 3.23.

3.16 Making your own package (optional)

A *package* is a group of classes in the same folder. If you want to make a package of a group of classes, called say myClasses, do the following:

1. Create a folder called myClasses and place the .java files into the folder.
2. Edit each Java file so that the first line reads:

       package myClasses;

3. Compile all the files.
4. Create a *jar* file of your package. A jar file is an archive of class files. Using jar files is a convenient way for others to use your package. To create a jar file, open a DOS box and change to the folder *above* myClasses. Type in the following command (note: jar is part of the Java SDK):

       jar cf myClasses.jar myClasses

   This will create a file called myClasses.jar
5. Copy myClasses.jar into the following directory:

       c:\jdk1.3.1\jre\lib\ext

   If your version of Java is stored somewhere else, then copy it to the equivalent \jre\lib\ext folder.

You can now use the classes from anywhere on your computer by importing the package:

```
import myClasses.*;
```

Summary

- Structuring code logically into classes leads to programs that are easier to understand and re-use.
- As a programmer, you will be continually switching roles from *class provider* to *class user* to *end user*.
- Objects *encapsulate* both data and methods.
- *Handles* are references to objects stored in memory. When a handle is empty it is called a *null reference*.
- `Strings` in Java are proper objects.
- A method is a block of statements inside a class, which has a name.
- Methods have arguments (data sent *to* the method) and return values (data sent *out* of the method).
- A value sent to a method is known as an *actual parameter*, whereas the declaration of an argument inside a method is known as a *formal parameter*.
- Constructors are special methods that are used for creating objects in memory and initializing the data members.
- The *scope* of a variable is the region of code within which the variable can be referred to by its name.
- The approach we recommend to solving a problem through a class is:

    1. Decide on data members.
    2. Decide on methods needed.
    3. Write a `main` method to test how the class can be used.
    4. Write the methods.
    5. Test the class by running the `main` method.

- A `private` element of a class can only be accessed from within the class, whereas a `public` element can be accessed from anywhere.
- When a primitive variable is passed to a method, it cannot be changed by the method. On the other hand, when an object is passed to a method, the values inside the object can be changed by the method.
- When one object handle is assigned to another object handle, they will both point to the same object in memory.
- The keyword `static` indicates that an element belongs to the class, rather than to individual objects of that class.
- Constants are `static final` data members and are used to store values that do not change or vary between objects.
- The Java API is a useful source of information on the standard Java classes.

Exercises

3.1 Write a program which uses the `Square` class from Section 3.4 to draw a square of size 10, using the character `'x'`.

3.2 Modify your program above, so that it prompts the user to enter the size and pattern character to use, before drawing the square. (**Hint:** Use the `readChar` method of `Keyboard` for reading in a single character. Also, ask the user to enter the size and pattern on the same line.)

3.3 Modify the Square class to include a data member called fill, which is of type boolean. The default value of fill should be set to true. If the value of fill is true, the square shape should be drawn with characters filling up the square (as it has been until now). If the value of fill is false, then the square should be drawn as an outline of characters. For example, if size is 6, pattern is '*', and fill is set to false, the following shape should be drawn:

```
******
*    *
*    *
*    *
*    *
******
```

3.4 Write a main method to test your modified Square class.

3.5 Study the following program:

```
import essential.*;
public class TurtleExercise
{
  public static void main (String[] args)
  {
    Turtle t1;
    Turtle t2;
    t1.forward(100);
    t2.backward(100);
  }
}
```

What will happen when you compile this program? If there are any errors, modify the program until you can run it and see the output.

3.6 What is the output of the following statements?

```
String s1 = "polo";
String s2 = "call";
System.out.print(s2.charAt(0));
System.out.print(s1.charAt(3));
System.out.print(s1.charAt(1));
System.out.print(s2.charAt(2));
System.out.println("!");
```

3.7 Write a program that prompts the user for two strings. If the two strings entered are equal, then print the message: 'The strings are the same', otherwise print the message: 'The strings are different'.

3.8 Write a program that asks the user to enter a string and then prints out that string backwards. (Hint: remember that the length method will tell you how many characters there are in the string.)

3.9 For the following statements, give the name of the method, the data in (arguments), data out (return value) and side effect (assume that t and g refer to existing Turtle and Graph objects respectively):

(a) String s = Keyboard.readLine();
(b) t.home();

    (c) `g.setAxes(0,10,0,6);`
    (d) `Turtle t = new Turtle(Color.green);`

3.10 In the `grow()` method of the `RabbitColony` class (Section 3.8), the `adults` variable is updated first, followed by `young` and `babies`.

    (a) Explain what would happen if the statements were reordered as followed:

```
young = babies;    // all the current babies become young
adults += young;   // all the young become adults
babies = adults;   // all adult pairs produce a baby pair
```

    (b) Explain what would happen if the statements were reordered as follows:

```
babies = adults;   // all adult pairs produce a baby pair
young = babies;    // all the current babies become young
adults += young;   // all the young become adults
```

3.11 Using the `RabbitColony` class defined in Section 3.8, write a program which prints out the total number of rabbits every year for 15 years.

3.12 Change the `RabbitColony` class to reflect that 1 in 4 of the baby rabbit pairs die at birth. Round this value down to the nearest pair of rabbits. For example, if there are 10 pairs of babies born, only 8 will survive.

3.13 Using your modified `RabbitColony` class from Exercise 3.12, write a program which prints out the total number of rabbits every year for 15 years. How does this program differ from the one in Exercise 3.11?

3.14 Modify the `Tree` class from Section 3.10 so that the growth rate is reduced by 10% every year once the tree is taller than 1 m. Run the `main` method again to see what impact it has on the heights of the three trees.

3.15 Add a default constructor to the `Tree` class, which sets the height to 0.1 m and the growth rate to 10 cm per year. Write a `main` method which creates a `Tree` object using the default constructor and prints out the height of the tree, to test that it works correctly.

3.16 Add a parameterized constructor to your modified `Square` class from Exercise 3.3, which takes three arguments for setting the `size`, `pattern` and `fill` data members. Modify your class so that the class user can still use the default constructor as an alternative. Write a `main` method to test both constructors.

3.17 Does the following code compile? If not, explain why not.

```
public class TryThis
{
  private int memberX = 150;

  public void method1( )
  {
    int local1 = memberX;
    local2 = 5;
    System.out.println(local1);
  }
  public void method2( )
  {
    int memberX = 20;
    int local2 = 6;
    method1( );
```

```
        System.out.println(memberX);
    }
} // end of class TryThis
```

What would be the output if `method2` was invoked? (Assume that any lines that cause errors are commented out.)

3.18 Add methods to the `Convert` class defined in Section 3.13 to convert acres to hectares and vice versa (see Exercise 2.10 for conversion factors).

3.19 Add methods to the `Convert` class defined in Section 3.13 to convert pounds to kilograms and vice versa (see Exercise 2.10 for conversion factors).

3.20 Write a main method to test the new methods you wrote in the above two exercises.

3.21 Using the Java API, find out how to use the `endsWith` and `substring` methods of the `String` class. Now write a program which reads in from the user a weight in kilograms. Store the weight as a string, rather than a number. You should check if the user typed in the value followed by 'kg' or not. If they did type in 'kg', you should create a new string which has the 'kg' part removed. Print the final string (which should just be a number) to check that your program works correctly.

3.22 In the `Float` class, there is a `static` method called `parseFloat`, which takes a `String` as an argument and returns a `float`. Use this method to change the `String` you created in Exercise 3.21 to a `float`.

3.23 Modify your program from Exercise 3.22 to print out the value of the weight in pounds. In other words, the final program should read in a weight in kilograms and print it out in pounds. Your program should not generate an error if the user types in 'kg' after the weight, but should simply ignore it. Use the `Convert` class from Exercise 3.19 to do the conversion.

4
More on loops

Objectives

By the end of this chapter you should be able to

- identify two distinct types of repetition in program design: determinate and indeterminate;
- write more general programs involving the `for` loop;
- write short programs involving indeterminate repetition with the `while` construct.

This chapter will also give you more experience in developing object-oriented solutions to science and engineering problems.

In Chapter 2 we introduced the powerful `for` statement, which is used to repeat a block of statements a fixed number of times. This type of structure, where the number of repetitions must be determined in advance, is sometimes called *determinate repetition*. However, it often happens that the condition to end a loop is only satisfied *during the execution of the loop itself*. Such a structure is called *indeterminate*. This chapter is mainly about indeterminate loops; first, however, we will look at some more general examples of `for` loops.

4.1 Determinate repetition with `for`

Binomial coefficient

The *binomial coefficient* is widely used in mathematics and statistics. It is defined as the number of ways of choosing r objects out of n without regard to order, and is given by

$$\binom{n}{r} = \frac{n!}{r!(n-r)!}. \tag{4.1}$$

If this form is used, the factorials can get very big, causing an overflow. But a little thought reveals we can simplify Equation (4.1) as follows:

$$\binom{n}{r} = \frac{n(n-1)(n-2)\cdots(n-r+1)}{r!}, \tag{4.2}$$

$$\text{e.g.} \quad \binom{10}{3} = \frac{10!}{3! \times 7!} = \frac{10 \times 9 \times 8}{1 \times 2 \times 3}.$$

Equation (4.2) is computationally much more efficient. We would like to implement it as a method, so that we can easily use it from any program. Since the method will be the kind that has data passed to it (rather than using data member variables), it makes sense for it to be static. A logical 'home' for this method could be a class which contains common mathematical and statistical methods. We will call the class `EssentialMath` (so that it does not conflict with Java's `Math` class).

```java
import essential.*;              //needed in due course

public class EssentialMath
{
    public static double ncr(int n, int r)
    {
        double ncr = 1;

        for (int k = 1; k <= r; k++)
        {
            ncr = ncr*(n - k + 1)/k;
        }

        return ncr;
    }
}
```

The binomial coefficient is sometimes pronounced 'n-see-r'. Work through the method by hand with some sample values. Here's how to use `ncr` in a main method:

```java
public static void main(String[] args)
{
    System.out.println( ncr(10, 3) );
}
```

`for` *loops with non-unit increments*

Up to now, we have used a `for` loop where the counter always increases in steps of 1. Here's an example where the increment is 2:

```java
for (int i = 1; i <= 20; i += 2)
    System.out.print( i + "   " );
```

The output is

```
1   3   5   7   9   11   13   15   17   19
```

The increment can in fact be any expression, even a decrement. The following code prints the numbers 1–10 in reverse order:

```java
for (int i = 10; i >= 1; i--)
    System.out.print(i + " ");
```

Now try Exercises 4.1 to 4.6 at the end of the chapter.

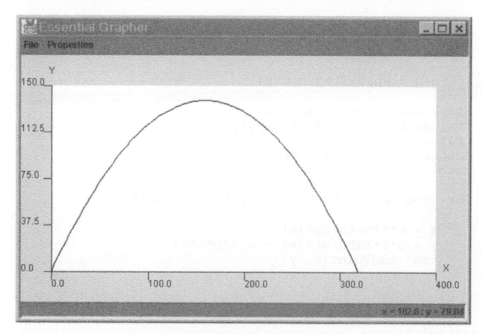

Figure 4.1 Projectile trajectory with Essential Grapher (launch velocity = 60 m/s, launch angle = 60°)

Plotting a projectile trajectory with Essential Grapher

Drawing graphs is easy with our handy graphics tool, Essential Grapher, which is part of the `essential` package. The following program shows how to use it to plot the trajectory of a projectile launched from the ground with a velocity u metres per second at an angle of a degrees to the horizontal. If there is no air resistance, the horizontal and vertical displacements of the projectile t seconds after launch are given by the formulae

$$x = ut \cos(a),$$

$$y = ut \sin(a) - gt^2/2,$$

where g is the acceleration due to gravity. Figure 4.1 shows a typical trajectory plotted with Essential Grapher. Here is a class to plot the trajectory, together with a `main` method that uses the class, followed by an explanation:

```
import essential.*;
import java.awt.Color;
public class Projectile
{
    public static double g = 9.8;  //acceleration due to gravity
    private double a;              //launch angle in radians
    private double u;              //launch velocity

    public Projectile( double a, double u )
    {
        this.a = a*Math.PI/180;  //convert to radians
        this.u = u;
    }

    public double getTimeOfFlight()
```

```
            {
                    return 2*u*Math.sin(a)/g;   // from applied maths!
            }

        public void displayTrajectory()
            {
                    Graph traj = new Graph();
                    traj.setAxes(0, 400, 0, 150);
                    traj.setColour(Color.black);
                    double tof = getTimeOfFlight();
                    double x, y;

                    for (double t = 0; t <= tof; t = t + 0.1)
                    {
                        x = u*t*Math.cos(a);
                        y = u*t*Math.sin(a) - 0.5*g*t*t;
                        traj.addPoint(x, y);
                    }
            }
        }

    import essential.*;

    public class UseProjectile
    {
        public static void main(String[ ] args)
        {
                System.out.print( "Enter launch angle (in degrees): " );
                double a = Keyboard.readDouble();
                System.out.print( "Enter launch velocity: " );
                double u = Keyboard.readDouble();
                Projectile p = new Projectile(a, u);
                p.displayTrajectory();
        }
    }
```

- The parameters of the `Projectile` constructor (a and u) have the same name as the data members being initialized. This simplification is made possible by the use of `this`.
  The constructor converts the launch angle from degrees to radians.
- If you have done some applied mathematics you will recognize the formula in the `getTimeOfFlight` method as the time of flight of the projectile.
- The `Graph` class in our `essential` package implements Essential Grapher in a class user-friendly fashion. The statement

      Graph traj = new Graph();

(in the `displayTrajectory` method of `Projectile`) creates an object `traj` of this class which will draw itself.
- The method `setAxes` sets the limits of the axes of the graph display. Its four parameters stand for `xmin`, `xmax`, `ymin` and `ymax` respectively.
- The `setColour` method (note the British spelling!) sets the drawing colour of our `traj` object. This method in turns selects a colour from the Java API class `Color` (US spelling!).
- The `for` statement repeats the calculation of the x and y coordinates of the trajectory as time increases and uses the `addPoint` method of the `Graph` class to plot the point.

Grapher joins each point plotted with a straight line, so if the points are close enough the resultant graph will look smooth.

Note that the index t in the `for` loop,

```
for (double t = 0; t <= tof; t = t + 0.01)
```

is no longer a simple counter as it has been in our previous examples of `for` loops, but represents the times at which the trajectory points are calculated. The increments in t are kept small, so that the graph looks smooth. The `for` loop stops when t reaches `tof` (the time of flight).

- The user can change the axis limits of the graph with Grapher's **Properties** menu.
- The trajectory looks remarkably like a parabola. This is not surprising since it *is* a parabola. You can prove this quite easily by eliminating t from the equations for x and y.

Use Grapher to find by trial-and-error the launch angle that gives the maximum range (applied mathematicians should know the answer).

Now try Exercise 4.7.

Update processes

Many problems in science and engineering involve modelling a process where the main variable is repeatedly updated over a period of time. Here is an example of such an *update process*. We are going to program the solution in an object-oriented way, to provide you with a useful template for similar problems in the future.

A can of beer at temperature 25 °C is placed in a fridge, where the ambient temperature F is 10 °C. We want to find out how the temperature of the beer changes over a period of time. A standard way of approaching this type of problem is to break the time period up into a number of small steps, each of length dt. If T_i is the temperature at the end of step i, we can use the following model to get T_{i+1} from T_i:

$$T_{i+1} = T_i - K \, dt \, (T_i - F), \tag{4.3}$$

where K is a constant parameter depending on the insulating properties of the can, and the thermal properties of beer. Assume that units are chosen so that time is in minutes.

To make the solution more general, we will introduce some more notation before developing the Java solution. Call the initial time a, and the final time b. Since our time steps are of length dt, the number m of such steps will be

$$m = (b - a)/dt$$

(where m must obviously be an integer). We will want the results to be displayed in some form. If dt is very small, it will be inconvenient to have output printed after every step, so the program below (`Fridge`) allows you to set the *output interval* `opInt`. This is the interval (in minutes) between successive rows of (printed) output. It checks that this interval is an integer multiple of dt and prints a warning if it is not. This device also enables you to compare results for different values of dt (simply use the same value of `opInt`).

The following program as it stands calculates and draws the cooling curves of two different types of beverage placed in the fridge: a can of beer and a can of OJ (orange juice). Explanation of the main points follows the program.

```java
import essential.*;
import java.text.*;    // for DecimalFormat

public class Fridge
{
    private double F;  // ambient temp in fridge
```

```java
    private double K;   // cooling constant
    private double T0;  // initial temp of beverage

    // constructor: put the beverage in the fridge
    public Fridge( double Fi, double Ki, double Ti )
    {
        F = Fi; K = Ki; T0 = Ti;
    }

    public void cool( double a, double b, double dt, int opInt )
    // cool the beverage for b minutes, in steps of dt,
    // starting at time a,
    // with results displayed every opInt minutes
    {
        int m;             // number of update steps
        double t = 0;      // time elapsed
        double T;          // current temperature of beverage
        DecimalFormat df = new DecimalFormat("00.00");
                           //format to 2 decimal places

        Graph coolDraw = new Graph();
        coolDraw.setTitle("K = " + K);
        coolDraw.setDrawTitle(true);
        coolDraw.setAxes(0, 100, 10, 30);

        m = (int) Math.floor((b-a)/dt);
        t = a;
        T = T0;

        if (Math.abs(Math.IEEEremainder(opInt,dt)) > 1e-6)
            System.out.println
                    ( "Warning: opInt not an integer multiple of dt!" );

        System.out.println("time    Model");
        System.out.println(df.format(t) + "   " + df.format(T0));
                                        //initial values

        for (int i = 0; i < m; i++)
        {
            t = t + dt;
            T = T - K*dt*(T-F);              // update model equation
            if (Math.abs(Math.IEEEremainder(t, opInt)) < 1e-6)
                System.out.println( df.format(t) + "   " +
                                    df.format(T) + "   ");
                coolDraw.addPoint(t, T);
        }
    }

    public static void main(String[ ] args)
```

```
    {
        Fridge beer = new Fridge( 10, 0.05, 25 );
        Fridge OJ = new Fridge( 10, 0.15, 25 );

        beer.cool( 0, 100, 0.1, 5 );
        OJ.cool( 0, 50, 0.1, 5 );
    }
}
```

- We use the object-oriented programming concepts introduced in Chapter 3. So a class `Fridge` is defined; beverages with different cooling properties will be placed in the fridge to cool.
- The data members of `Fridge` are the ambient temperature inside (F), K as defined in Equation (4.3), and the initial temperature of a beverage in the fridge, `T0`.
- The constructor for `Fridge` sets the properties that will affect a beverage placed in the fridge: the ambient temperature in the fridge, the beverage's constant K (which will be different for beer and OJ) and its initial (room) temperature.
- `Fridge` has one method, `cool`. Its parameters are the initial and final times, *dt* and the output interval `opInt`.
- For every time step *dt*, `cool` updates the temperature according to Equation (4.3), plots the current temperature against time with Essential Grapher.
  If time `t` is a multiple of `opInt`, `cool` prints the time and the temperature.
- Note that by creating a `Graph` object inside `cool` a cooling curve may be drawn with Essential Grapher for each `Fridge` object created in `main`. Figure 4.2 shows what to expect.

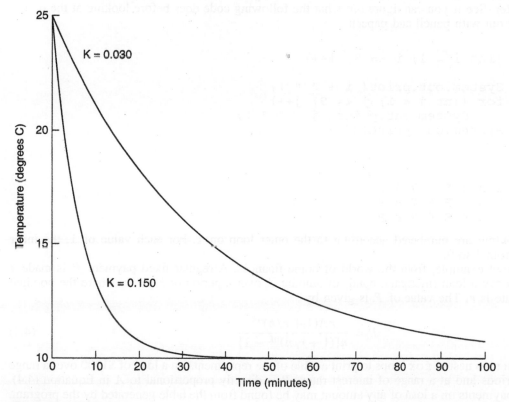

Figure 4.2 Cooling curves

- Graph has a method setTitle which labels the particular graph being plotted.

  Note how the string concatenation operator (+) is used in the argument of setTitle.

  The Graph method setDrawTitle(true) must be used to make the title visible.
- The Java API class DecimalFormat (in java.text) is used to format the output neatly with two decimal places. The DecimalFormat constructor has a string argument which provides a pattern for the required format. You create a DecimalFormat object for each type of format you want, and use its format method to output a correctly formatted string.

  The pattern "00.00" produces two decimal places over five columns altogether (one for the decimal point), filled with zeros from the left if necessary.

With values of K = 0.05, F = 10, initial temperature T0 = 25, b = 100, dt = 1 minute and opInt = 5 minutes, we get the following output:

```
time    Model
00.00   25.00
05.00   21.61
10.00   18.98
15.00   16.95
...
100.00  10.09
```

Try Exercises 4.8 and 4.9.

The nested for loop

A for loop may be 'nested' inside another for. The main point to note is that the counter of the *inner* for changes faster. See if you can figure out what the following code does before looking at the output below it (work it out with pencil and paper):

```
for (int i = 1; i <= 3; i++)
{
    System.out.print( i + " " );
    for (int j = 1; j <= 9; j++)
        System.out.print( j + " " );
    System.out.println();
}
```

Output:

```
1 1 2 3 4 5 6 7 8 9
2 1 2 3 4 5 6 7 8 9
3 1 2 3 4 5 6 7 8 9
```

The rows of output are numbered according to the outer loop on i. For each value of i, the inner loop on j runs from 1 to 9.

Here's a different example, from the world of home finances. A regular fixed payment P is made n times a year to repay a loan (mortgage bond) of amount A over a period of k years, where the nominal annual interest rate is r. The value of P is given by

$$P = \frac{rA(1 + r/n)^{nk}}{n[(1 + r/n)^{nk} - 1]}. \tag{4.4}$$

The next program uses nested for loops to print a table of the repayments on a loan of $1000 over a range of repayment periods and at a range of interest rates. P is directly proportional to A in Equation (4.4). Therefore the repayments on a loan of any amount may be found from the table generated by the program, by simple proportion.

```
import java.text.*;

public class Loan
{
    private double a = 1000;     //amount borrowed

    public double getPayment(int n, int k, double r)
    {
    //returns the regular fixed payment given the
    //payments per year (n), period (k years) and annual
    //interest rate (r)
        double N = r*a*Math.pow(1+r/n, n*k);
        double D = n*(Math.pow(1+r/n, n*k) - 1);
        return N/D;
    }

    public void printTable(int n, int y1, int y2,
                            double r1, double r2)
    {
        DecimalFormat dP = new DecimalFormat( "00.00" );
        DecimalFormat dr = new DecimalFormat( "00%" );

        //heading
        System.out.print( "rate" );
        for (int k = y1; k <= y2; k += 5)
            System.out.print( "\t" + k + " yrs" );
        System.out.println();

        for (double r = r1; r <= r2*(1+1e-6); r += 0.01)
                                    // watch out for rounding
        {
            System.out.print( dr.format(r) + "\t\t" );

            for (int k = y1; k <= y2; k += 5)
            {
                double P = getPayment(n, k, r);
                System.out.print( dP.format(P) + "\t" );
            }
            System.out.println();
        }
    }

    public static void main(String[] args)
    {
        Loan l = new Loan();
        l.printTable(12, 15, 30, 0.1, 0.2);
    }
}
```

Output:

rate	15 yrs	20 yrs	25 yrs	30 yrs
10%	10.75	09.65	09.09	08.78

11%	11.37	10.32	09.80	09.52
12%	12.00	11.01	10.53	10.29
13%	12.65	11.72	11.28	11.06
14%	13.32	12.44	12.04	11.85
15%	14.00	13.17	12.81	12.64
16%	14.69	13.91	13.59	13.45
17%	15.39	14.67	14.38	14.26
18%	16.10	15.43	15.17	15.07
19%	16.83	16.21	15.98	15.89
20%	17.56	16.99	16.78	16.71

Note:

- The `DecimalFormat` pattern `"00%"` multiplies by 100 and inserts the % symbol.
- Did you spot the odd condition `r <= r2*(1+1e-6)` in the outer `for` loop of `printTable`? If you use the more obvious `r <= r2` the loop may not execute for `r = r2`. This is because of rounding error: `r` is never exactly equal to `r2` for non-integer types. Rounding error, which can occur with non-integer types, is discussed in Chapter 5.

It is probably better to avoid using double type altogether when counting in a `for` loop. We, after all, learnt to count on our fingers, of which we have a whole number!

We want `r` to go from values `first` to `last` in steps of `increment`. The *iteration count* or *trip count* for the loop is then computed as

```
Math.floor((last-first)/increment)+1
```

The `for` loop for `r` must then be replaced by something like

```
for (i = 1; i <= Math.floor(...)+1; i++)
```

You will also need to increment `r` explicitly. As an exercise, see if you can rewrite the program using this counting device.

Now try Exercise 4.10, which uses nested `for` loops.
Exercises 4.11 to 4.22 provide some further practice with `for` loops generally.

4.2 Indeterminate repetition with `while`

Determinate loops all have in common the fact that you can work out in principle exactly how many repetitions are required *before the loop starts*. But in all the problems in this section there is no way *in principle* of working out the number of repeats, so a different structure is more appropriate.

Rolling a dice for a six

How many times do you have to roll a dice before you get a six (or any other number, for that matter)? Well, it depends, doesn't it? If we want to write a program to *simulate* rolling a dice until a six is thrown, we don't know in advance when the six will come up (if we did, we could win a fortune many times over at casinos which would be foolish enough to accept us!). We could use a `for` loop for this situation, but we will rather introduce a more appropriate loop structure for this problem—a `while` loop.

The structure plan for this problem is as follows:

1. Generate and display a random integer in range 1–6
2. While integer is not a six repeat:
   Generate and display a random integer in range 1–6
3. Display the total number of throws.

Step 1 is necessary before the loop in Step 2 begins; you must roll the die once before you can see whether any repeats are necessary. This plan translates into the following Java class (six is generalized to *n*), which is implemented in the program following it (it also counts how many throws are need to get the number *n*):

```java
public class Dice
{
    public int thro()
    {
        int numberOnDice = (int) Math.floor(6*Math.random())+1;
        return numberOnDice;
    }

    public void throwUntil( int n )
    {
        int numberOfThrows = 1;
        int numberOnDice = thro();
        System.out.print( numberOnDice + " " );

        while (numberOnDice != n)
        {
            numberOnDice = thro();
            numberOfThrows++;
            System.out.print( numberOnDice + " " );
        }

        System.out.println( "(" + numberOfThrows + " throws)" );
    }
}

public class UseDice
{
    public static void main(String[ ] args)
    {
        Dice d = new Dice();
        d.throwUntil(6);
    }
}
```

Output from two sample runs:

```
5 4 5 2 2 3 5 3 3 4 1 5 4 1 3 1 3 5 4 1 1 3 6 (24 throws)
3 6 (2 throws)
```

Try Exercise 4.23.

The while *statement*

In general the while statement looks like this:

```java
while (condition) {
    statements
}
```

The while construct repeats *statements* as long as its *condition* remains true. The condition is tested each time *before statements* are repeated. Since the condition is evaluated before *statements* are executed, it is possible to arrange for *statements* not to be executed at all under certain circumstances. Clearly, *condition* must depend on *statements* in some way, otherwise the loop will never end.

A guessing game

In this problem the program 'thinks' of an integer between 1 and 10 (i.e. generates one at random). You, the user, have to guess it. If your guess is too high or too low, the program must say so. If your guess is correct, a message of congratulations must be displayed.

Once again a structure plan is helpful here:

1. Generate random integer
2. Ask user for guess
3. While guess is wrong:
    If guess is too low
        Tell her it is too low
    Otherwise
        Tell her it is too high
    Ask user for new guess
4. Polite congratulations.

Here is the object-oriented implementation:

```java
import essential.*;
public class GuessingGame
{
    //generate random integer between 1 and 10:
    private int javaNum = (int) Math.floor(10*Math.random())+1;

    public void play()
    {
        System.out.print( "Your guess please: " );
        int userGuess = Keyboard.readInt();

        while (userGuess != javaNum)
        {
            if (userGuess > javaNum)
                System.out.println( "Too high" );
            else
                System.out.println( "Too low" );

            System.out.print( "Your next guess please: " );
            userGuess = Keyboard.readInt();
        }

        System.out.println( "At last!" );
    }

    public static void main(String[ ] args)
    {
        GuessingGame g = new GuessingGame();
        g.play();
    }
}
```

Try it out a few times. Note that the `while` loop repeats as long as `javaNum` is not equal to `userGuess`. There is no way in principle of knowing how many loops will be needed before the user guesses correctly. The problem is truly indeterminate.

Note that `userGuess` has to be input in two places: firstly to get the `while` loop going, and secondly during the execution of the `while`.

Try Exercises 4.24 and 4.25.

Prime numbers

Many people are obsessed with prime numbers, and most books on programming have to include an algorithm to test if a given number is prime. So here's ours.

A number is prime if it is not an exact multiple of any other number except itself and 1, i.e. if it has no factors except itself and 1. The easiest plan of attack then is as follows. Suppose P is the number to be tested. See if any numbers N can be found that divide into P without remainder. If there are none, P is prime.

Which numbers N should we try? Well, we can speed things up by restricting P to odd numbers, so we only have to try odd divisors N.

When do we stop testing? When $N = P$? No, we can stop a lot sooner. In fact, we can stop once N reaches $\sqrt{P}$, since if there is a factor greater than $\sqrt{P}$ there must be a corresponding one less than $\sqrt{P}$, which we would have found.

And where do we start? Well, since $N = 1$ will be a factor of any P, we should start at $N = 3$.

The structure plan is as follows:

1. Input P
2. Initialize N to 3
3. Find remainder R when P is divided by N
4. While $R \neq 0$ and $N < \sqrt{P}$ repeat:
    Increase N by 2
    Find R when P is divided by N
5. If $R \neq 0$ then
    P is prime
Else
    P is not prime.

Note that there may be no repeats—R might be zero the first time. Note also that there are *two* conditions under which the loop may stop. Consequently, an `if` is required after completion of the loop to determine which condition stopped it.

We implement the algorithm as a `static boolean` method of the `EssentialMath` class proposed at the beginning of the chapter. The method screens out the special cases $P = 1$ and $P = 2$, as well as even values of P.

```
public class EssentialMath
{
    public static boolean isPrime(int p)
    {

    //first screen out some tricky and obvious ones:
        if (p == 1 || p == 2)  //prime by definition
            return true;
        else if (p%2 == 0)      //even
            return false;
        else {
            long n = 3;
            long r = p % n;
```

```
        while (r != 0 && n < Math.sqrt(p))
        {
            n += 2;
            r = p % n;
        }

        if (r != 0)
            return true;
        else
            return false;
    }
}
    ...

public static void main(String[] args)
{
    System.out.println( isPrime(17) );
}
}
```

Try it out on the following numbers: 4058879 (not prime), 193707721 (prime) and 2147483647 (prime). If such things interest you, the largest *known* prime number at the time of writing was $2^{6972593} - 1$ (discovered in June 1999). It has 2098960 digits and would occupy about 70 pages if it was printed in a newspaper. Obviously our algorithm cannot test such a large number, since it's unimaginably greater than the largest number which can be represented by Java. Ways of testing such huge numbers for primality are described in D.E. Knuth, *The Art of Computer Programming. Volume 2: Seminumerical Algorithms* (Addison-Wesley, 1981). This particular whopper was found by the GIMPS (Great Internet Mersenne Prime Search). See http://www.utm.edu/research/primes/largest.html for more information on the largest known primes.

Try Exercise 4.26.

Projectile trajectory

In Section 4.1 we considered a program (Projectile) to plot the trajectory of a projectile, given the usual equations of motion (assuming no air resistance). Although this problem can be solved with a determinate loop, as it was there—if you know enough applied mathematics—it is of interest also to see how to solve it with an indeterminate while loop. The idea is to calculate the trajectory repeatedly with increasing time, *while* the vertical displacement (y in the program below) remains positive. The only changes that need to be made to Projectile are in the displayTrajectory method:

```
public void displayTrajectory()
{
    Graph traj = new Graph();
    traj.setAxes(0, 400, 0, 150);
    traj.setColour(Color.black);
    double t = 0;
    double dt = 0.5;      //time step
    double x = 0;
    double y = 0;

    while (y >= 0)
```

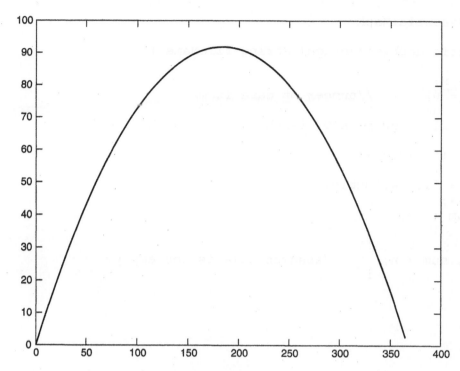

Figure 4.3 Projectile trajectory using a `while` loop

```
        {
                traj.addPoint(x, y);
                t += dt;            //update time
                x = u*t*Math.cos(a);
                y = u*t*Math.sin(a) - 0.5*g*t*t;
        }
    }
```

Figure 4.3 shows the trajectory for a launch angle of 45° and a launch velocity of 60 m/s. Note in particular how the trajectory stops above the x axis.

Note also that when the loop finally ends, the value of y will be negative. However, the position of the `proj.addPoint` statement ensures that only points with positive y components are plotted. If for some reason you need to record the last value of t, say, before y becomes negative, you will need an `if` statement inside the `while`, e.g.

```
        if (y >= 0)
          tmax = t;
```

Reading an unknown amount of data

In Section 2.6 we saw how to read a *known* amount of data from a text file (**Reading data from a text file**). In reality we are unlikely to know exactly how much data we have. The next example uses a `while` loop to read an unknown amount of data from the file nums.txt and to compute their average. You can test it, if you like, on the following data, which has an average of 6.19:

```
        3.1 7.2 4.5 9.9 6.0 7.9 3.7 9.2 6.5 3.9
```

The code is written as another `static` method of `EssentialMath`:

```
public class EssentialMath
{
    public static double average( String fileName )
    {
        double x;
        int n = 0;          //number of data items
        double sum = 0;
        FileIO f1 = new FileIO( fileName, FileIO.READING );

        while (!f1.isEof())
        {
            x = f1.readDouble( );
            n++;
            sum += x;
        }

        return sum / n;     //assumes file is not empty!
    }

    ...

}
```

Note:

- The crucial device here is the `FileIO.isEof` method in the `essential` package. This method is true for a `FileIO` object as long as there is more input in the file waiting to be read.

Try Exercises 4.27 to 4.31 for some general practice using `while` loops.

The `do-while` statement

Java has an alternative to the `while statement: do-while`. Here's how to use it to code the `throwUntil` method of the `Dice` class at the beginning of this section—rolling a dice until a particular number comes up:

```
public void throwUntil( int n )
{
    int numberOfThrows = 0;
    int numberOnDice;

    do
    {
        numberOnDice = thro();
        numberOfThrows++;
        System.out.print( numberOnDice + " " );
    }
    while (numberOnDice != n);

    System.out.println( "(" + numberOfThrows + " throws)" );
}
```

Note the subtle difference here: the dice does not have to be rolled *before* the loop starts.

The `do-while` loop has the form

```
do {
    statements
} while (condition);
```

The block markers are not strictly necessary when there is only one statement; however, they improve readability.

The `do-while` repeats *statements* while the expression *condition* remains true (i.e. until it becomes false). The condition is tested after each repeat before making another repeat. Since the condition is at the end of the loop, *statements* will always be executed *at least once*.

`while` *versus* `do-while`

A problem coded with `while` can logically always be rewritten with `do-while`, and vice versa (try it if you are skeptical—see Exercise 4.32). The question then arises: when should we use `do-while` and when should we use `while`?

This is a matter of taste. There is, however, a large body of opinion among programmers which maintains that it is good programming style for conditions under which loops are repeated to be stated at the *beginning* of the loop. This favours the `while` construct, since its condition is stated at the beginning. However, in situations where at least one repeat must be made, it often seems more natural to use the `do-while` construct.

Summary

- A `for` statement should be used to program a determinate loop, where the number of repeats is known to the program (i.e. in principle to the programmer) *before* the loop is encountered. This situation is characterized by the structure plan:

    Repeat *N* times:
        Block of statements to be repeated

    where *N* is known or computed *before* the loop is encountered for the first time, and is not changed by the block.
- A `while` or a `do-while` statement should be used to program an indeterminate repeat structure, where the exact number of repeats is *not* known in advance. Another way of saying this is that these statements should be used whenever the truth value of the condition for repeating is changed in the body of the loop. This situation is characterized by the following structure plan:

    While *condition* is true repeat:
        statements to be repeated (reset truth value of *condition*).

  or

    Repeat:
        statements to be repeated (reset truth value of *condition*)
    while *condition* is true.

- The statements in a `while` construct may sometimes never be executed.
- The statements in a `do-while` construct are always executed at least once.
- Loops may be nested to any depth.

Exercises

4.1 Write some statements which print the odd integers $99, 97, 95, \ldots, 3, 1$.

4.2 Write some statements to find and print the sum of the successive even integers $2, 4, \ldots, 200$. (Answer: 10100)

4.3 Generate a table of conversions from degrees (first column) to radians (second column). Degrees should go from $0°$ to $360°$ in steps of $10°$. Recall that π radians $= 180°$.
Code your solution as a `static` method `degrees2Radians` which you can add to the `Convert` class suggested in Section 3.13.

4.4 Set up a table with degrees in the first column from 0 to 360 in steps of 30, sines in the second column, and cosines in the third column.
Now try to add tangents in the fourth column. Can you figure out what's going on?

4.5 Write some statements that display a list of integers from 10 to 20 inclusive, each with its square root next to it.

4.6 If C and F are Celsius and Fahrenheit temperatures respectively, the formula for conversion from Celsius to Fahrenheit is $F = 9C/5 + 32$.

(a) Write a program which will ask you for the Celsius temperature and display the equivalent Fahrenheit one with some sort of comment, e.g.

```
The Fahrenheit temperature is: ...
```

Try it out on the following Celsius temperatures (answers in brackets): 0 (32), 100 (212), -40 (-40!), 37 (normal human temperature: 98.6).

(b) Change the program to use a `for` loop to compute and display the Fahrenheit equivalent of Celsius temperatures ranging from $20°$ to $30°$ in steps of $1°$, in two columns with a heading, e.g.

```
Celsius     Fahrenheit
  20.00        68.00
  21.00        69.80
    ...
  30.00        86.00
```

4.7 It has been suggested that the population of the United States may be modelled by the formula

$$P(t) = \frac{197273000}{1 + e^{-0.03134(t - 1913.25)}}$$

where t is the date in years. Write a program to compute and display the population every *ten* years from 1790 to 2000. **Hint:** Use `Math.exp(x)` for the exponential function e^x.
Use Essential Grapher to plot a graph of the population against time (Figure 6.5, accompanying Exercise 6.6 in Chapter 6, shows this graph compared with actual data).
Use your program to find out if the population ever reaches a 'steady state', i.e. whether it stops changing.

4.8 (a) The cooling problem in Section 4.1 has an exact mathematical solution. The temperature $T(t)$ at time t is given by the formula

$$T(t) = F + (T_0 - F)e^{-Kt}, \tag{4.5}$$

where T_0 is the initial temperature.
Insert this formula into the `cool` method of `Fridge` and display it alongside the numerical solution. Your enlarged table of output should look something like this:

```
time    Model   Exact
00.00   25.00   25.00
05.00   21.61   21.68
10.00   18.98   19.10
15.00   16.95   17.09
. . .
```

(b) The numerical solution generated by Equation (4.3) gets more accurate as dt gets smaller. That is because Equation (4.5) (the exact solution) is derived from Equation (4.3) *in the limit* as $dt \to 0$.

Table 4.1 Model of cooling: effect on temperature of changing the step-length *dt*

time	$dt = 1$	$dt = 0.1$
00.00	25.00	25.00
05.00	21.61	21.67
10.00	18.98	19.09
15.00	16.95	17.07

Table 4.1 compares results for $dt = 1$ and $dt = 0.1$, with opInt $= 5$.

On the other hand, as dt gets larger, the numerical solution becomes less and less accurate and eventually becomes meaningless. Experiment with a few larger values of dt.

4.9 In a model of bacteria growth, time is broken up into a number of small steps each of length dt hours. If we define N_i as the number of bacteria present at the end of step i, we can get N_{i+1} from N_i as follows:

$$N_{i+1} = N_i + r \, dt \, N_i,$$

where r is the growth rate per hour. At time $t = 0$ there are 1000 bacteria.

Using the example of Section 4.1 (**Update processes**) as a guide, write a program to generate the bacteria numbers from time $t = 0$ to 12 hours, given $r = 0.1$ and $dt = 1$ hour.

Hint: Set up a class Bacteria with a constructor Bacteria(N0, r) where N0 is the initial number of bacteria, and a method grow(tend, dt, opInt), where tend is the final time, and opInt is the time interval at which results are displayed.

Paste your results in a text file results.txt, with time in the first column and bacteria numbers in the second.

Now run the program with $dt = 0.5$, and place the bacteria numbers, at hourly intervals, in the third column of results.txt.

The exact number of bacteria at time t hours is given by the formula

$$N(t) = 1000 \, e^{rt}.$$

Use this formula to put the exact number of bacteria, also at hourly intervals, into the fourth column of results.txt.

Your results should be something like this:

```
    0       1000.00     1000.00     1000.00
 1.00       1100.00     1102.50     1105.17
 2.00       1210.00     1215.51     1221.40
 . . .
12.00       3138.43     3225.10     3320.12
```

4.10 A person deposits $1000 in a bank. Interest is compounded monthly at the rate of 1 per cent per month. Write a program which will compute the monthly balance, but write it only *annually* for 10 years (use nested `for` loops, with the outer loop for 10 years, and the inner loop for 12 months). Note that after 10 years, the balance is $3300.39, whereas if interest had been compounded annually at the rate of 12 per cent per year the balance would only have been $3105.85.

4.11 There are many formulae for computing π (the ratio of a circle's circumference to its diameter). The simplest is

$$\frac{\pi}{4} = 1 - 1/3 + 1/5 - 1/7 + 1/9 - \cdots \qquad (4.6)$$

which comes from putting $x = 1$ in the series

$$\arctan x = x - \frac{x^3}{3} + \frac{x^5}{5} - \frac{x^7}{7} + \frac{x^9}{9} - \cdots \qquad (4.7)$$

(a) Write a program to compute π using Equation (4.6). Use as many terms in the series as your computer will reasonably allow (start modestly, with 100 terms, say, and re-run your program with more and more each time). You should find that the series converges very slowly, i.e. it takes a lot of terms to get fairly close to π.

(b) Rearranging the series speeds up the convergence:

$$\frac{\pi}{8} = \frac{1}{1 \times 3} + \frac{1}{5 \times 7} + \frac{1}{9 \times 11} \cdots$$

Write a program to compute π using this series instead. You should find that you need fewer terms to reach the same level of accuracy that you got in (a).

(c) One of the fastest series for π is

$$\frac{\pi}{4} = 6 \arctan \frac{1}{8} + 2 \arctan \frac{1}{57} + \arctan \frac{1}{239}.$$

Use this formula to compute π. Don't use `Math.atan` to compute the arctangents, since that would be cheating. Rather use Equation (4.7).

4.12 The following method of computing π is due to Archimedes:

    1. Let $A = 1$ and $N = 6$
    2. Repeat 10 times, say:
        Replace N by $2N$
        Replace A by $[2 - \sqrt{(4 - A^2)}]^{1/2}$
        Let $L = NA/2$
        Let $U = L/\sqrt{1 - A^2/2}$
        Let $P = (U + L)/2$ (estimate of π)
        Let $E = (U - L)/2$ (estimate of error)
        Print N, P, E.

Write a program to implement the algorithm.

4.13 Write a program to compute a table of the function

$$f(x) = x \sin \left[\frac{\pi(1 + 20x)}{2} \right]$$

over the (closed) interval $[-1, 1]$ using increments in x of (a) 0.2 (b) 0.1 and (c) 0.01.

Use your tables to sketch graphs of $f(x)$ for the three cases (by hand), and observe that the tables for (a) and (b) give totally the wrong picture of $f(x)$.

Get your program to draw the graph of $f(x)$ for the three cases, superimposed.

Hint: to draw multiple graphs in the same window with Essential Grapher simply create a different Graph object for each graph to be drawn.

4.14 The transcendental number e (2.71828182845904...) can be shown to be the limit of

$$(1 + x)^{1/x}$$

as x tends to zero (from above). Write a program which shows how this expression converges to e as x gets closer and closer to zero.

4.15 The formula

$$F(t) = \frac{4}{\pi} \sum_{k=0}^{\infty} \frac{1}{2k+1} \sin\left[\frac{(2k+1)\pi t}{T}\right]$$

represents the *Fourier series* of square waves like the one shown in Figure 4.4.

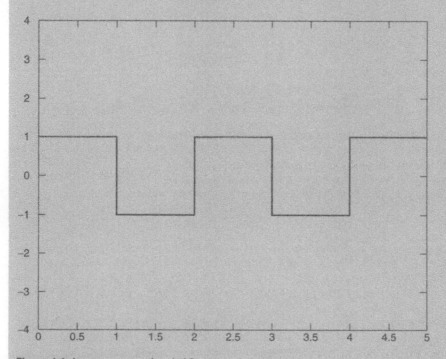

Figure 4.4 A square wave of period 2

It is of interest to know how many terms are needed for a good approximation to the infinite sum in the formula. Taking $T = 1$, write a program to compute and plot $F(t)$ summed to n terms for t from -1.1 to 1.1 in steps of 0.01, say. Run the program for different values of n, e.g. 1, 3, 6, etc.

Superimpose plots of $F(t)$ against t for a few values of n.

On each side of a discontinuity a Fourier series exhibits peculiar oscillatory behaviour known as the Gibbs phenomenon. Figure 4.5 shows this clearly for the above series with $n = 20$ (and

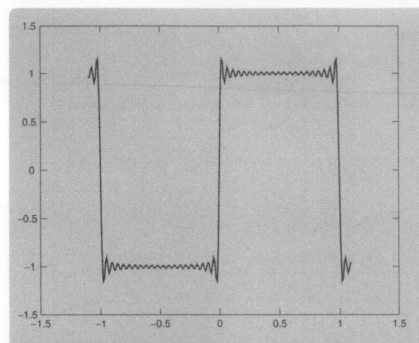

Figure 4.5 Fourier series: Gibbs phenomenon

increments in t of 0.01). The phenomenon is much sharper for $n = 200$ and t increments of 0.001.

(A Fourier series reconstructs a given function as an infinite series of sinusoidal terms. This exercise involves evaluating one such series; you do not need to know the theory involved in order to write the program—a common experience for programmers!)

4.16 If an amount of money A is invested for k years at a nominal annual interest rate r (expressed as a decimal fraction), the value V of the investment after k years is given by

$$V = A(1 + r/n)^{nk}$$

where n is the number of compounding periods per year. Write a class Investment to compute V as n gets larger and larger, i.e. as the compounding periods become more and more frequent, like monthly, daily, hourly, etc. Take $A = 1000$, $r = 4$ per cent and $k = 10$ years. You should observe that your output gradually approaches a limit. **Hint**: use a for loop which doubles n each time, starting with $n = 1$.

Also compute the value of the formula Ae^{rk} for the same values of A, r and k (use Math.exp), and compare this value with the values of V computed above. What do you conclude?

4.17 The Spiral of Archimedes (Figure 4.6) may be represented in polar co-ordinates by the equation

$$r = a\theta,$$

where a is some constant. (The shells of a class of animals called nummulites grow in this way.) Write a program which uses Essential Grapher to draw the spiral for some values of a.

4.18 Another type of spiral is the *logarithmic* spiral (Figure 4.6), which describes the growth of shells of animals like the periwinkle and the nautilus. Its equation in polar co-ordinates is

$$r = aq^{\theta},$$

where $a > 0$, $q > 1$. Draw this spiral.

Archimedes   Logarithmic

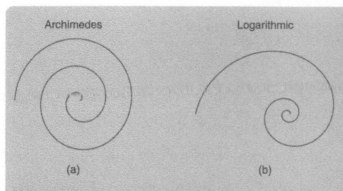

(a)   (b)

Figure 4.6 Spirals

Figure 4.7 A perfect sunflower?

4.19   The arrangement of seeds in a sunflower head (and other flowers, like daisies) follows a fixed
       mathematical pattern. The nth seed is at position

$$r = \sqrt{n},$$

with angular co-ordinate $\pi dn/180$ radians, where d is the constant angle of divergence (in
degrees) between any two successive seeds, i.e. between the nth and $(n+1)$th seeds. A perfect
sunflower head (Figure 4.7) is generated by $d = 137.51°$. Write a program to draw the seeds
in a sunflower head; use a circle for each seed. A remarkable feature of this model is that the
angle d must be exact to get proper sunflowers. Experiment with some different values, e.g.
137.45° (spokes, from fairly far out), 137.65° (spokes all the way), 137.92° (Catherine wheels).
Hint: If your Essential Grapher Graph object is sunF, the statement

```
sunF.setPointShape(new CirclePoint(PointShape.UNFILLED));
```

will plot small open circles instead of points, and the statement

```
sunF.setDrawingStyle(Graphable.PLOTPOINTS);
```

will plot the circles only, without joining them with lines (the default).

4.20 The equation of an ellipse in polar co-ordinates is given by

$$r = a(1 - e^2)/(1 - e \cos\theta),$$

where a is the semi-major axis and e is the eccentricity, if one focus is at the origin, and the semi-major axis lies on the x-axis.

Halley's Comet, which visited us in 1985/6, moves in an elliptical orbit about the Sun (at one focus) with a semi-major axis of 17.9 A.U. (A.U. stands for Astronomical Unit, which is the mean distance of the Earth from the Sun: 149.6 million km.) The eccentricity of the orbit is 0.967276. Write a program which draws the orbit of Halley's Comet and the Earth (assume the Earth is circular).

4.21 The following very interesting iterative relationship is often used to model population growth in cases where the growth is not unlimited, but is restricted by shortage of food, living area, etc.:

$$y_{k+1} = r y_k (1 - y_k)$$

(this is a discrete form of the well-known *logistic model*). Given y_0 and r, successive y_k's may be computed very easily, e.g. if $y_0 = 0.2$ and $r = 1$, then $y_1 = 0.16$, $y_2 = 0.1334$, and so on. Fascinating behaviour, known as *mathematical chaos*, is shown by y_k for values of r between 3 and 4 (independent of y_0). Write a class Population which plots y_k against k as individual points; use the essential package Graph method

```
setDrawingStyle(Graphable.PLOTPOINTS).
```

Values of r that give particularly interesting graphs are 3.3, 3.5, 3.5668, 3.575, 3.5766, 3.738, 3.8287, and many more that can be found by patient exploration.

4.22 A rather beautiful *fractal* picture can be drawn by plotting the points (x_k, y_k) generated by the following difference equations

$$x_{k+1} = y_k(1 + \sin 0.7x_k) - 1.2\sqrt{|x_k|},$$

$$y_{k+1} = 0.21 - x_k,$$

starting with $x_0 = y_0 = 0$. Write a program to draw the picture (plot individual points; do not join them).

4.23 Write a program to estimate the number of throws needed on average to get a six.
Hints: Use the principles introduced in Section 2.7 (**Rolling dice**). Repeat n times the basic process of rolling a dice until a six comes up. Count the number of throws in total. Divide the number of throws by n. (You can guess what the theoretical answer is: 6.)

4.24 Write a program to compute the sum of the series $1^2 + 2^2 + 3^2 \ldots$ such that the sum is as large as possible without exceeding 1000. The program should display how many terms are used in the sum.

4.25 Consider the following structure plan, where M and N represent Java variables:

1. Set $M = 44$ and $N = 28$
2. While M not equal to N repeat:
    While $M > N$ repeat:
        Replace value of M by $M - N$

> While $N > M$ repeat:
>> Replace value of N by $N - M$
>> 3. Display M.

    (a)   Work through the structure plan by hand, sketching the contents of M and N during execution. Give the output.

    (b)   Repeat (a) for $M = 14$ and $N = 24$.

    (c)   What general arithmetic procedure does the algorithm carry out (try more values of M and N if necessary)?

    (d)   Write a program to implement the structure plan.

4.26   Adapt the program for the prime number algorithm in Section 4.2 to find all the prime factors of a given positive integer (even or odd).

       Write your solution as a method of `EssentialMath` to print out prime factors.

4.27   Use the Taylor series

$$\cos x = 1 - \frac{x^2}{2!} + \frac{x^4}{4!} - \frac{x^6}{6!} + \cdots$$

to write a program to compute $\cos x$ correct to four decimal places (x is in radians). See how many terms are needed to get 4-figure agreement with `Math.cos`. Don't make x too large; that could cause rounding error.

4.28   A student borrows $10000 to buy a used car. Interest on her loan is compounded at the rate of 2 per cent per month while the outstanding balance of the loan is more than $5000, and at 1 per cent per month otherwise. She pays back $300 every month, except for the last month, when the repayment must be less than $300. She pays at the end of the month, *after* the interest on the balance has been compounded. The first repayment is made one month after the loan is paid out. Write a class `LoanShark` which displays a monthly statement of the balance (after the monthly payment has been made), the final payment, and the month of the final payment.

4.29   When a resistor (R), capacitor (C) and battery (V) are connected in series, a charge Q builds up on the capacitor according to the formula

$$Q(t) = CV(1 - e^{-t/RC})$$

if there is no charge on the capacitor at time $t = 0$. The problem is to monitor the charge on the capacitor every 0.1 seconds in order to detect when it reaches a level of 8 units of charge, given that $V = 9$, $R = 4$ and $C = 1$. Write a class `Charge` which displays the time and charge every 0.1 seconds until the charge first exceeds 8 units (i.e. the last charge displayed must exceed 8). Once you have done this, rewrite the program to display the charge only while it is strictly less than 8 units.

4.30   Using the `RabbitColony` class defined in Section 3.8 and modified in Exercise 3.12, write a program which will work out how many months it will take before the rabbit colony reaches 1000 rabbits in total.

4.31   Write a program which uses the `Tree` class from Section 3.10 to create a tree with a height of 50 cm and a growth rate of 10 cm per year. You program should calculate how many years it will take before the tree reaches a height of 4 m.

4.32   Rewrite the guessing program in Section 4.2 to use a `do-while` loop instead of `while`.

5
Debugging

Objectives

By the end of this chapter you should be able to

- distinguish between the following sorts of errors encountered in programming: compilation, run-time, logic, rounding;
- correct or avoid many of these errors.

Even experienced programmers seldom get programs to run correctly the first time. In computer jargon, an error in a program is called a *bug*. The story is that a moth short-circuited two thermionic valves in one of the earliest computers. This primeval (charcoaled) 'bug' took days to find. The process of detecting and correcting such errors is called *debugging*. There are four main types of errors:

- *compilation* errors
- *run-time* errors
- errors of *logic*
- *rounding* errors.

In this chapter we deal with examples of these sort of errors that can arise with the programming we have done so far.

5.1 Compilation errors

Compilation errors are errors in syntax and construction, like spelling mistakes, that are picked up by the `javac` compiler during compilation (the process whereby your `.java` source code is translated to `.class` byte-code files). The compiler displays a message, which may or may not be helpful, when it encounters such an error.

There are a large number of compiler error messages. Since a compiler is nowhere near as intelligent as you are, the error messages can sometimes be rather confusing. A few common examples which tend to be generated by beginners (using the Java SDK compiler) are given below.

You should bear in mind that compilation errors tend to 'cascade' (see below). If there is more than one error, start by correcting the first one, and then recompile. With a bit of luck quite a few of the rest will have gone away.

The line numbers in the examples below are references to the programs we ran to generate the errors.

Error: `';' expected`

- ```
  D:\EJSE\Junk.java:6: ';' expected
                  double bal, finBal, rate
                                          ^
  ```

  What could be clearer than that! Semi-colon left out after statement?

- This one is also quite helpful—can you spot the error?

  ```
  C:\EJSE\Junk.java:7: ';' expected
          for (int i = 1, i <= 10; i++;)
                                  ^
  ```

  (comma used instead of semi-colon in `for`:

- But these are not so clear:

  ```
  D:\EJSE\Junk.java:10: ';' expected
                  elseif (bal < 10000)
                                      ^
  D:\EJSE\Junk.java:12: 'else' without 'if'
                  else
                      ^
  D:\EJSE\Junk.java:10: cannot resolve symbol
  symbol  : method elseif  (boolean)
  location: class Junk
                  elseif (bal < 10000)
                  ^
  3 errors
  ```

  These rather curious errors are all due to writing `elseif` incorrectly as one word in the code

  ```
      if (bal < 5000)
          rate = 0.09;
      elseif (bal < 10000)
          rate = 0.12;
      else
          rate = 0.15;
  ```

Error: `')' expected`

- ```
  D:\EJSE\Junk.java:9: ')' expected
                  for (k = 1; k <= 10; k++;)
                                          ^
  ```

  Semi-colon incorrectly inserted after *increment* clause of `for` loop.

Error: `cannot resolve symbol`

- ```
  D:\EJSE\Junk.java:9: cannot resolve symbol
  symbol   : variable rate
  location: class Junk
                    rate = 0.15;
                    ^
  ```

  Variable `rate` not declared.

- ```
  D:\EJSE\Junk.java:9: cannot resolve symbol
  symbol   : variable random
  location: class java.lang.Math
                    bal = 15000*Math.random;
                    ^
  ```

  Left out `()` after `Math.random`. But look what happened to one of our students:

- ```
  D:\EJSE\Junk.java:9: cannot resolve symbol
  symbol   : method random ()
  location: class Math
                    bal = 15000*Math.random();
                    ^
  ```

  Nasty one this! The student had created her own class `Math` in the current directory, which *hid* the Java API class `Math`!

This error also occurs if you forget to import a package.

Another source of the same error is if you call your class by the same name as a different class you are using, for example, if you call your class `Turtle` and also expect to use the `essential.Turtle` class. To fix the error, rename your class to something different and delete the old files (*both* `Turtle.java` *and* `Turtle.class`).

Error: `'class' or 'interface' expected`

- ```
  D:\EJSE\Junk.java:2: 'class' or 'interface' expected
  public static void main(String[] args)
                    ^
  ```

  Left out `public class ...` declaration at start of program.

Error: `class ... is public, should be declared in a file named ...`

- ```
  D:\EJSE\junk.java:2: class Junk is public, should be declared
  in a file named Junk.java
  public class Junk
           ^
  ```

  This one can take a while to sort out. Program was saved with filename `junk.java` instead of `Junk.java`!

Error: `illegal start of expression`

- ```
  D:\EJSE\junk.java:10: illegal start of expression
                    if (b*b >= 4*a*c) && (a != 0)
                    ^
  ```

  This one's also rather subtle. The entire logical expression in an `if` statement must be enclosed in parentheses:

  ```
  if ((b*b >= 4*a*c) && (a != 0))
  ```

Error: `illegal start of type`

- `C:\EJSE\Junk.java:8: illegal start of type`
  ```
              if (bal < 5000)
                      ^
  ```

Left out `public static void main`. Compiler expected this statement to be a declaration of a method or a data member. This single mistake can generate a vast number of different compiler errors.

Error: `not a statement`

- `D:\EJSE\Junk.java:6: not a statement`
  ```
              double, bal, finBal, rate;
                    ^
  ```

Incorrect comma after `double`.

Error: `operator - cannot be applied to java.lang.String ...`

- `D:\EJSE\Junk.java:9: operator - cannot be applied to`
  `java.lang.String,double`
  ```
          System.out.println( x + "   " + x-0.2 );
                                            ^
  ```

If you want to concatenate the result of an expression to a string in `println()` you have to enclose it in parentheses:
```
          System.out.println( x + "   " + (x-0.2) );
```

Error: `possible loss of precision`

- `D:\EJSE\Junk.java:9: possible loss of precision`
  `found    : double`
  `required: int`
  ```
          numberOnDice = Math.floor(6*Math.random())+1;
                                                      ^
  ```

Although `Math.floor()` returns a 'mathematical integer', according to the JDK documentation, it is nevertheless a `double` value, and must therefore be typecast with `(int)` in this case.

Error: `variable ... might not have been initialized`

- `C:\EJSE\Junk.java:9: variable rate might not have been`
  `                    initialized`
  ```
          bal = bal + rate*bal;
                      ^
  ```

`rate` was declared but not initialized.

Now try Exercise 5.1.

5.2 Run-time errors

Errors occurring when you attempt to run a compiled program with the Java Virtual Machine `java` are called run-time errors (or more correctly *exceptions* in Java), and are generally *fatal*, i.e. the program terminates. Java has facilities for intercepting run-time errors. This process is referred to as *exception handling*, and is discussed in Chapter 10.

Here are a few examples of run-time errors.

Error: `java.lang.ArithmeticException: / by zero`

- `java.lang.ArithmeticException: / by zero`
  `    at Junk.main(Junk.java:7)`
  `Exception in thread "main"`

  The culprit in line 7 is

  ```
  int n = 13/(1/2);
  ```

  (1/2) is evaluated first, using integer arithmetic, yielding 0.

Error: `java.lang.StringIndexOutOfBoundsException:`

- `java.lang.StringIndexOutOfBoundsException:`
  `    String index out of range: 3`
  `    at java.lang.String.charAt(String.java:507)`
  `    at Junk.main(Junk.java:8)`
  `Exception in thread "main"`

  A common problem with beginners. Here's the offending code extract: can you spot the error?

  ```
  String s = "abc";
  System.out.print( s.charAt(3) );
  ```

  Characters in strings are indexed from 0, so the index of the last character in the string `"abc"` is 2.

Error: `java.lang.NoClassDefFoundError: ...`

- `java.lang.NoClassDefFoundError: Junk`
  `Exception in thread "main"`

  Also common with beginners. Probably attempted to run program before compiling it. Could also arise because of an incorrect CLASSPATH setting—basically `java` can't find the `.class` file.

Error: `java.lang.NullPointerException:`

- `java.lang.NullPointerException`
  `    at Junk.main(Junk.java:8)`
  `Exception in thread "main"`

  Occurs if a string, for example, is not properly initialized, as in

  ```
  String s = null;
  int l = s.length();
  ```

Error: `java.lang.NumberFormatException:`

- `java.lang.NumberFormatException: 34,5`
  `    at java.lang.FloatingDecimal.readJavaFormatString`
  `                              (FloatingDecimal.java:1176)`

```
        at java.lang.Double.parseDouble(Double.java:184)
        at Junk.main(Junk.java:8)
Exception in thread "main"
```

Occurs, for example, when parsing strings, as in

```
        String s = "34,5";
        double d = Double.parseDouble(s);
```

5.3 Errors in logic

These are errors in the actual algorithm you are using to solve a problem, and are the most difficult to find; the program runs, but gives the wrong results! For example, the following code was meant to print five asterisks, but instead prints only one (can you see why?):

```
        for (int i = 1; i <= 5; i++);
            System.out.print( '*' );
```

(semi-colon incorrectly inserted after the `for` header).

It's even worse if you don't realize the answers are wrong. The following tips might help you to check out the logic.

- Try to run the program for some special cases where you know the answers.
- If you don't know any exact answers, try to use your insight into the problem to check whether the answers seem to be of the right order of magnitude.
- Try working through the program by hand, or with the Java Debugger (see below), or by using lots of `println` statements, to see if you can spot where things start going wrong.

Debugging logical errors

Java has a simple command-line debugger called `jdb` which you can use to find and fix run-time errors. See under `/docs/tooldocs/tools.html#basic` (**Tool Documentation**) in your Java SDK documentation.

Try Exercise 5.2.

5.4 Rounding errors

At times, as we have seen, a program will give numerical answers which we know are wrong. This can also be due to *rounding error*, which results from the finite precision available on the computer, i.e. eight bytes per variable, instead of an infinite number.

As an example, run the following code:

```
        double x = 0.1;

        while (x != 0.2) {
            x += 0.001;
            System.out.println( x );
        }
```

You will find that you need to crash the program to stop it, i.e. with **Ctrl-break** on a PC. The variable x never has the value 0.2 *exactly*, because of rounding error. In fact, x misses 0.2 by about 8.3×10^{-17}, as can be seen from displaying the value of x - 0.2. It would be better to replace the while clause with

```
while (x <= 0.2)
```

or, even better, with

```
while (Math.abs(x-0.2) > 1e-6)
```

In general, it is always better to test for 'equality' of two non-integer expressions as follows:

```
if (Math.abs((a-b)/a) > 1e-6)
    System.out.println( "a practically equals b" );
```

or

```
if (Math.abs((a-b)/b) > 1e-6)
    System.out.println( "a practically equals b" );
```

Note that this equality test is based on the *relative* difference between a and b, rather than on the *absolute* difference.

Rounding error may sometimes be reduced by a mathematical re-arrangement of a formula. Recall yet again the common quadratic equation

$$ax^2 + bx + c = 0,$$

with solutions

$$x_1 = (-b + \sqrt{b^2 - 4ac})/(2a),$$
$$x_2 = (-b - \sqrt{b^2 - 4ac})/(2a).$$

Taking $a = 1$, $b = -10^7$ and $c = 0.001$ gives $x_1 = 10^7$ and $x_2 = 0$. The second root is expressed as the difference between two nearly equal numbers, and considerable significance is lost. However, as you no doubt remember, the product of the two roots is given by c/a. The second root can therefore be expressed as $(c/a)/x_1$. Using this form gives $x_2 = 10^{-10}$, which is more accurate.

Try Exercises 5.3 and 5.4.

Summary

- Compilation errors are mistakes in syntax (coding), and are reported by javac.
- Run-time errors (exceptions) occur while the program is executing.
- The Java Debugger may be used to work through a program, statement by statement.
- Logical errors are errors in the algorithm used to solve the problem.
- Rounding error occurs because a computer can store numbers only to a finite accuracy.

Exercises

5.1 Try to spot the errors in the following code before running it (and fixing the errors).

```
public class Debug
{
    public static void main(String args)
```

```
            {
                int x, z = 10;
                System.out.print(x + z];
                for (int i = 0, i < z, z++)
                    if (i%2 = 0)
                        System.out.println(i);
            } \\end of for
            System.out.println( The End );
        }
    } \\end of Debug
```

5.2 Consider the following program:

```
        import essential.*;

        public class NumberTriangle
        {
            public static void main(String[] args)
            {
                System.out.print( "Enter size of number triangle: " );
                int size = Keyboard.readInt();
                for (int row = size; row < 0; row--)
                    for (int num = row; num < 0; num--)
                        System.out.print( num );
                    System.out.println();
            }
        }
```

If the user enters 5, for example, it is meant to produce the output

```
        54321
        4321
        321
        21
        1
```

However, it prints out nothing at all. Find out why, and correct it.

5.3 The Newton quotient

$$\frac{f(x+h) - f(x)}{h}$$

may be used to estimate the first derivative $f'(x)$ of a function $f(x)$, if h is 'small'. Write a program to compute the Newton quotient for the function

$$f(x) = x^2$$

at the point $x = 2$ (the exact answer is 4) for values of h starting at 1, and decreasing by a factor of 10 each time (use a `for` loop). The effect of rounding error becomes apparent when h gets 'too small', i.e. less than about 10^{-12}.

5.4 The solution of the two linear simultaneous equations

$$ax + by = c$$
$$dx + ey = f$$

is given by

$$x = (ce - bf)/(ae - bd),$$
$$y = (af - cd)/(ae - bd).$$

If $(ae - bd)$ is small, rounding error may cause quite large inaccuracies in the solution. Consider the system

$$0.2038x + 0.1218y = 0.2014,$$
$$0.4071x + 0.2436y = 0.4038.$$

(a) Write a program to compute the solutions x and y of this system. With double type you should find that $x = -2$ and $y = 5$, which is indeed the exact solution.

(b) With four-figure floating point arithmetic the solution obtained is quite different: $x = -1$, $y = 3$. This level of accuracy may be simulated in your solution to part (a) with some statements like

```
ae = Math.floor( a*e*1e4 )/1e4
```

and appropriate changes in the coding. Rewrite your program to implement four-figure accuracy in this way.

If the coefficients in the equations are themselves subject to experimental error, the 'solution' of this system using limited accuracy is totally meaningless.

See Chapter 12 for our class to solve linear equations directly.

6
Arrays and matrices

Objectives

By the end of this chapter you should be able to

- decide when it is appropriate to use an array structure;
- create and manipulate one- and two-dimensional arrays for use in various applications;
- sort an array using insertion sort.

6.1 Introduction

Situations often arise in real problem solving where we need to handle a large amount of data in the same way, e.g. to find the mean of a set of numbers, to sort a list of numbers or names, to analyse a set of students' test results, or to solve a system of linear equations. To avoid an enormously clumsy program, where perhaps hundreds of identifiers are needed, we can use *arrays*. An array is used to hold a collection of items of the *same* data type.

Why bother with arrays?

Say we want to write a program that reads in four numbers from the user, calculates the mean and then prints out the number which is furthest in absolute value from the mean. To do this we have to store all four numbers as variables so that we can compare each one later to the mean. Here is a first attempt:

```
import essential.*;

public class FurthestFromMean1
{
  public static void main(String[] args)
  {
    System.out.println("Enter four whole numbers:");
    int x1, x2, x3, x4;
    x1 = Keyboard.readInt();
    x2 = Keyboard.readInt();
    x3 = Keyboard.readInt();
```

```
    x4 = Keyboard.readInt();
    double mean = (x1 + x2 + x3 + x4)/4.0;
    System.out.println("The mean is: " + mean);
    double gap1 = Math.abs(mean - x1);
    double gap2 = Math.abs(mean - x2);
    double gap3 = Math.abs(mean - x3);
    double gap4 = Math.abs(mean - x4);
    int furthest;
    if ((gap1 >= gap2) && (gap1 >= gap3) && (gap1 >= gap4))
            furthest = x1;
    else if ((gap2 >= gap3) && (gap2 >= gap4))
            furthest = x2;
    else if (gap3 >= gap4)
            furthest = x3;
    else furthest = x4;
    System.out.println("Number furthest from the mean: " + furthest);
  }
}
```

Rather clumsy, not so? What would the program look like if we wanted to do the same thing with 20 numbers? Clearly, this solution is unworkable for large amounts of data.

Arrays allow us to declare multiple data values (of the same type) as a *single variable*, which is a much more elegant way of working with data. Here is a second attempt at calculating the mean, which uses arrays:

```
import essential.*;

public class FurthestFromMean2
{
  public static void main(String[] args)
  {
    System.out.println("Enter four whole numbers:");
    int x[] = new int[4];    // declares 4 ints as one variable
    int sum = 0;
    for(int i=0; i<4; i++)  // reads in 4 integers and adds them
    {
      x[i] = Keyboard.readInt();
      sum += x[i];
    }
    double mean = sum/4.0;    // calculates the mean
    System.out.println("The mean is: " + mean);

    double furthestGap = Math.abs(mean - x[0]);
    int item = 0;
    for(int i=1; i<4; i++)
    {
      double gap = Math.abs(mean - x[i]);
      if (gap > furthestGap)
      {
        furthestGap = gap;
        item = i;
      }
    }
```

```
      System.out.println("Number furthest from the mean: " + x[item]);
   }
}
```

Although it may seem just as complicated as the first version of the program, the same program (with very minor changes) can work with any number of integers. We will explain the details of the program as the chapter progresses.

6.2 The basics of arrays

Declaring and initializing an array

An array is set up in two distinct stages.

1. Firstly, the array name (reference), and the fact that it is an array, is declared with

   ```
   int[] r;    // int r[] also works
   ```

   In this case, we have declared an array of ints called r. We can declare an array of any type: primitive or object. For example, the following are all valid array declarations:

   ```
   double[] nums;
   Graph[] g;
   char[] c;
   ```

   When we declare an array, the name of the array is a *handle* to the array object. In all the examples above, the handles (nums, g, or c) are pointing nowhere. To create the array object, we have to allocate memory for it.
2. Secondly, memory for each element of the array is allocated, by using the new keyword and specifying a size:

   ```
   r = new int[n];    // creates an array of n ints
   nums = new double[100];   // creates an array of 100 doubles
   ```

The two stages can be combined in one statement, for example:

```
int[] r = new int[n];
```

Once the array is set up, we need to initialize it with data. One of the ways of doing this is to provide all the values when the array is declared, as shown in the following examples:

```
int[] n = {10,-5,6,12,9,54};
char[] whiteSpace = {' ','\n','\t'};
```

Note that if we initialize an array this way, we do not specify the size of the array—it is deduced from the number of elements provided.

As always, it is useful to have a mental picture of how memory works to understand how variables behave. Figure 6.1 shows some sample statements involving arrays with corresponding pictures of how memory would look.

Indexing elements of an array

The individual components of an array are called *elements*, and are written in the normal way, except that a subscript is enclosed in square brackets after the array name, e.g. x[3], y[i+2*n].

Statement	Memory after statement is executed

```int [ ] num;```
 	
```int n;```
	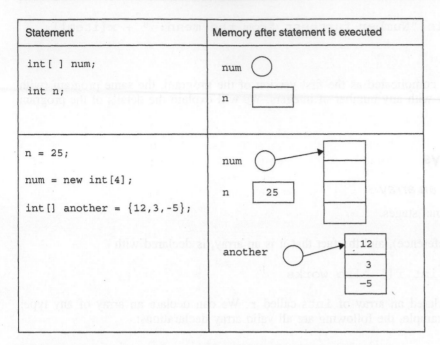

```n = 25;```
 	
```num = new int[4];```
 	
```int[] another = {12,3,-5};```	

Figure 6.1 Sample array statements showing how memory would be allocated

The first element of an array in Java always has the subscript 0.

The subscript of the last element will therefore be one less than the value used when the array is created. For example, consider the following statements:

```
int[] n = {31,12,6,-2,8,19,7,0};
System.out.println(n[0]);
System.out.println(n[2]);
System.out.println(n[1] + n[3] + n[5]);
System.out.println(n[7]);
```

The output would be:

```
31
6
29
0
```

Unlike its predecessors C and C++, Java implements range checking of array subscripts. Any attempt to subscript an element beyond the end of an array, or to use a negative subscript, generates the run-time exception (we will cover exceptions in Chapter 10):

```
java.lang.ArrayIndexOutOfBoundsException
```

In the array n above, attempting to print out n[8] would generate such an exception.

Looping through an array

Loops (in particular `for` loops) are very useful for accessing and manipulating arrays. Consider the following statements from the `FurthestFromMean2` program in Section 6.1:

```
int x[] = new int[4];    // declares four integers as one variable
int sum = 0;
for(int i=0; i<4; i++)   // read in four integers and add them
{
  x[i] = Keyboard.readInt();
  sum += x[i];
}
```

The for loop starts at 0 (the index of the first element of the array) and ends before 4 (i.e. at 3, which is the index of the last element of the array). Through each iteration of the loop, the particular array element is initialized by the value read in from the keyboard and is added to sum. Here is a second example of looping through an array, which generates an array of 10 random integers in the range 1 to 100:

```
public class RandomInts
{
  public static void main(String[ ] args)
  {
    int n = 10;
    int[ ] r;
    r = new int[n];

    for (int i = 0; i < n; i++)
    {
      r[i] = (int)(100*Math.random())+1;
    }

    //now print the whole array:
    for (int i = 0; i < n; i++)
    {
      System.out.print( "   " + r[i] );
    }
  }
}
```

Note:

- The code sets up the array r with 10 random elements, named r[0] to r[9].
  In a sample run the ten elements of the array looked like this:

r[0]	r[1]	r[2]	...	r[9]
27	65	31	...	41

- Note the standard way above of working through all the subscripts of an array with n elements, *starting at 0*:

```
for (int i = 0; i < n; i++) ...
```

- Technically, an array is an *object*. It knows how long it is by means of its field length, e.g. r.length in the above program has the value 10.

Now do Exercises 6.1 to 6.6.

6.3 Passing arrays to methods

Arrays, just like other objects, can be passed as arguments to methods. We pass the entire array by passing the *handle* to the array. For example, one of the constructors of String takes an array of characters as an argument and creates a String object from the array. The header of the method looks like this:

```
public String(char[] value)
```

Notice that the type of the argument is char[], meaning a handle that references an array of chars. Here are some sample statements that use this constructor:

```
char[] c = {'a','b','c','d'};
String s = new String(c);
```

As a further example, suppose you want to write a method to return the mean of the data in its parameter x (which is an array). The method header could look like this:

```
public static double mean( double[ ] x )
```

To use this method, assuming the actual data is in the array data, you simply pass its name to mean, e.g.

```
System.out.println( "Mean is " + mean(data) );
```

Now do Exercises 6.7 and 6.8.

6.4 Frequency distributions: a simple bar chart

In this section we present a program that simulates the random movement of an ant. Without the use of arrays, this example would be very difficult to implement.

Imagine an ant walking along a straight line, e.g. the x-axis. She starts at $x = 40$. She moves in steps of one unit along the line. Each step is to the left or the right with equal probability. We want to know how much time she spends at each position.

Run the following program:

```
public class Ant
{
  int [] f = new int[80]; // frequencies

  public Ant()
  {
    for (int i = 0; i < 80; i++)
      f[i] = 0;            // initialize all frequencies to zero
  }

  public int[] randomSteps(int numSteps)
  {
    int x = 40;               // start at position 40

    for (int i = 1; i <= numSteps; i++)
    {
      double r = Math.random();
      if (r < 0.5)
        x++;
      else
```

```
        x--;

      if (x < 0 || x > 79)      // on the edge
        x = 40;

      f[x]++;                   // another time at x
    }
    return f;
  }

  public void printFreq(int start, int end)
  {
    for (int i = start; i <= end; i++)
      System.out.print( " " + f[i]);
  }

  public static void main(String[] args)
  {
    Ant sue = new Ant();
    sue.randomSteps(500);
    sue.printFreq(35,45);
  }
}
```

Note:

- In the `randomSteps` method, we use `Math.random`. This method returns a random number in the range 0–1. If it's greater than 0.5, the ant moves right (x++), otherwise she moves left (x--).
- The array f has 80 elements, initially all zero. We define f [x] as the number of times the ant lands at position x. Suppose her first step is to the right, so x increases to 41. The statement

      f[x]++

  then increases the value of f [41] to 1, meaning that she has been there once. When she next wanders past this value of x, f [41] will be increased to 2, meaning she's been there twice.
- f [x] is called a *frequency distribution*. Sample output of `printFreq(35,45)` was:

      39 43 53 59 51 40 33 24 12 5 1

  So, for example, the ant was at position 44 a total of 5 times, and at position 45 only once.
- This program *simulates* the random movement of the ant. If you re-run it, you will get a different frequency distribution, because `Math.random` will generate a different sequence of random numbers. Simulation is discussed more fully in Chapter 11.

Now do Exercise 6.9.

6.5 Multi-dimensional arrays

The arrays we have been declaring until now have been one-dimensional. In this section, we look at two-dimensional arrays.

Consider the following array declaration:

```
int[][] twoD = new int[3][5];
```

This statement creates an array of arrays called twoD. The array contains three elements. Each element is an array of five ints. We therefore have $3 \times 5 = 15$ integers stored in total. To loop through the 15 elements, we need a nested for loop. For example, the following code initializes the elements to consecutive numbers:

```
int n = 0;
for(int i = 0; i < 3; i++)
   for(int j = 0; j < 5; j++)
      twoD[i][j] = n++;
```

Figure 6.2 shows two representations of the array twoD in memory. The first representation is the more accurate way of visualizing memory, where each element of twoD is a handle to an array. Using this picture, it is clear that twoD[2], for example, is an array of five values.

The second representation is often the more practical one, where we visualize the array as a table of values with three rows and five columns. **Remember that subscripts start at zero!** So, for example, the element in row 3 and column 2 of the table (i.e. 11) must be referenced as twoD[2][1]. The first subscript represents the row, the second represents the column, both starting at zero.

The array twoD can also be printed using a nested for loop. The following code prints twoD one row per line:

```
for(int i = 0; i < 3; i++)
{
   for(int j = 0; j < 5; j++)
      System.out.print(twoD[i][j] + "\t");
   System.out.println();
}
```

A concrete example

Multi-dimensional arrays may be used to represent tables (and matrices—see below), as this example illustrates.

A ready-mix concrete company has three factories (S1, S2 and S3) which must supply three building sites (D1, D2 and D3). The costs, in some suitable currency (hundreds of dollars, say), of transporting a load of concrete from any factory to any site are given by the cost table in Table 6.1.

The factories can supply 4, 12 and 8 loads per day respectively, and the sites require 10, 9 and 5 loads per day respectively. The real problem is to find the cheapest way to satisfy the demands at the sites, but we are not considering that here.

Suppose the factory manager proposes the transportation scheme in Table 6.2 (each entry represents the number of loads of concrete to be transported along that particular route).

Table 6.1 Cost table

	D1	D2	D3
S1	3	12	10
S2	17	18	35
S3	7	10	24

Table 6.2 Solution table

	D1	D2	D3
S1	4	0	0
S2	6	6	0
S3	0	3	5

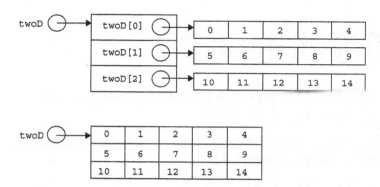

Figure 6.2 Alternative visualisations of the same two-dimensional array in memory. The first representation is the more accurate, while the second is the more practical

This sort of scheme is called a *solution* to the transportation problem. The cost table (and the solution) can then be represented by tables **C** and **X**, say, where c_{ij} is the entry in row i and column j of the cost table, with a similar convention for **X**.

To compute the cost of the above solution, each entry in the solution table must be multiplied by the corresponding entry in the cost table. (This operation is not to be confused with matrix multiplication, which is entirely different.) We therefore want to calculate

$$3 \times 4 + 12 \times 0 + \cdots + 24 \times 5.$$

The table in Table 6.2 can be set up in Java as follows:

```
int[][] x = {{4, 0, 0},
             {6, 6, 0},
             {0, 3, 5}};
```

Exercise 6.10 implements this example further. Try it now.

Matrix multiplication

A (two-dimensional) matrix looks just like the tables introduced in the previous section. Certain mathematical properties are, however, defined for matrices, which makes them a cut above mere tables. Matrix *multiplication* is probably the most important such property. It is used widely in such areas as network theory, coordinate transformation in computer graphics, solution of linear systems of equations, transformation of co-ordinate systems, and population modelling, to name but a very few. The rules for multiplying matrices look a little weird if you've never seen them before, but will be justified by the applications that follow (in Chapter 12).

When two matrices **A** and **B** are multiplied together their product is a third matrix **C**. The operation is written as

$$\mathbf{C} = \mathbf{AB},$$

and the element c_{ij} in row i and column j of **C** is formed by taking the *scalar product* of the ith row of **A** with the jth column of **B**. (The scalar product of two *vectors* **x** and **y** is $x_1 y_1 + x_2 y_2 + \cdots$, where x_i and y_i are the components of the vectors.)

It follows that **A** and **B** can only be successfully multiplied (in that order) if the number of columns in **A** is the same as the number of rows in **B**.

The general definition of matrix multiplication is as follows: If **A** is a $n \times m$ matrix and **B** is a $m \times p$ matrix, their product **C** will be a $n \times p$ matrix such that the general element c_{ij} of **C** is given by

$$c_{ij} = \sum_{k=1}^{m} a_{ik} b_{kj}.$$

Note that in general **AB** is not equal to **BA** (matrix multiplication is not *commutative*).

For example,

$$\begin{bmatrix} 1 & 2 \\ 3 & 4 \end{bmatrix} \times \begin{bmatrix} 5 & 6 \\ 0 & -1 \end{bmatrix} = \begin{bmatrix} 5 & 4 \\ 15 & 14 \end{bmatrix}$$

$$\begin{bmatrix} 5 & 6 \\ 0 & -1 \end{bmatrix} \times \begin{bmatrix} 1 & 2 \\ 3 & 4 \end{bmatrix} = \begin{bmatrix} 23 & 34 \\ -3 & -4 \end{bmatrix}$$

Since a vector is simply a one-dimensional matrix, the definition of matrix multiplication given above also applies when a vector is multiplied by an appropriate matrix, e.g.

$$\begin{bmatrix} 1 & 2 \\ 3 & 4 \end{bmatrix} \times \begin{bmatrix} 2 \\ 3 \end{bmatrix} = \begin{bmatrix} 8 \\ 18 \end{bmatrix}.$$

The following program uses a `static` method `multiplyMatrix` to multiply two matrices a and b, returning their product c. It is tested on the two matrices **A** and **B** above. (Note: we provide a temporary solution here in the form of a class `MultiplyTest`. A complete `Matrix` class is defined in the `essential` package and will be used in Chapter 12 on **Modelling with matrices**).

```java
public class MultiplyTest
{
  public static double[][] multiplyMatrix(
                      double[][] a, double[][] b )
  {
    int n = a.length;      //rows in a
    int m = a[0].length;   //cols in a
    int p = b[0].length;   //cols in b

    double [][] cTemp = new double[n][p];

    for (int i = 0; i < n; i++)
    {
      for (int j = 0; j < p; j++)
      {
        cTemp[i][j] = 0;
        for (int k = 0; k < m; k++)
          cTemp[i][j] += a[i][k]*b[k][j];
      }
    }
    return cTemp;
  }
  public static void main(String args[])
  {
    double [][] a = {{1,2},{3,4}};
    double [][] b = {{5,6},{0,-1}};

    double [][] c = multiplyMatrix(a, b);

    for (int i = 0; i < c.length; i++)
    {
      for (int j = 0; j < c[0].length; j++)
        System.out.print(c[i][j] + "\t");
```

```
            System.out.println();
        }
    }
}
```

Note:

- Inside `multiplyMatrix` the number of rows in a is returned by `a.length`. This is consistent with a being an array of arrays (a has `length` elements—rows—each of which is an array).

  The number of elements in a row is returned by `a[0].length`, for example—this will be the number of columns.

- `multiplyMatrix` returns a two-dimensional array. The actual size of the product c is only determined when the method returns.

- It is assumed that a and b have the right number of rows and columns in order to be successfully multiplied. (You could build in a test to check that the number of columns of a equals the number of rows of b.)

- In the `main` method, matrices a and b are initialized and then passed to `multiplyMatrix`. Notice that we use `c.length` to determine the number of rows in c and `c[0].length` to determine the number of columns.

Experiment with different matrices and see if you get the same answers as the program.

6.6 Arrays of objects

Just as we can have arrays of arrays, we can have arrays of any other objects.

Suppose we have defined a class `Student`, with two data members, age and name:

```
public class Student
{
    private int age;
    private String name;
    public Student( int a, String n )
    {
        age = a; name = n;
    }
    public void print()
    {
        System.out.println(name + " " + age);
    }
}
```

To set up an array of `Student` objects we declare the array name and size in the same way as we have been doing. But now there is a third stage: we have to call a constructor for *each object in the array*. The following code creates an array group of `Student` objects and instantiates all the objects in the array:

```
Student[ ] group;
group = new Student[4];        // 4 in the group
group[0] = new Student( 21, "Jack" );   // starting at 0
group[1] = new Student( 18, "Ann" );
group[2] = new Student( 25, "Jim" );
group[3] = new Student( 23, "Mary" );   // last one
group[3].print();    // print Mary's details
```

Note:

- In the second line (group = new Student[4]), the new statement is calling the constructor for an array object *not* a Student object. Only in the line after that are we calling the Student constructor. As in Figure 6.2, the handle group is pointing to an array of *handles*. Before the objects are created, these handles are pointing nowhere.
- To call one of the Student methods, you have to index a particular element in the array.

In the case of arrays of Strings, we can initialize the array without calling new for each string as follows:

```
String[] words = {"one", "two", "three", "four"};
```

This is an exceptional case and does not apply to other types of objects.

Now do Exercises 6.11 to 6.12.

6.7 Sorting an array

Sometimes you will need to sort the elements of an array before you can use them. There are many different sorting algorithms, some more efficient than others (entire books have been written on sorting and searching algorithms). We will present one that is fairly easy to understand, called *insertion sort*.

The basic idea of insertion sort is that we start with an empty array and add each element one-by-one into the correct position. In this way we build up an ordered array. For example, say we have the following unsorted elements:

```
56   -167   5   78   -10
```

The process is:

1. Starting with an empty array, we insert the first element (56):

   ```
   56
   ```

2. Insert the second element (-167) in the correct position. We start at the end of the array (at 56) and move each element that is larger than -167 to the right, in this way making a space for the new element:

   ```
   -167   56
   ```

3. Insert the third element (5) in the correct position. Start with the last element (56) and move it to the right (because it is larger than 5). The next element -167 is smaller, so leave it in the first position and insert 5 to the right of -167:

   ```
   -167   5   56
   ```

4. This process continues until all elements are inserted.

Here is code that implements the insertion sort on an array of integers:

```
public class TestSort
{
  public static int[] sort(int[] unsorted)
  {
    int[] sorted = new int[unsorted.length];
    int numElts = 0;  // number of elements currently sorted
```

```
   for(int i = 0; i < unsorted.length; i++)
   {
      int elt = unsorted[i]; // pick up next element to insert
      int pos = numElts;  // start at the end of sorted array
      while((pos > 0)&&(sorted[pos-1]>elt))
      {
         // move the element up:
         sorted[pos] = sorted[pos-1];
         pos--;
      }
      sorted[pos] = elt;  // insert element
      numElts++;
   }  // next element to insert
   return sorted;
}

public static void main(String[] args)
{
   int[] test = {3,-5,12,18,5,-45,8,34};
   int[] sorted = sort(test);
   System.out.println("Unsorted:");
   for(int i=0; i<test.length;i++)
      System.out.print(test[i] + "\t");
   System.out.println();
   System.out.println("Sorted:");
   for(int i=0; i<sorted.length;i++)
      System.out.print(sorted[i] + "\t");
}
}
```

Do a trace of the variables on paper to see how the program works (use a small array as a sample).

Note that we have shown you the insertion sort because it is a relatively simple algorithm to program. However, there are other sorting algorithms which are more *efficient*, both in terms of time and space. This means that if you had to sort a large data set using the insertion sort, it would take a longer time to run than in the case of some other algorithms. The sort method above also uses a second array to sort the elements. This is not usually needed when sorting an array, so we say that it is inefficient in its use of space. If you are sorting a large number of elements you should use one of the built-in Java sorting methods, for example, Arrays.sort in the java.util package.

Now do Exercise 6.13.

Summary

- Arrays are useful for representing and processing large amounts of data of the same type.
- An array is created in two stages: the array name must be declared, and then memory must be allocated for each element in the array. The two stages can be combined in one statement, e.g. the declaration

```
      int[ ] x = new int[10];
```

sets up an array of ten int elements x[0], x[1],...., x[9]. *The first element of an array in Java always has the subscript 0.*

- An array may be initialized at declaration, e.g.

  ```
  double[ ] x = {5.2, 6.8, -1.2, 0, 13};
  ```

- A Java array is an object.
  The number of elements in an array is stored in the array's special data member `length`, e.g. `x.length`.
- Java checks array subscripts during runtime and throws an exception if an array subscript goes out of range.
- Arrays can be sent to methods by passing the array handles as arguments.
- Two-dimensional arrays may be set up as arrays of arrays, e.g.

  ```
  double [][] a = new double[3][4];
  Tree[][] forest = new Tree[100][200];
  ```

  The number of rows is given by `a.length`, and the number of columns by `a[0].length` (or `a[i].length` in general).
- Matrices can be modelled as two-dimensional arrays of numbers.
- When an array of objects is created, a constructor must be called for each element in the array.
- Arrays can be sorted using a sorting algorithm such as the *insertion sort*.

Exercises

6.1 If `num` is an `int` array with 100 elements write lines of code which will
  (a) put the first 100 positive integers (1, 2, ..., 100) into the elements `num[0]`, ..., `num[99]`;
  (b) put the first 50 positive even integers (2, ..., 100) into the elements `num[0]`, ..., `num[49]`;
  (c) assign the integers in *reverse* order, i.e. assign 100 to `num[0]`, 99 to `num[1]`, etc.

6.2 When you were at school you probably solved hundreds of quadratic equations of the form

$$ax^2 + bx + c = 0.$$

A structure plan of the *complete* algorithm for finding the solution(s) x, given any values of a, b and c, is shown in Figure 6.3. Note that the structure plan caters for all possible situations, e.g. no solution, indeterminate solution, complex roots, etc. Figure 6.4 shows the graph of a quadratic equation with real unequal roots.
Write a method (in your `EssentialMath` class):

```
public static double[] solveQuadratic(
                    double a, double b, double c)
```

to solve a quadratic equation, with the following specifications:

  - if the roots are real and unequal, return an array with the roots as its two elements;
  - if the roots are real and equal, return an array with the root as its single element;
  - for all other situations, return `null`.

Returning `null` does not distinguish between the cases of complex roots, an indeterminate solution or no solution. To handle these cases properly you should use exceptions (see Chapter 10).

```
1. Declare array called roots
2. If a = 0 then
       If b = 0 then
           If c = 0 then
               return null (solution indeterminate)
           else
               return null (no solution)
       else
           x = -c/b
           Add x to roots (only one root: equation is linear)
   else if b² < 4ac then
       return null (complex roots)
   else if b² = 4ac then
       x = -b/(2a)
       Add x to roots (equal roots)
   else
       x₁ = (-b + √b² - 4ac) / (2a)
       x₂ = (-b - √b² - 4ac) / (2a)
       Add x₁ and x₂ to roots
3. return roots.
```

Figure 6.3 Quadratic equation structure plan

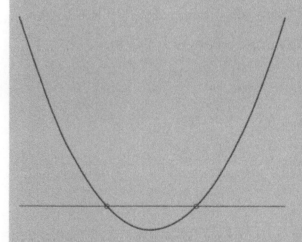

Figure 6.4 Graph of a quadratic equation with real unequal roots indicated by o

6.3   The numbers in the sequence

$$1, 1, 2, 3, 5, 8, 13, \ldots$$

are known as Fibonacci numbers. Can you work out what the next term is, before looking at the generating equation below?

Fibonacci numbers are defined by the relationship

$$F_n = F_{n-1} + F_{n-2}.$$

Starting with $F_0 = F_1 = 1$ gives the sequence above.

Write a program to put the first 30 Fibonacci numbers into an array `f[0]`, `f[1]`, ... Print out the array to check that your program works correctly.

6.4 The sample mean of a set of N observations is defined as

$$\overline{X} = \frac{1}{N} \sum_{i=1}^{N} X_i,$$

where X_i is the ith observation. The standard deviation s of the data is defined with the formula

$$s^2 = \frac{1}{N-1} \sum_{i=1}^{N} (X_i - \overline{X})^2.$$

Write a program to compute the mean and standard deviation of the data in the following array x:

```
double[ ] x = {5.1, 6.2, 5.7, 3.5, 9.9, 1.2,
                7.6, 5.3, 8.7, 4.4};
```

(Answers: $\overline{X} = 5.76, s = 2.53$)

6.5 Salary levels at an educational institution are (in thousands of dollars): 9, 10, 12, 15, 20, 35 and 50. The number of employees at each level are, respectively, 3000, 2500, 1500, 1000, 400, 100, 25. Write a program which finds and prints:

(a) the average salary *level* ($21571.4);
(b) the number of employees above and below the average level (125 above, 8400 below);
(c) the *average salary earned* by an individual in the institution ($11466.3).

6.6 Draw a graph of the population of the USA from 1790 to 2000, using the (logistic) model

$$P(t) = \frac{197\,273\,000}{1 + e^{-0.03134(t-1913.25)}}$$

where t is the date in years.

Actual data (in 1000s) for every decade from 1790 to 1950 are as follows: 3929, 5308, 7240, 9638, 12 866, 17 069, 23 192, 31 443, 38558, 50 156, 62 948, 75 995, 91 972, 105711, 122775, 131 669, 150 697. Create an array initialized with this data, and use the array to superimpose the data on the graph of $P(t)$. Plot the data as discrete circles (i.e. do not join them with lines) as shown in Figure 6.5.

Hints:

1. To superimpose the graphs on the same axes, create one Essential Grapher `Graph` object to plot the model, and a separate `Graph` object to plot the data.

2. If your `Graph` object to plot the data is `dataPlot`, the statement

```
dataPlot.setPointShape(new CirclePoint(
                 PointShape.UNFILLED));
```

will use small open circles instead of points for plotting, and the statement

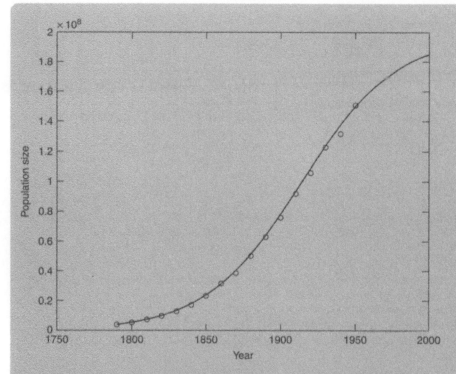

Figure 6.5 USA population: model and census data (o)

```
dataPlot.setDrawingStyle(Graphable.PLOTPOINTS);
```

will prevent the circles from being joined with lines.

6.7 In Chapter 3, we created an `EssentialMath` class. Add two `static` methods to this class, called `mean` and `std`, which return the mean and standard deviation of the elements in an array of any length passed to them as a parameter. Test your methods on the data in Exercise 6.4. **Hint:** remember that the number of elements in an array `x` is given by `x.length`.

6.8 Write a `static` method of `EssentialMath` called `furthestFromMean` that takes an array of `doubles` (of any length) as an argument and returns the element of the array that is furthest in absolute value from the mean. **Hint:** Modify the code in `FurthestFromMean2` (Section 6.1) to work with an array of any length. You should also call the `mean` method written in Exercise 6.7, rather than duplicating the code for calculating the mean.

6.9 Write a new method of `Ant` (from Section 6.4) called `printBarChart` that prints a rough 'bar chart' depicting the frequencies `f`. The method should take two arguments giving the range of frequencies to plot. Given the frequencies (for the range 35 to 45):

```
39 43 53 59 51 40 33 24 12 5 1
```

your output should look something like this:

```
35: ************************************
36: **************************************
37: *****************************************************
38: ***************************************************************
39: ***********************************************************
40: *********************************************
41: **********************************
42: ************************
43: *************
44: *****
45: *
```

i.e. each asterisk represents landing once in that column. If you generate much more than 500 steps you may need to scale the frequencies down to avoid printing more than one row of asterisks per frequency.

6.10 Write a program which:

- sets up two-dimensional arrays to represent the cost and solution tables in the concrete transportation problem specified in Section 6.5;
- prints the cost and solution tables one row per line;
- computes the cost of this transportation scheme as described.

6.11 Create a `Card` class which stores the suit and value of a playing card. The methods should include the following:

- a parameterized constructor for setting the suit and value;
- a `toString` method which returns a `String` representation of the card.

In a separate class create a `main` method which declares an array of 52 cards and initializes them to be a sorted pack of cards. Loop through the array and print the card details.

6.12 Successive points in the set (X_i, Y_i) are joined by straight lines. The y co-ordinate of a point on the line joining the two points (X_i, Y_i) and (X_{i+1}, Y_{i+1}) with x co-ordinate X is given by

$$Y = Y_i + (X - X_i)\frac{(Y_{i+1} - Y_i)}{(X_{i+1} - X_i)}.$$

This process is called *linear interpolation*. Suppose 100 sets of data pairs are stored, in ascending order of X_i, in a text file. Write a program which will read the data and compute an interpolated value of Y given an arbitrary value of X keyed in at the keyboard. It is assumed that X is in the range covered by the data. Note that the data must be sorted into ascending order with respect to the X_i values. If this were not so, it would be necessary to sort them first. (**Hint:** create a class called `Point` that stores a single (X,Y) pair, and then create an array of `Points`).

Test your program on some sample data.

6.13 Modify your program from Exercise 6.12 to assume that the file of data is not sorted and sort it first. (**Hint:** modify the insertion sort code from Section 6.7 to compare the X values of `Point` objects.)

Part II
More advanced topics

Part I has been concerned with those aspects of Java which you need in order to get to grips with the essentials of the language and of scientific programming. Parts II and III contain more advanced topics and applications which don't really fall under the heading of 'essentials'.

7
Inheritance

Objectives

By the end of this chapter, you should be able to do the following:

- reduce redundancy in code by applying generalization;
- apply the concept of specialization, by extending and overriding existing Java classes;
- implement solutions in Java using inheritance.

7.1 Introduction

Inheritance is a very powerful feature of object-oriented programming. It is integral to the way that Java works, therefore it is important that you understand how to use inheritance to move beyond the basics of programming in Java.

What is inheritance?

Inheritance is about describing one class in terms of another class. There are two ways that classes can be used to describe other classes:

1. *Inheritance*. This form of a relationship occurs when once class is a *specialized* version of a different class. For example, if we had a Student class and a Person class, then Student would be a specialized form of Person, since a student *is a* person, with some extra features. To emphasise the nature of this relationship, we sometimes refer to inheritance as an '*is a*' relationship.
2. *Aggregation* (also known as *composition*). This is a relationship between classes when one class A *contains* a reference to another class B, for example, if A contains a data member which is of type B. In other words, class B is *part of* class A. For example, say we are defining classes to model a pack of cards. If Card is a class and PackOfCards is a class, then Card is part of PackOfCards, so Card is being used to describe PackOfCards. To emphasise the nature of this relationship, we sometimes refer to aggregation as a '*has a*' relationship.

When we are describing the relationships between classes, it is sometimes helpful to draw a diagram to illustrate these relationships. This can be either a *parts hierarchy*, showing the aggregation relationships between classes, or a *class hierarchy*, showing the inheritance relationships between classes. For example,

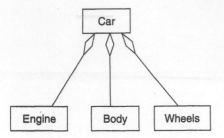

Figure 7.1 A parts hierarchy of a car

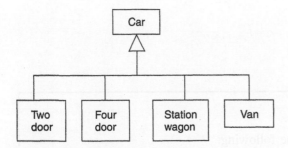

Figure 7.2 A class hierarchy of a car

when describing a car, we can either describe it in terms of a hierarchy of parts or a hierarchy of classes. A motor mechanic is somebody who would be interested in a parts hierarchy. Figure 7.1 shows such an example. A car is made up of an engine, a body and wheels. A car therefore *has a* engine, body and wheels. We call car a *super-part* and the lower classes *sub-parts*.

In contrast, Figure 7.2 shows an example of a class hierarchy. A car rental company would be interested in such a classification. The types of car represent *specializations* of a car. A van *is a* car, but is more specialized than a car. In object-oriented terminology, we say that class Car is a *superclass* of classes TwoDoor, FourDoor, StationWagon and Van. The 'lower' four classes are *subclasses* of Car. A superclass is sometimes also referred to as a *base class* and the subclasses as *derived classes*.

The notation used in both Figures 7.1 and 7.2 is UML (Unified Modelling Language) notation. UML is a popular modelling language used for designing and specifying software.

Now do Exercise 7.1.

Generalization and specialization

Inheritance can be seen in two directions: *up* or *down* the class hierarchy. Suppose we want to write a computer game for young children, which simulates a farmyard scene. In the scene, animals are scattered around. A child can click on any animal and it will make the particular sound of that animal. Animals can also be moved around the scene. Figure 7.3 shows a class hierarchy with FarmyardAnimal as the superclass. For now, we only have cows, chickens and ducks in our farmyard.

Generalization is the process of identifying features which are common to different classes and combining them into a new common superclass. For example, assuming we started with classes Cow, Duck and Chicken. In these separate classes we may have found features or behaviour that were duplicated in all three classes, such as the fact that they have a position on the screen and can be moved. Generalization involves *taking out* these common features from the individual classes and putting them into a new superclass with an appropriate general name (FarmyardAnimal). In the same way, Chicken and Duck have shared features (such as, they both have wings), so are generalized to a superclass Fowl.

Specialization, on the other hand, involves identifying additional features which make a class a more specialized form of an existing class (which then becomes the superclass). For example, say we wanted to add bantam chickens to our scene. Bantams are very similar to chickens, except that they have the

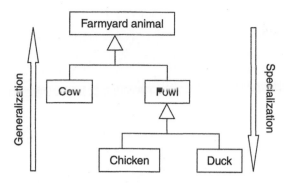

Figure 7.3 Class hierarchy of a farmyard scene

additional feature of having feathers on their feet. In our model, a Bantam therefore *is a* Chicken, but is more specialized, so will be placed as a subclass of Chicken in Figure 7.3.

Now do Exercise 7.2

7.2 Inheritance in Java

Inheritance is implemented in Java using the keyword extends. When class B is a subclass of class A, we say B *extends* A. The word 'extends' is descriptive, because inheritance means that class B 'adds on' extra features over and above what class A provides. The following simple example will show how extends works:

```java
public class Person
{
  private String name;
  public void setName(String n)
  {
    name = n;
  }
  public void print()
  {
    System.out.println(name);
  }
}

public class Student extends Person
{
  private String studentNo;
  public void setStudentNo(String s)
  {
    studentNo = s;
  }
  public void print()
  {
    super.print();
    System.out.println(studentNo);
  }
}

public class UseStudent
```

```
{
  public static void main(String[] args)
  {
    Student s = new Student();
    s.setName("Jill Hope");
    s.setStudentNo("HPXJIL003");
    s.print();
  }
}
```

In the above program, notice the following:

- `Student extends Person`: this statement means that the class `Student` implicitly incorporates the data members and methods of class `Person`. We say that `Student` *inherits* the data member `name` and the methods `setName` and `print` from class `Person`.
- Although `Student` inherits the method `print` from `Person`, it also defines its own `print` method. To call the `print` method of the `Person` class from within `Student`, it is preceded by the keyword `super`. The keyword `super` refers to the superclass `Person`. If we left out the keyword `super`, we would be referring to the `Student` `print` method, so the method would continue to call itself indefinitely!
- In the `main` method, when a `Student` object is created, it contains both `name` (from `Person`) and `studentNo` (from `Student`) inside memory. Methods of the `Person` class can be called using the `Student` object handle.
- When the `print` method is called using the `Student` handle `s`, the method inside `Student` is called, which in turn calls the `print` method of the `Person` class.

Now do Exercise 7.3.

Reusing code through specialization

Inheritance allows us to take the form of an existing class and add code to it, through specialization, *without* modifying the existing class. This is a very powerful and convenient way of reusing code written by somebody else—if their code does not meet all your requirements, you can simply extend it. In this section we will show you how to 'add' additional methods and attributes to an existing class without needing to see the source code.

We start by implementing a class called `CleverTurtle` that can do everything that a `Turtle` object can do and more. We would like `CleverTurtle` objects to draw entire shapes with a single command. Here is our first version of `CleverTurtle`, which extends `Turtle` and defines an additional method for drawing a square of a given size:

```
import essential.*;

public class CleverTurtle extends Turtle
{
  public void square(int size)
  {
    for(int i=1; i<=4; i++)
    {
      forward(size);
      right(90);
    }
  }
}
```

If we create a CleverTurtle object, we can call any of the existing Turtle methods, or the new square method. Here is an example of a main method that uses the CleverTurtle class to draw a pattern of multiple squares.

```java
public class UseCleverTurtle
{
  public static void main(String[] args)
  {
    CleverTurtle zap = new CleverTurtle();
    for(int i=1; i<=360/5; i++)
    {
      zap.square(60);
      zap.right(5);
    }
  }
}
```

The output of the above program is shown in Figure 7.4. Notice in the program how we call both the square method and the right method (inherited from the Turtle class) with the CleverTurtle object handle.

Now do Exercises 7.4 to 7.7.

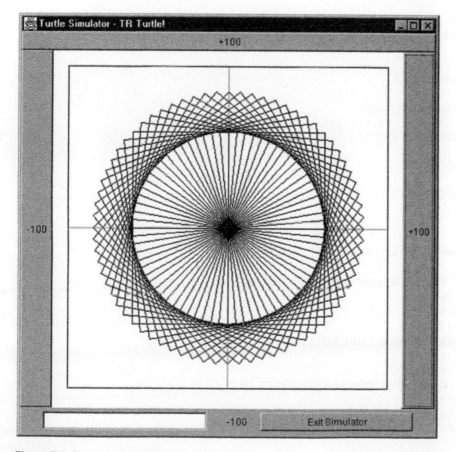

Figure 7.4 Output from running UseCleverTurtle.java

Overriding methods

Sometimes we will want to replace existing methods (which we inherit from the superclass) by ones which are more suited to the subclass. To illustrate this concept, we will write a class called ZigZagTurtle, which always walks in a zigzag. Here is a ZigZagTurtle class with a main method for testing the class:

```java
import essential.*;

public class ZigZagTurtle extends CleverTurtle
{
  private int size = 4;  // the size of one line of the zigzag

  public void setSize(int s)
  {
    size = s;
  }

  public void forward(double distance)
  {
    while(distance > size)
    {
      zigzag();
      distance -= size;
    }
    if(distance > 0)
      super.forward(distance);
  }

  private void zigzag()
  {
    // draw a single zigzag:
    left(60);
    super.forward(size/2);
    right(120);
    super.forward(size);
    left(120);
    super.forward(size/2);
    right(60);
  }

  public static void main(String[] args)
  {
    ZigZagTurtle ziggy = new ZigZagTurtle();
    ziggy.square(80);
    ziggy.left(45);
    ziggy.forward(100);
    Turtle straight = new Turtle();
    straight.right(135);
    straight.forward(100);
    ZigZagTurtle bigZig = new ZigZagTurtle();
    bigZig.setSize(10);
    bigZig.right(225);
    bigZig.forward(100);
  }
}
```

The output from this program is shown in Figure 7.5. Note the following about the program:

- ZigZagTurtle inherits from CleverTurtle. This means that objects of type ZigZagTurtle can use any methods of CleverTurtle, which includes any methods of Turtle.
- An additional data member called size is defined, with an associated setSize method.
- A forward method is defined. This essentially *redefines* the forward method of the superclass (or in this case the supersuperclass!). We say that the forward method of ZigZagTurtle *overrides* the forward method of Turtle. Inside the method, it calls a private method called zigzag, which draws a single zigzag. We declare zigzag as private, because it is just a *helper* method and we do not expect the class user to call it directly.
- In the forward and zigzag methods, when we want to call the forward method of Turtle (rather than the ZigZagTurtle method), we use the keyword super.
- In the main method, we define three turtles. The turtles ziggy and bigZig are of type ZigZagTurtle, whereas straight is of type Turtle. When we tell ziggy to draw a square, the object draws a zigzag square. The square method inside CleverTurtle calls the forward method, and since this has been overridden, it will call the new 'zigzagged' forward method.

By overriding the forward method, we have defined a different way for a ZigZagTurtle to move forward. A ZigZagTurtle can now only move forward in zigzags—it can no longer walk straight using the Turtle's forward method. One important point to remember about overriding methods is that the *signature* of the new method has to be *identical* to the signature of the method to be overridden in the superclass. In addition, the return types must be the same. If the signatures or return types differ

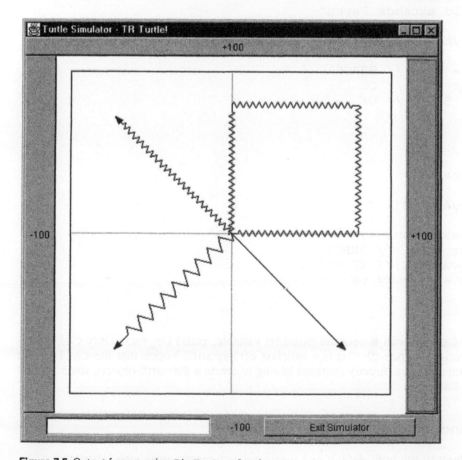

Figure 7.5 Output from running ZigZagTurtle.java

in any way, you will simply be adding a different method and not overriding (or replacing) the method of the superclass. Data members can also be overridden (there is an example of this in Exercise 7.8).

Now do Exercises 7.8 to 7.10.

The protected *keyword*

If you want a data member or method to be accessible to any subclasses, then you should use the protected access modifier. (Elements declared as protected are also visible to other non-subclasses in the same package. Remember that if no package is specified, your class is part of the package with no name.) The following example will illustrate how protected works. (All three classes are stored in different files. Classes Child and Orphan are stored in the same folder, while Parent is stored in a subfolder called tester)):

```
package tester;
public class Parent
{
  private int private_var;
  protected int protected_var;
  public int public_var;
}

import tester.*;
public class Child extends Parent
{
  public void tryAccess()
  {
    private_var = 5;    // ERROR!
    protected_var = 5;  // OK
    public_var = 5;     // OK
  }
}

import tester.*;
public class Orphan
{
  public void tryAccess()
  {
    Parent p = new Parent();
    p.private_var = 5;   // ERROR!
    p.protected_var = 5;// ERROR!
    p.public_var = 5;    // OK
  }
}
```

Both classes (Child and Orphan can access the public variable, public_var. Only Child can access the protected variable, since Child is a subclass of Parent. Notice that the Child class can access the Parent data members directly (without having to create a Parent object), since Child is simply an extension of Parent.

7.3 Constructors and inheritance

This section will explain how to use both default and parameterized constructors with inheritance.

Default constructors

In our `CleverTurtle` example from Section 7.2, `CleverTurtle` is a subclass of `Turtle`. When we create a `CleverTurtle` object by calling the default constructor, Java will automatically call the `Turtle` constructor first. The general rule is therefore: in the case of default constructors, the compiler always calls the superclass constructor *before* calling the current constructor. The following example illustrates this principle:

```
class Mammal
{
  public Mammal()
  {
    System.out.println("Making a mammal");
  }
}
class Rodent extends Mammal
{
  public Rodent()
  {
    System.out.println("Making a rodent");
  }
}
class Rat extends Rodent
{
  public Rat()
  {
    System.out.println("Making a rat");
  }
}
```

The statement:

```
Rat r = new Rat();
```

will print the following output:

```
Making a mammal
Making a rodent
Making a rat
```

What would be the output if you created a `Rodent` object, or a `Mammal` object?

The super keyword

In the `Rat` and `Rodent` example above, the superclass constructor is called implicitly by the compiler. You can, however, put in the call to the superclass constructor explicitly, using the `super` keyword, as in the example below:

```
class Rat extends Rodent
{
  public Rat()
  {
    super();   // call to the superclass (Rodent) default constructor
    System.out.println("Making a rat");
  }
}
```

The call to the superclass constructor must be the *first* statement of the method. The compiler will generate an error if it is not the first statement.

Parameterized constructors

In the case of a subclass constructor with arguments, you have to call the superclass constructor explicitly. As in the case of the default constructor, the call to the superclass constructor must be the first statement in the subclass constructor. Look at the following example:

```java
class Publication
{
  protected String authorName, title;

  public Publication(String a, String t)
  {
    authorName = a;
    title = t;
  }
}
class Book extends Publication
{
  private String publisher;

  public Book(String a, String t, String p)
  {
    super(a, t);    // calls the superclass constructor
    publisher = p;
  }
}
```

When a `Book` object is created, we would need the class user to specify the `authorName`, `title` and `publisher`, for example:

```java
Book b = new Book("J.R.R. Tolkein", "The Hobbit", "HarperCollins");
```

The constructor should therefore have three arguments. Since two of these attributes belong to the superclass, they should be initialized in the superclass. It would be possible to initialize the data members of `Publication` in the `Book` constructor, because they are declared as `protected`. It is, however, better programming practice to initialize data in the class in which they are declared. We therefore pass the first two parameters to the superclass constructor so that the values can be initialized in that class. Lastly, the `publisher` data member is initialized.

Now do Exercises 7.11 to 7.13.

7.4 The `Object` class

The standard Java classes are organized in a huge hierarchy of classes. In the Java API, you can view this hierarchy as a sideways 'tree'. Open the Java API and do the following:

- Click on **Tree** at the top of the page.
- Scroll down to the section called **Class Hierarchy**. You will see a list of classes starting with `java.lang.Object`. This class is the root of the tree and the 'branches' are the nested sub-lists to the right.
- Click on the `Object` class. Look at the methods that are provided by the class.

The class Object is the 'supreme' class from which all classes inherit. Any class in Java that does not explicitly inherit from another class, is by default a subclass of Object. Therefore, every class that you have defined in Java is either a direct subclass of Object (by default), or an indirect subclass of Object. This means that you can call any of the methods of the Object class from any object handle.

Now do Exercise 7.14.

The toString method

One of the methods of the Object class is the toString method. This method returns a string made up of the name of the class, followed by some characters (more precisely, the unsigned hexadecimal representation of the hash code of the object, but you need not worry about it). Although the toString method is defined in Object, it is recommended that subclasses override it. Where it makes sense, classes should have a toString method that returns a string that textually represents the object. We return to the Person and Student classes to illustrate how toString works. We have modified the classes slightly.

```
public class Person
{
  protected String name;
  public Person(String n)
  {
    name = n;
  }
}

public class Student extends Person
{
  private String studentNo;
  public Student(String n, String s)
  {
    super(n);
    studentNo = s;
  }
}

public class UseStudent
{
  public static void main(String[] args)
  {
    Student jill = new Student("Jill Hope","HPXJIL003");
    String s = jill.toString();
    System.out.println(s);
    System.out.println(jill);
  }
}
```

The output from this program is:

```
Student@1fcc69
Student@1fcc69
```

In the main method, we create a Student object, called jill. When we call the toString method, Java first looks in the Student class. It finds no toString method, so it looks in the superclass Person. There is no toString method defined in Person, so it looks in the superclass, which by default is the class `Object`. In the `Object` class Java finds a `toString` method and executes it. The result is therefore the name of the class followed by some characters. Notice that the output of the last statement is the same as the output of the second last statement. When we call `print` or `println` and pass it an object handle, Java will automatically call the first `toString` method that it finds in the class hierarchy. The last line is therefore equivalent to the two lines above it.

To generate more meaningful output, we would have to override the `Object` `toString` method. Here is a `toString` method for `Student`:

```java
public String toString()
{
    return name + ", " + studentNo;
}
```

The statement: `System.out.println(jill)` will now generate the following output:

```
Jill Hope, HPXJIL003
```

In the same way, you should add `toString` methods to your classes, where it is appropriate.
Now do Exercise 7.15.

7.5 Abstract classes and interfaces

We return to the farmyard example from Section 7.1 to illustrate the concepts of *abstract* methods, abstract classes and *interfaces*.

Every farmyard animal must be able to make a noise. We should therefore have a method called, for example `makeNoise`, inside the `FarmyardAnimal` class. However, we cannot say what kind of noise a farmyard animal should make before we know what type of animal it is. The details of the `makeNoise` method would therefore have to be left blank in the `FarmyardAnimal` class. The appropriate way to handle such methods, is to declare them as `abstract`. An abstract method has no body; it exists only so that it can be overridden. In other words, the *implementation is left to the subclass*. A class containing `abstract` methods is called an abstract class and must be specified as such, using the `abstract` keyword. Here is the basic form of our farmyard classes so far:

```java
abstract class FarmyardAnimal
{
    protected int positionX, positionY;
    public abstract void makeNoise(); // no method body
    public void move(newX, newY)
    {
        positionX = newX;
        positionY = newY;
    }
}
class Duck extends FarmyardAnimal
{
    public void makeNoise()
    {
        // code to go quack quack
    }
...
}
class Pig extends FarmyardAnimal
{
    public void makeNoise()
```

```
    {
        // code to go oink oink
    }
    ...
}
```

Note the following about our program:

- `FarmyardAnimal` defines two data members and a concrete (i.e. non abstract) method `move`. It also declares an `abstract` method `makeNoise`, which has no body.
- Classes `Duck` and `Pig` extend `FarmyardAnimal`, so inherit the two data members and the `move` method. In addition, they are each *forced* to define a `makeNoise` method. (An error will be generated if they do not provide the method definition.)

Although it does make sense to create a `Duck` or `Pig` object, it does not make sense to create a `FarmyardAnimal` object. Java, in fact, does not allow objects to be created from abstract classes. This is because an abstract class is not yet completely defined.

Why bother with abstract classes?

Abstract classes establish a basic form, so that it is clear what is in common between all subclasses. If you create a class which extends `FarmyardAnimal`, you would want it to be able to make a noise. Abstract methods *force* the subclasses to provide these method definitions. Say we had an array of `FarmyardAnimals` called `animals`:

```
FarmyardAnimal[] animals = new FarmyardAnimal[50];
```

The variable `animals` could be initialized to contain a variety of different types of farmyard animals. We might want all the animals in the farmyard to make a noise at the same time—the pig should oink, the duck quack, the cow moo, etc. This could be done in a simple statement:

```
for(int i=0; i<animals.length; i++)
    animals[i].makeNoise();
```

We can do this because we are assured that *each* subclass of `FarmyardAnimal` has a `makeNoise` method.

Interfaces

An interface is a *pure* abstract class. Interfaces contain no data variables or method bodies, only constants and method headers. The purpose of an interface is to specify the form of a class. An interface says: 'This is what all classes that implement this particular interface will look like'. Classes do not inherit from interfaces (because there is nothing to inherit), but they *conform* to the specification. To create an interface, we use the `interface` keyword instead of the `class` keyword. To make a class which conforms to the interface, we use the `implements` keyword (instead of `extends`). A class can implement many interfaces, but only extend a single class.

To illustrate the use of interfaces, we return to the farmyard example. In the farmyard, we would like to add some animals which do not make a noise (like tortoises and rabbits), and some other farmyard objects which make a noise, but do not move (like windmills). To implement this change, we create an `interface` called `CanMakeNoise` which specifies the `makeNoise()` method. This method declaration is then taken out of the `FarmyardAnimal` class. The animals which make a noise then extend `FarmyardAnimal` and implement `CanMakeNoise`. Animals which do not make a noise only extend `FarmyardAnimal`. Objects which can make a noise, but cannot move implement `CanMakeNoise`. Here is our modified code (like classes interfaces are stored in files of their own):

```
class FarmyardAnimal
{
  public void move(newX, newY) { ...}
  protected int positionX, positionY;
}
interface CanMakeNoise
{
  public abstract void makeNoise();
}
class Duck extends FarmyardAnimal implements CanMakeNoise
{
  public void makeNoise() {  /* code to go quack quack */  }
  ...
}
class Rabbit extends FarmyardAnimal
{
  public void wriggleEars() { ...}
  ...
}
class Windmill implements CanMakeNoise
{
  public void makeNoise() {  /* code to go squeak squeak */  }
}
```

In the Java API, in the list of **All Classes** (bottom left frame), you will notice some of the class names are in italics. These are in fact not classes, but interfaces. Find the interface called `Comparable` and click on it. The only method specified by `Comparable` is `compareTo`. At the top, there is a list of **All Known Implementing Classes**. The class `String` is among those classes. Because `String` implements `Comparable`, we know that `String` has a method called `compareTo`. Check that this is so, by looking inside the `String` class. We will work more with interfaces in the next chapter on graphical user interfaces.

Summary

- *Inheritance* is one of the most powerful features of object-oriented programming. Inheritance is a relationship between classes where one class is a *more specialized* version of another class.
- *Aggregation* is a relationship between classes where one class is *part of* another class.
- Inheritance is implemented in Java using the `extends` keyword.
- A *subclass* inherits (can use) the attributes and behaviour of its *superclass*, can add its own attributes and methods and can change the behaviour of the superclass by *overriding* the superclass methods.
- A programmer can also use inheritance to factor out common elements of classes into superclasses (*generalization*). This results in better code (less redundancy and more logical structure).
- A programmer can use an existing class by extending it, without even needing to see the source code (*specialization*). In this way, reusability is maximized.
- The `protected` access modifier allows elements to be accessed directly by subclasses.
- In the case of default constructors, the compiler automatically calls the superclass constructor *before* calling the current constructor.
- In the case of parameterized constructors, the superclass constructor has to be called explicitly.
- Every class in Java is a subclass of the class `Object`. Where appropriate, classes should override the `toString` method of `Object`.

- An *abstract class* is a class which contains at least one abstract method (a method without a body). Abstract classes establish a basic form to which all subclasses must conform.
- An *interface* is a pure abstract class, i.e. it contains no data variables or method bodies, only constants and method headers.

Exercises

7.1 For each of the following, give any example of a subpart, a superpart, a subclass and a super-class.

 (a) House
 (b) CD

7.2 Apply the concept of generalization to the following classes, by describing a suitable super-class:

 - class Book with attributes: title, authorName, publisher.
 - class ConferencePaper with attributes: authorName, title, location.
 - class JournalPaper with attributes: authorName, title, journal, volume.

7.3 Based on your modified class descriptions in Exercise 7.2, show how these would be implemented in Java code.

7.4 Modify the square method of class CleverTurtle (defined in Section 7.2) so that the square is drawn with the starting position of the turtle as the centre of the square. After drawing the square, the turtle should be moved back to the same position and direction as when it started. For example, if the turtle is in the centre facing North and a square of size 200 is drawn, then the shape should match the outlines of the drawing area.

7.5 Use your modified CleverTurtle class from Exercise 7.4 to draw 15 nested squares, with the inner circle of size 5 and each consecutive square 10 units larger than the previous square.

7.6 Add a method to the CleverTurtle class defined in Section 7.2 that draws a circle shape of a given radius. The circle should be drawn with the current position of the turtle as the centre of the circle. After the circle has been drawn, the turtle should be back in the same position and direction as when it started. (Hint: Use the radius to calculate the circumference and divide this distance by 360°). Write a main method to test your new method.

7.7 There is a class called Complex defined in the essential package. Use the essential API to find out what the class contains. Using the Complex class, write a new class called MyKeyboard that extends Keyboard to read in complex numbers. Show how you would use MyKeyboard for reading in both complex numbers and real numbers.

7.8 Study the following classes before answering the questions below.

```
public class Base
{
  public int num = 100;
  public void printNumber()
  {
    System.out.println("Number from Base: " + num);
  }
}
public class Subclass extends Base
{
  private int num = 20;
```

```
        private int extra = 6;
        public void printNumber()
        {
          System.out.println("Number from Subclass: " + num);
          System.out.println("Extra number: " + extra);
        }
      }
    public class Driver
    {
      public static void main(String[] args)
      {
        Base b = new Base();
        Subclass s = new Subclass();
        b.printNumber();
        s.printNumber();
      }
    }
```

(a) What is the output of the program?

(b) How would the output change if you changed the name of the variable num in Subclass to Num?

(c) How would the output change if you changed the name of the method in Subclass to printNumbers (the main method stays the same)?

(d) How would the output change if you added the following statements to the end of the main method:

```
        b = s;
        b.printNumber();
```

7.9 Add a method to the ZigZagTurtle class, defined in Section 7.2, which overrides the backward method of Turtle to also draw in zigzags. Write a main method to check that your method works as it should.

7.10 In the ZigZagTurtle class, defined in Section 7.2, change the type of the argument in the forward method from double to float. The start of the method should look like this:

```
    public void forward(float distance){
```

Re-compile and run the main method and notice that the output has changed. Explain how it has changed and why.

7.11 Change the CleverTurtle class to include a parameterized constructor for setting the drawing colour.

7.12 Change the ZigZagTurtle class to include two parameterized constructors. The first constructor should initialize only the size of the zigzag. The second constructor should initialize both the size and the drawing colour. Make sure both of the new constructors work by writing an appropriate main method.

7.13 Write a new class called FertilisedTree, which is a more specialized version of the Tree class defined in Chapter 3, and modified in Exercise 3.14. A FertilisedTree differs from a Tree only in the way it grows. In the case of a FertilisedTree, when the height of the tree is greater than 1 metre, the growth rate decreases by 5% (as opposed to 10% in the case of a Tree). Only when a FertilisedTree reaches a height of 3 metres or more, does the growth rate decrease by 10%. Write a main method which creates one Tree and one FertilisedTree object, both with an initial height of 0.1 metres and growth rate of 20 cm/year. Allow both trees to grow for 30 years. Print out the height of both trees after the

30 years. (**Hint:** to access the height and rate attributes of Tree, change them to have protected access in class Tree.)

7.14 Study the following program before answering the questions below:

```
class MyObject
{
}

public class TestObject
{
  public static void main(String[] args)
  {
    MyObject m = new MyObject();
    System.out.println(m.getClass());
    Object o = new Object();
    System.out.println(o.getClass());
  }
}
```

(a) Explain why it is possible to call the method getClass with MyObject handle m if the method is not defined inside class MyObject?

(b) What do you expect to be the output?

7.15 We would like to write a program for managing bank accounts in a bank. There are two types of accounts: savings accounts and credit accounts (described below). For this exercise you are required to do the following:

(a) Design classes, using inheritance techniques, to model the data described below;

(b) Write a driver class, which will test these classes thoroughly;

(c) Implement the classes.

Description of a savings account:

- All savings accounts have an account number, a branch and a current balance.
- All savings accounts have the same interest rate.
- There must be the ability to withdraw money (if there are sufficient funds) and deposit money, set a new interest rate and add interest to the balance on a monthly basis.
- The details of the savings account (account number, branch and current balance) should be returned using the standard toString method.

Description of a credit account:

- All credit accounts have an account number, a branch, a current balance and a credit limit.
- All credit accounts have a set interest rate on debit balances and a set rate on credit balances.
- There must be the ability to withdraw (as long as it does not exceed the credit limit) and deposit money, set new interest rates and add interest to the balance on a monthly basis.
- The details of the credit account account (account number, branch, current balance and credit limit) should be returned using the standard toString method.

8

Graphical user interfaces (GUIs)

Objectives

By the end of this chapter, you should be able to do the following:

- write a simple graphical user interface in Java using Swing;
- find out how to use components by browsing the Swing Tutorial and the Java API;
- program listeners to respond to user generated events;
- use layout managers to arrange components attractively in windows;
- do simple graphics painting.

8.1 Introduction

Up till now you have written programs that communicate with the user through a text-based interface, using `System.out` for output and `Keyboard` for input. In this chapter you will learn how to communicate with the user through a graphical user interface (GUI) instead. In addition, we will show you how to do simple graphics painting.

GUIs in Java

Java provides two sets of facilities for developing GUIs: the *Abstract Window Toolkit (AWT)* and *Swing*. AWT is part of the core Java classes, whereas Swing is part of the Java Foundation Classes (JFC). The JFC software extends the original AWT by adding a set of graphical user interface class libraries. Both AWT and Swing are included in Java 2 (in packages `java.awt` and `javax.swing` respectively). Notice the `javax` prefix to the Swing package. It indicates that this is a package that was initially developed as an extension for JDK 1.1, and has migrated into the core for JDK 1.2. From a programmer's perspective, Swing is an alternative to using the AWT, although technically Swing extends (but does not replace) the AWT.

Graphical components of different operating systems look and operate differently. For example, a window in Microsoft Windows has the exit button on the top *right* corner, whereas a window on a Macintosh computer has the exit button on the top *left* corner. The advantage of using Java to program GUIs is that the *same* Java window component can look like a Microsoft window when running on a Microsoft platform and a Macintosh window when running on a Macintosh. (With Swing, you can in fact choose a 'look and feel' for your program.) In this way, the same Java GUI can run on many platforms. In other programming languages, a GUI would normally have to be completely rewritten to run on a different platform.

Understanding events

In the case of a text-based interface, there is a *predetermined* sequence of events. The program pauses execution when it expects input from the user and continues on the same set path after it receives the input. With graphical interfaces, on the other hand, there is no set sequence of events. The user can do any number of things at any time, such as type in a text box, resize the window or press a button. These responses from the user are called *events*. The central feature of a graphical program is an *event loop*, where the program is ready for any event and responds accordingly. We say the program is *event-driven*. You can imagine the event loop as a massive `switch` statement enclosed in a `while` loop. Each `case` of the `switch` corresponds to a single event. The event loop is part of the code that implements the AWT, so we (thankfully!) do not have to write it.

In Java, when an event happens, it is received by one or more *listeners*. A listener is an object that responds to a particular event and contains code that is executed when that event occurs. To program a GUI, we therefore decide which graphical components we want and write listeners to handle the events of these components.

8.2   Building a Swing application

In this section we will show you some of the basics of using Swing, by building a simple application from scratch.

A first version

Here is the first version of our program. Try compiling and running it and see what happens:

```
import javax.swing.*;
public class FirstGUI
{
  public static void main(String[] args)
  {
    JFrame f = new JFrame();
    f.setVisible(true);
  }
}
```

Notice the *tiny* window in the top left corner of the screen. Play around with resizing and maximizing/minimizing it. There is a problem with our window—if we exit the program (by pressing the ⊠ button), the window disappears, but notice that our Java program is still running. You have to press **Control-C** in the DOS box to stop the application. We will soon see how to fix this.

To program GUIs using Swing, we import `javax.swing.*`. JFrame is the Swing class that implements an independent window on the screen. The method `setVisible` displays the `JFrame` object `f` and enters the event loop, waiting for events to occur. With a `JFrame` we get all the basic functionality of a window, such as the ability to move the window and resize it in various ways. Behind these events are listeners that have been provided as part of the class `JFrame`.

Shutting down the application properly

To program our application to shut down properly, we have to add a single statement. Here is our modified code:

```
import javax.swing.*;
public class FirstGUI
{
    public static void main(String[] args)
    {
        JFrame f = new JFrame();
        f.setDefaultCloseOperation(JFrame.EXIT_ON_CLOSE);
        f.setVisible(true);
    }
}
```

Compile and run the program and notice that the application is now shutting down properly. If you are using an earlier version of Java (prior to version 1.3) you will have to insert the following code instead:

```
f.addWindowListener(new WindowAdapter()
{
    public void windowClosing(WindowEvent e)
    {
        System.exit(0);
    }
});
```

Now do Exercise 8.1.

Components and containers

A component is any GUI element, such as a window, button or label. A container is a type of component that has the purpose of containing other components (which can be containers themselves). Every Swing program contains at least one *top-level container* (JFrame, JDialog, or JApplet). Top-level containers cannot be added to other containers.

Other than top-level containers, there are two other types of components: *intermediate containers* and *atomic components* (also called *basic controls*). Intermediate containers are used to group components so that they can be handled as a single component for layout purposes. Examples are JPanel and JTabbedPane. Atomic components, on the other hand, cannot contain other components. Examples include JButton, JTextField, JComboBox and JList.

Now do Exercise 8.2.

Adding a button to the application

We want to add a button and a label to our application. We start by adding the button. Here is our modified code:

```
import javax.swing.*;
public class FirstGUI
{
    public static void main(String[] args)
    {
        JFrame f = new JFrame();
        JButton button = new JButton("Press me!");  // create a button
        f.getContentPane().add(button); // add the button to the frame
        f.setDefaultCloseOperation(JFrame.EXIT_ON_CLOSE);
        f.setVisible(true);
    }
}
```

The JButton class is used for creating standard buttons that can be pressed. The JButton constructor takes a string as an argument, which is the label to be displayed on the button. Every JFrame contains an intermediate container, known as a *content pane*. We use the `getContentPane` method to access this container, and use the `add` method to add the button to the content pane (thus adding it to the frame).

If you compile and run this program, the button is hidden—you have to resize the window to see the button. To avoid this, we can tell the frame to organize itself, so that the components will be visible when the window is opened. This is done by calling the `pack` method just before setting the frame to be visible:

```
f.pack();
f.setVisible(true);
```

In summary, to add a button to our frame, we did the following:

- created an instance of `JButton`;
- added it to the content pane of the frame;
- before we set the frame to visible, we called the `pack` method.

Organizing the code in a better way

As we start adding more components, the `main` method will become larger and larger and will end up getting rather messy. A better way to organize our code is to put all components into a class, rather than in the `main` method. Components are made into data members of the class and any initialization is done in the constructor. The `main` method then only creates the object and sets it to be visible—the bulk of the work is done in the class. Here is our reorganized program, which will result in better code in the long run:

```
import javax.swing.*;
public class SimpleFrame extends JFrame
{
  private JButton button = new JButton("Press me!");

  public SimpleFrame()
  {
    getContentPane().add(button);
    setDefaultCloseOperation(JFrame.EXIT_ON_CLOSE);
    pack();
  }
}
```

Here is a program which uses `SimpleFrame`:

```
public class FirstGUI
{
  public static void main(String[] args)
  {
    SimpleFrame s = new SimpleFrame();
    s.setVisible(true);
  }
}
```

Note the following:

- `SimpleFrame` extends `JFrame`. Therefore, when we create a `SimpleFrame` object, we are also creating a `JFrame` object.
- `button` is a data member of the class `SimpleFrame`. `SimpleFrame` therefore defines a specialization of `JFrame` by adding an additional component.

- The default constructor of `SimpleFrame` adds the button to the frame, programs the frame to shut down properly and packs the components.
- To call methods of `JFrame` (such as `getContentPane` or `pack`), we no longer need an object handle, since these methods are now inherited from `JFrame`.

Adding a label

We now want to add a label to our application. We do this by creating a background, which has both components on it. We then add this background to our frame. In Swing such a background is a component called a panel (more specifically a `JPanel`). The layout of the components is shown as a hierarchy in Figure 8.1. The diagram shows which components contain other components.

Here is our modified code:

```java
import javax.swing.*;
public class SimpleFrame extends JFrame
{
  private JButton button = new JButton("Press me!");
  private JLabel label = new JLabel("Go on, press the button");
  private JPanel background = new JPanel();

  public SimpleFrame()
  {
    background.add(button);  // add button to background
    background.add(label);   // add label to background

    getContentPane().add(background); // add background to frame
    setDefaultCloseOperation(JFrame.EXIT_ON_CLOSE);
    pack();
  }
}
```

The `JLabel` class can be used for placing plain text on a GUI. In our class, we declare a `JLabel` object as a data member. The constructor for `JLabel` takes a string, which is the text to be displayed.

The `JPanel` class is an intermediate container and is used for grouping the components into one component. The `button` and `label` components are added to the `background` panel, which in turn is added to the content pane of the frame.

Now do Exercises 8.3 to 8.4.

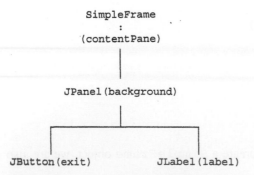

Figure 8.1 Layout of components of `SimpleFrame`. The `JPanel` component (background) contains a `JButton` and a `JLabel` component

Getting the button to do something

When we press the button, nothing happens. If we want something to happen, we have to write code to respond to the event of the button being pressed. Here is a the modified `SimpleFrame` class that responds to the button being pressed:

```java
import javax.swing.*;
import java.awt.event.*;
public class SimpleFrame extends JFrame
{
  private JButton button = new JButton("Press me!");
  private JLabel label = new JLabel("This is a label: ");
  private JPanel background = new JPanel();

  public SimpleFrame()
  {
    button.addActionListener( new ActionListener()
    {
      public void actionPerformed(ActionEvent e)
      {
        // code to be executed when button is pushed
        label.setText(" Ouch ... that hurt! ");
      }
    });
    background.add(button);
    background.add(label);

    getContentPane().add(background);
    setDefaultCloseOperation(JFrame.EXIT_ON_CLOSE);
    pack();
  }
}
```

Run the modified program and see what happens when you press the button. Notice that we have imported `java.awt.event.*`. This package contains most of the code related to event handling (we will later see that some of the event handling code is in `javax.swing.event`). When the user clicks the mouse on our button, an event is generated. The code that responds to that event is called the *listener* for the button. In this case, the code that is executed is:

```java
label.setText(" Ouch ... that hurt! ");
```

This changes the text of the label component to the given string. We will now explain the new Java code around the `label.setText` statement.

Listeners as nested classes

To specify a listener for a button, we use the `addActionListener` method:

```java
button.addActionListener(...);
```

Look in the Java API for the `JButton` class. Find the `addActionListener` method. (Hint: it could be inherited from a superclass, in which case you will have to look in the superclass to find the method). What is the type of the argument in the `addActionListener` method?

To use the `addActionListener` method, we have to pass it an `ActionListener` object. Click on **ActionListener** and see what it says. `ActionListener` is an interface. This is what it looks like:

```
public interface ActionListener extends EventListener
{
   public void actionPerformed(ActionEvent e);
}
```

We have to send the `addActionListener` method an `ActionListener` object. However, remember that we can't create an object from an interface, because it is not a real class—the implementation is incomplete. We therefore first have to create a concrete class that implements `ActionListener`, and then we can create an `ActionListener` object to send to the method. Here is a possible structure for the concrete class:

```
class ButtonListener implements ActionListener
{
   public void actionPerformed(ActionEvent e)
   {
      \\ code to be executed when button is pushed
      label.setText(" Ouch ... that hurt! ");
   }
}
```

Because listeners are often applicable to only one class and they frequently need to access other components defined in the class (such as `label`), we normally define them inside the class as *nested classes*. One of the ways to do this is to declare the listener class as a member, as we do with methods:

```
public class SimpleFrame extends JFrame
{
   private JButton button = new JButton("Press me!");
   ...

   public SimpleFrame()
   {
      button.addActionListener(new ButtonListener());
      ...
   }

   class ButtonListener implements ActionListener
   {
      public void actionPerformed(ActionEvent e)
      {
         \\ code to be executed when button is pushed:
         label.setText(" Ouch ... that hurt! ");
      }
   }

}
```

In the code above, class `ButtonListener` is a member of class `SimpleFrame`. Notice how we use the `ButtonListener` class by creating a `ButtonListener` object and passing it to the `addActionListener` method of `button`. In this way, we are telling Java to call the `actionPerformed` method of `ButtonListener` when `button` is pressed.

Listener methods are different from other methods that we have been writing until now. Although we have defined a method called `actionPerformed`, we will never call this method ourselves. We are providing the body of the method, so that *Java* can call it from the event loop. Since Java will be calling the method, you must be sure to define it in exactly the right way (correct name, arguments and return type), otherwise your method will not be called when the event happens. Java ensures this through interfaces. For example, if you left out the `ActionEvent` argument by mistake, your code would not compile.

An alternative way of defining a nested class, is to use an *anonymous class*. An anonymous class has no name and is defined at the point at which the object is created. You can use anonymous classes when you will only ever create one object of that class. This is what we did in the previous version of our program. Here is the code again:

```
button.addActionListener( new ActionListener()
{
  public void actionPerformed(ActionEvent e)
  {
    label.setText(" Ouch ... that hurt! ");
  }
});
```

Notice the parentheses (i.e. round brackets). Can you see where the method call to `addActionListener` starts and when it ends? Inside the parentheses of `addActionListener`, we are defining an anonymous class and creating an object of that class at the same time. The class is an implementation of the `ActionListener` interface, with the body of the `actionPerformed` method specified. If we choose to use this approach, then we will no longer need the definition of class ButtonListener as a member of class `SimpleFrame`.

The `ActionEvent` argument e is an object that is created by `button` when it is pressed. The object e is sent to the `actionPerformed` method and can be queried for information such as whether the **CTRL** key was down at the same time as the button was pressed.

Now do Exercises 8.5 to 8.6.

8.3   Arranging components

If you have been doing all the exercises, you will notice that the layout of `SimpleFrame` is getting a bit out of hand. We would like to organize our components in a better way. *Layout managers* are used to control the size and position of components in containers. The Java platform provides a number of layout managers, including `BorderLayout`, `FlowLayout` and `GridLayout`.

The `FlowLayout` *manager*

The following program uses a `FlowLayout` manager:

```
import javax.swing.*;
import java.awt.*;

public class TestFlowLayout extends JFrame
{
  private JButton button1 = new JButton("One");
  private JButton button2 = new JButton("Two");
  private JButton button3 = new JButton("Three");
  private JButton button4 = new JButton("Four");
  private JPanel background = new JPanel();

  public TestFlowLayout()
  {
    background.setLayout(new FlowLayout());
    background.add(button1);
    background.add(button2);
    background.add(button3);
```

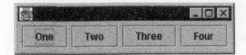

Figure 8.2 Buttons positioned using a `FlowLayout` manager

```
        background.add(button4);
        getContentPane().add(background);
        setDefaultCloseOperation(JFrame.EXIT_ON_CLOSE);
        pack();
    }

    public static void main(String[] args)
    {
        TestFlowLayout frame = new TestFlowLayout();
        frame.setVisible(true);
    }
}
```

The output of the above program is shown in Figure 8.2. Note the following:

- To use layout managers, you have to import `java.awt.*`.
- To use a particular layout manager, you use the `setLayout` method.
- The `FlowLayout` manager positions buttons from left to right as they are added to the panel. If you resize the window, the buttons are not resized, but they are repositioned to be in the centre at the top. (Try this.)
- If you do not specify a layout manager for a panel, the default is `FlowLayout`. Therefore, in the program above, if the `setLayout` statement was left out, the window would still look the same.

The `BorderLayout` *manager*

The following program uses the `BorderLayout` manager instead:

```
import javax.swing.*;
import java.awt.*;

public class TestBorderLayout extends JFrame
{
    private JButton buttonN = new JButton("North");
    private JButton buttonS = new JButton("South");
    private JButton buttonE = new JButton("East");
    private JButton buttonW = new JButton("West");
    private JButton buttonC = new JButton("Center");
    private JPanel background = new JPanel();

    public TestBorderLayout()
    {
        background.setLayout(new BorderLayout());
        background.add(buttonN, BorderLayout.NORTH);
        background.add(buttonS, BorderLayout.SOUTH);
        background.add(buttonE, BorderLayout.EAST);
        background.add(buttonW, BorderLayout.WEST);
        background.add(buttonC, BorderLayout.CENTER);
```

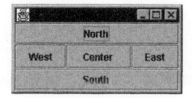

Figure 8.3 Buttons positioned using a `BorderLayout` manager

```
      getContentPane().add(background);
      setDefaultCloseOperation(JFrame.EXIT_ON_CLOSE);
      pack();
   }

   public static void main(String[] args)
   {
      TestBorderLayout frame = new TestBorderLayout();
      frame.setVisible(true);
   }
}
```

The output of this program is shown in Figure 8.3. When we add components using a `BorderLayout`, we specify a particular position (NORTH, SOUTH, EAST, WEST or CENTER). If the position is left out, it defaults to `BorderLayout.CENTER` (note the American spelling of centre!). Try resizing the window and see how the buttons change. Notice that the size of the buttons change to fill up the entire area of the window. The **North** and **South** buttons stay at the same height, but become wider to fill the window. The **West** and **East** buttons stay at the same width, but become taller to fit the window and the **Center** button becomes both wider and taller.

Although `BorderLayout` is not suitable for buttons (`FlowLayout` is more appropriate), `BorderLayout` is very useful for positioning panels of components. You don't have to fill all the positions in a `BorderLayout`. You could, for example, use the CENTER area for placing a background of components and SOUTH for a panel of buttons (which in turn could use the `FlowLayout`). Note that the default layout manager for the content pane of a `JFrame` is the `BorderLayout`, so you could add components directly to a frame, without having to create a background.

Now do Exercises 8.7 to 8.8.

Adding borders to components

A further way of influencing the positions of components is to use borders. Borders (empty borders in particular) can be used to put spaces between components, so that they do not look all squashed together. Some layout managers automatically put space between components; others do not. A border can be defined for any component. The following statement illustrates how empty borders can be created:

```
      background.setBorder(
         BorderFactory.createEmptyBorder(30, //top
                                          30, //left
                                          10, //bottom
                                          30) //right
      );
```

Now do Exercise 8.9.

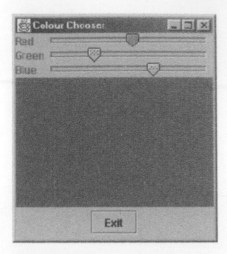

Figure 8.4 Screen shot of the ColourChooser application. The sliders can be moved by the user to change the colour of the box in the middle

8.4 A colour chooser application

We will now build a more interesting Swing application. The purpose is to illustrate how components can be organised using layout managers, as well as to introduce a new component (JSlider). Figure 8.4 shows what the final application will look like. The sliders can be moved by the user to change the colour of the box in the middle.

Planning the GUI

Before you start coding, it is often useful to plan how the components will fit together. We do this by dividing the screen up into areas. One way of dividing the area would be as three main panels: top (with the sliders), middle (with the colour box) and bottom (with the exit button). The top panel could be further divided into two panels (one for the labels and the other for the sliders). To show how the components fit together, we can draw a component hierarchy (see Figure 8.5). This makes it easier to program the interface. When GUIs become more complex and you are buried in the details of your code, it is often tricky to remember which component must be added to which container. In these situations, the component hierarchy serves as a useful reference.

Defining the colour

To define the colour, we use the same Color class we used before with Turtle objects. The class Color defines set colours (such as red, blue, etc), but can also create any colour using values for red, green and blue (values 0-255). For example, a purplish colour can be created with the following values:

```
Color currentColour = new Color(134,71,169);
        // mostly red and blue, with a bit of green
```

Color(255,255,255) is black and Color(0,0,0) is white. To change the colour of a panel (called thePanel), we use the setBackgound method:

```
thePanel.setBackground(currentColour);
```

Adding the components

To add the components, we are going to use three types of layout managers. The main background panel and topPanel (see Figure 8.5) will use a BorderLayout, bottomPanel will use a

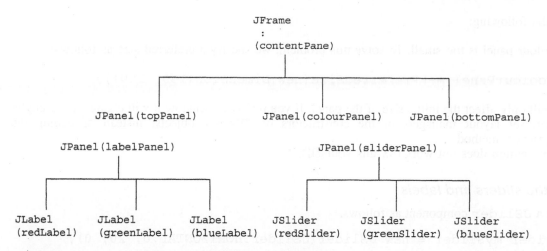

Figure 8.5 Component hierarchy of the colour chooser application

FlowLayout, and sliderPanel and labelPanel will use GridLayouts. Let's start by adding the colourPanel and the exit button:

```java
import java.awt.*;
import javax.swing.*;
import java.awt.event.*;

public class ColourChooser extends JFrame
{
    JPanel background = new JPanel(new BorderLayout());
    JButton exit = new JButton("Exit");
    JPanel colourPanel = new JPanel();
    Color theColour = new Color(134, 71, 169);  // purple
    // use FlowLayout for positioning the button
    JPanel bottomPanel = new JPanel(new FlowLayout());

    public ColourChooser()
    {
        colourPanel.setBackground(theColour);
        bottomPanel.add(exit);
        background.add(colourPanel,BorderLayout.CENTER);
        background.add(bottomPanel,BorderLayout.SOUTH);
        getContentPane().add(background);
        setDefaultCloseOperation(JFrame.EXIT_ON_CLOSE);
        pack();
    }

    public static void main(String[] args)
    {
        ColourChooser app = new ColourChooser();
        app.setVisible(true);
    }
}
```

Notice the following:

- The colour panel is too small. To solve this problem, we specify a preferred size as follows:

```
colourPanel.setPreferredSize(new Dimension(150, 150));
```

This will only affect the initial size of the panel. If you resize the window it will change accordingly.
- We can set layout managers in the constructors of JPanel objects, instead of calling the setLayout method.
- The exit button does not work (fix this yourself).

Adding the sliders and labels

We create a JSlider component as follows:

```
JSlider mySlider = new JSlider(JSlider.HORIZONTAL,0, 20, 0);
```

The first argument is a constant defined in the JSlider class to specify whether the slider should be horizontal or vertical. The second and third arguments give the minimum and maximum values of the slider. (In the above example, if the slider is dragged all the way to the left, the value will be 0 and if it is dragged all the way to the right, the value will be 20.) The last argument gives the initial value (where the slider position should be when it is first displayed). Here is the code for adding the sliders and labels as components to the class (as always, try to do this yourself, before looking at the code below):

```
public class ColourChooser extends JFrame
{
    // 3 colour sliders with initial positions making up purple:
    JSlider redSlider = new JSlider(
                    JSlider.HORIZONTAL,0, 255, 134);
    JSlider greenSlider = new JSlider(
                    JSlider.HORIZONTAL,0, 255, 71);
    JSlider blueSlider = new JSlider(
                    JSlider.HORIZONTAL,0, 255, 169);
    // specify 3 rows (columns don't matter):
    JPanel sliderPanel = new JPanel(new GridLayout(3,0));

    JLabel redLabel = new JLabel("Red");
    JLabel greenLabel = new JLabel("Green");
    JLabel blueLabel = new JLabel("Blue");
    JPanel labelPanel = new JPanel(new GridLayout(3,0));

    JPanel topPanel = new JPanel(new BorderLayout());
    ...
    public ColourChooser()
    {
        sliderPanel.add(redSlider);
        sliderPanel.add(greenSlider);
        sliderPanel.add(blueSlider);
        topPanel.add(sliderPanel,BorderLayout.CENTER);

        labelPanel.add(redLabel);
        labelPanel.add(greenLabel);
        labelPanel.add(blueLabel);
        topPanel.add(labelPanel,BorderLayout.WEST);
```

```
      background.add(topPanel,BorderLayout.NORTH);
      ...
  }
  ...
}
```

Remember to refer to the component hierarchy in Figure 8.5. This diagram indicates which containers contain which components. Based on the diagram, we did the following:

- added the slider components to `sliderPanel`;
- added the label components to the `labelPanel`;
- added `labelPanel` and `sliderPanel` to `topPanel`;
- and finally added the `topPanel` to `background`.

We used the `GridLayout` manager for positioning the labels and sliders, because we wanted them to line up perfectly.

Programming the behaviour

How do we program the application so that when the sliders change, the colour in the box will change? Find out (by browsing the API) what the relevant listener is for a `JSlider` component (Hint: look for a method stating with `add`).

The listener that we have to program for our sliders is `ChangeListener`. To implement `ChangeListener`, we have to provide the code for the method called `stateChanged`. Here is the code for the `redSlider`:

```
import javax.swing.event.*;
...

  redSlider.addChangeListener(new ChangeListener()
  {
    public void stateChanged(ChangeEvent e)
    {
      Color newCol = new Color(redSlider.getValue(),
                  greenSlider.getValue(),blueSlider.getValue());
      colourPanel.setBackground(newCol);
    }
  });
```

Notice the following:

- The interface `ChangeListener` is defined in the package `javax.swing.event`, so we have to import this package.
- The `stateChanged` method is called when the user moves a slider. By implementing the method, we are giving Java code to execute when the slider is moved.
- In the `stateChanged` method, we are creating a new colour based on the current values of the sliders. Note that we use the `getValue` method to determine the current position of any slider. The value returned will be in terms of the maximum and minimum values specified when the `Slider` object was created (i.e. a value between 0 and 255).
- Using the `setBackground` method, we change the background colour of `colourPanel` to be the new colour.

The same code must be implemented for the `greenSlider` and `blueSlider` components (otherwise nothing will happen when the user drags these sliders). If we simple copy this code, there will be unnecessary duplication. If we decide to change the code later, we would have to change it in three separate places. For this reason, it is better to have *one copy* of the code. Here is a better solution, which implements `ChangeListener` as a member class:

```
...
public class ColourChooser extends JFrame
{
    ...
    public ColourChooser()
    {
        redSlider.addChangeListener(new SliderListener());
        greenSlider.addChangeListener(new SliderListener());
        blueSlider.addChangeListener(new SliderListener());
        ...    // the rest of the code
    }

    class SliderListener implements ChangeListener
    {
        public void stateChanged(ChangeEvent e)
        {
            Color newCol = new Color(redSlider.getValue(),
                    greenSlider.getValue(),blueSlider.getValue());
            colourPanel.setBackground(newCol);
        }
    }
    ...
}
```

Now do Exercises 8.10 to 8.11.

8.5 Painting

The aim of this section is to develop a demonstration of interacting objects, and to show you how to paint graphics. The concepts are similar to those involved in moving a mouse around a screen to click on various items, e.g. how does an icon 'know' it has been clicked on?

We begin with a simple program to paint (draw) a filled circle. Painting is a fairly advanced topic, which we will just touch on here. The following program draws a red disk in a window with a pleasantly coloured background. Run it, and then look at the explanations below.

```
import javax.swing.*;
import java.awt.*;
import java.awt.event.*;

public class Drawing extends JFrame
{
    DrawPanel drawArea = new DrawPanel();
    int winWidth;
    int winHeight;

    public Drawing()
    {
        setTitle("My First Drawing");
        getContentPane().add(drawArea);
        drawArea.setBackground(new Color(200,200,255));
```

```
            setDefaultCloseOperation(JFrame.EXIT_ON_CLOSE);
            pack();
      }

      class DrawPanel extends JPanel
      {

            public DrawPanel()
            {
                  winWidth = 400;
                  winHeight = 400;

                  setPreferredSize (new Dimension(winWidth,winHeight));
            }

            protected void paintComponent (Graphics g)
            {
                  super.paintComponent (g);

                  int centreX = 200;
                  int centreY = 200;
                  int radius = 50;

                  g.setColor(Color.red);
                  g.fillOval(centreX-radius, centreY-radius,
                             radius*2, radius*2);

            }
      }

      public static void main(String[] args)
      {
            Drawing d = new Drawing();
            d.setVisible(true);
      }

}
```

Note:

- Painting (drawing) in Java with Swing classes is done on an extended JPanel object. This object must override a method called paintComponent to do the actual drawing with methods of the Graphics class (which is passed as a parameter). We therefore have to extend JPanel by defining a new (inner) class DrawPanel. DrawPanel overrides the paintComponent method, which calls the Graphics method fillOval to draw a red circle.
In general,

```
      fillOval(x, y, width, height)
```

draws a circle inscribed inside a rectangle with a width and height of width and height respectively, and with top left corner at the point (x, y), where x is the horizontal distance in pixels from the left border of the panel, and y is the vertical distance from the *top* border. The coding in paintComponent above shows how to draw a circle of radius radius centred at the point (centreX, centreY).

- The `DrawPanel` object `drawArea` is a data member of the `Draw` class and is added to the content pane. The `setBackground` method paints `drawArea` with a pleasant pastel colour. The `paintComponent` method of `drawArea` is automatically called when the program runs.

PacMan and the Blocks

We now begin an extended example which will culminate in a program where you can move an object (PacMan) around the screen to gobble up randomly moving objects (Blocks). We encourage you to try to write the code yourself before looking at the solutions provided.

A `Point` class

1. Start by designing a class `Point` for a 'point' object. We will need to distinguish between the point's *location* on the screen, and *displaying* the point at its location. Include the following features:

   - data members to represent the point's location: x (horizontal displacement in pixels) and y (downward vertical displacement in pixels). These data members should be declared `protected` (accessible only to all *sub*classes, i.e. 'descendants').
   Also define data members for the `size` of the point (the diameter of the circle which will represent the point) and its colour.
   - a general constructor which initializes all the data members.
   - a method `public void show( Graphics g )` which draws a circle of diameter `size` centred at the point's location.

   Try to write such a `Point` class before looking at our solution below.

```
import java.awt.*;
import javax.swing.event.*;

public class Point
{
  protected int x, y;  // position to draw the point
  protected Color col;
  protected int size = 8;

  public Point(int x, int y, int s, Color c)
  {
    this.x = x;
    this.y = y;
    size = s;
    col = c;
  }

  public void show(Graphics g)
  {
    // draw the point
    g.setColor(col);
    g.fillOval (x-size/2, y-size/2, size, size);
  }
}
```

2. Write a program, PacMan, based on Drawing at the beginning of this section, which draws at least two Point objects.

```java
import javax.swing.*;
import java.awt.*;
import java.awt.event.*;

public class PacMan extends JFrame
{
  DrawPanel drawArea = new DrawPanel();
  int winWidth;
  int winHeight;
  Point pt1, pt2;

  public PacMan()
  {
    setTitle("PacMan");
    getContentPane().add(drawArea);
    drawArea.setBackground(new Color(200,200,255));
    setDefaultCloseOperation(JFrame.EXIT_ON_CLOSE);
    pack();
  }

  class DrawPanel extends JPanel
  {

    public DrawPanel()
    {
      winWidth = 400;
      winHeight = 400;
      pt1 = new Point(winWidth/2, winHeight/2, 8, Color.blue);
      pt2 = new Point(winWidth/4, winHeight/2, 8, Color.red);
      setPreferredSize (new Dimension(winWidth,winHeight));
    }

    protected void paintComponent (Graphics g)
    {
      super.paintComponent (g);

      //draw the points
      pt1.show(g);
      pt2.show(g);
    }
  }

  public static void main(String[] args)
  {
    PacMan pm = new PacMan();
    pm.setVisible(true);
  }
}
```

A `Pac` class

1. Now we want to start designing an object (PacMan, after the cute electronic game which was popular in the later part of the last century) which we will be able to move around the screen using the arrow keys. Since it is also going to have a location on the screen, it might as well inherit our `Point` class. So start designing a class `Pac` (the subclass) which inherits `Point` (the superclass).

   It needs no new data members, does it? However, PacMan will *look* different, so a `Pac` object needs a new `show` method to override `Point`'s `show` method. You can use the `Graphics` method `fillArc` to draw a PacMan-like shape:

   ```
   g.fillArc (x, y, size, size, 45, 290);
   ```

   Try to write the `Pac` class before looking at our solution.

   ```java
   import java.awt.*;
   import javax.swing.event.*;

   public class Pac extends Point
   {
     public Pac(int x, int y, int s, Color c)
     {
       super(x, y, s, c);
     }

     public void show(Graphics g)
     {
       g.setColor(col);
       g.fillArc (x, y, size, size, 45, 290); //draw PacMan

     }
   }
   ```

2. Update your `PacMan` program to create and show some `Point` *and* `Pac` objects at different locations.

A `Block` class

Now we want to introduce another screen object with which PacMan will eventually be able to interact (to demonstrate the principle of interactive screen objects, e.g. windows which interact with a mouse.)

Let's call the new object a Block. Since Blocks will have locations, they should inherit `Point` in the same way that `Pac` does.

Write such a class `Block` which inherits `Point`. Use the `Graphics` method

```
fillRect(x, y, size, size)
```

to represent a Block.

Test it by creating and showing objects of all three types—`Point`, `Pac` and `Block`.

An array of Blocks

The next step is to create and show an *array* of Blocks. Can you remember how to instantiate an array of objects? See Chapter 6 (**Arrays of objects**) if you can't.

Update your `PacMan` program to show PacMan and a few Blocks.

Random Blocks

The previous exercise was pretty easy. See if you can initialize your army of Blocks at random locations on the screen ...

You'll need some statements like this in your `PacMan` program:

```
for (int i = 0; i < numBlocks; i++)
{
    int x = (int) (winWidth*Math.random());
    int y = (int) (winHeight*Math.random());
    blockArmy[i] = new Block(x,y,15,Color.black,winWidth,winHeight);
}
```

Moving PacMan

At last the moment we have been waiting for ... moving PacMan around the screen.

1. Since it is the *location* of PacMan objects we wish to move, it makes sense to enable the superclass Point objects to move. This ability will then automatically be inherited by subclass PacMan objects, and also by Block objects, which will want to run around in a random way, so that PacMan struggles to catch them.

   Write four new `Point` methods—`up()`, `down()`, `left()` and `right()`—which will change the data members `x` and `y` by an amount `dx` and `dy` respectively. (If we change `x` and `y` by only one pixel at a time, movement will be too slow. Set the additional data members `dx` and `dy` to 10, say—and make them `proteced`.)

   Remember that up will have to *decrease* `y`, and down will have to increase it.
2. If our user program has a Pacman object named `pc`, we now want it to call `pc.up()`, `pc.down()` etc. in response to the arrow keys on the keyboard.

   - We therefore have to specify a listener for a key, in the same way that we specified a listener for a button in Section 8.2. The `addKeyListener` method (listed as an inherited method of `JFrame`) is used for this purpose.

     We pass the `addKeyListener` method a `KeyAdapter` object, which defines a `keyPressed` method. This method is called whenever a key is pressed. We override the `keyPressed` method to determine which key has been pressed, and to decide on appropriate action. This can all be implemented as an anonymous class object passed to `addKeyListener`:

     ```
     addKeyListener(new KeyAdapter()
     {
       public void keyPressed(KeyEvent e)
       {
         int key = e.getKeyCode();
         if (key ==  KeyEvent.VK_UP) pc.up();
         if (key ==  KeyEvent.VK_DOWN) pc.down();
         if (key ==  KeyEvent.VK_LEFT) pc.left();
         if (key ==  KeyEvent.VK_RIGHT) pc.right();
         repaint();
       }
     }
     });
     ```

     Note that `keyPressed` calls the `repaint` method, which in turn automatically calls the `paintComponent` method to draw the objects.

     The key codes for the keyboard keys are fields of the `KeyEvent` class, which you can look up in the Java API.
   - Insert the above code for the `addKeyListener` method into the constructor of the `PacMan` user program and check that PacMan responds correctly to the keys.

Zapping the Blocks

You will have noticed, if you have been doing these exercises, that although PacMan can walk all over the Blocks they remain on the screen. We therefore need to let a Block *know* when PacMan zaps it. In other words, we want PacMan to be able to *interact* with Blocks, in much the same way that an icon 'knows' when you click the mouse on it.

The easiest way to do this is to run through the whole array of Blocks (with a `for` loop) each time PacMan moves, and to ask each Block if it has been 'touched' by PacMan. If it has been touched, kill it!

We need to extend our `Block` class.

- Introduce a new `private boolean` data member `alive` which is initially set to `true`.
  In keeping with good OOP principles we are insisting that the `alive` data member is `private`, to protect Blocks from being murdered at will by any old class user.
  The `alive` data member must be used in the `show` method of the Block class to make sure that only living Blocks are shown when the panel is repainted after each move by PacMan.
- Write a new method

```
public void tryKill( Pac p )
```

which kills a Block if PacMan touches it. Let's say that PacMan is deemed to have touched a Block if the distance between their respective locations is less than some critical value, `zapRange`. This requires some elementary coordinate geometry. If two points have coordinates (x_1, y_1) and (x_2, y_2) respectively, the distance d between them is

$$d = \sqrt{(x_1 - x_2)^2 + (y_1 - y_2)^2}.$$

Note again how we are using the principles of OOP. The Blocks decide if they have been touched by PacMan, and then wipe themselves out. It is the objects which are in the limelight.

Update your `Block` class, and test it with `PacMan`.

Moving the Blocks with a timer

At the moment the Blocks are sitting ducks for PacMan—they need to be able to get away. You may have your own ideas about various evasion strategies they can use to escape, which you could have fun implementing. One possible strategy is for the Blocks to move randomly at regular intervals. This requires the use of a *timer* object, which can be made to 'fire' regularly. When it fires, it generates an `ActionEvent` object which is passed to the `ActionPerformed` method of an `ActionListener` object.

The following code implements a timer to move Blocks randomly every 100 milliseconds. Insert it in the constructor of the `PacMan` class:

```
Timer t = new Timer(100, new ActionListener()
{
  public void actionPerformed(ActionEvent e)
  {
    for(int i=0; i< numBlocks; i++)
      if (blockArmy[i].isAlive())
      {
        double r = Math.random();
        if (r < 0.25) blockArmy[i].left();
        else if (r < 0.5) blockArmy[i].right();
        else if (r < 0.75) blockArmy[i].up();
```

```
          else blockArmy[i].down();
          blockArmy[i].tryKill(pc);
        }
      repaint();
    }
  });
  t.start();
```

Note:

- The Timer class is in the javax.swing package.
- The first argument of the Timer constructor is the interval in milliseconds at which the timer fires.
- The response to the timer's firing is implemented as an anonymous class object in the second argument of the Timer constructor.
- Start the timer with the Timer method start.
- Since only living Blocks should move when the timer fires, Block needs a public method isAlive to return the state of health of Blocks.

Final version

You might like to arrange for the Blocks to 'wrap around' when they move out of the frame, e.g. if one disappears on the right of the frame it should reappear on the left with the same vertical coordinate (Block and Pacman).

The final version of PacMan, listed below with the Point, Pac and Block classes, shows you how to display a message when all the Blocks have been killed.

```java
import java.awt.*;
import javax.swing.event.*;

public class Point
{
  protected int x, y;   //location of the point
  protected Color col;
  protected int size = 8;
  protected int dx = 10;    //amount to move left and right
  protected int dy = 10;    //amount to move up and down

  public Point (int x, int y, int s, Color c)
  {
    this.x = x;
    this.y = y;
    size = s;
    col = c;
  }

  public void show(Graphics g)
  {
    //draw the point
    g.setColor(col);
    g.fillOval (x-size/2, y-size/2, size, size);
  }
```

```java
  public void up()    { y -= dy;  }
  public void down()  { y += dy;  }
  public void left()  { x -= dx;  }
  public void right() { x += dx;  }


}



import java.awt.*;
import javax.swing.event.*;

public class Pac extends Point
{
  public Pac(int x, int y, int s, Color c)
  {
    super(x, y, s, c);
  }

  public void show(Graphics g)
  {
    //draw PacMan
    g.setColor(col);
    g.fillArc (x, y, size, size, 45, 290);

  }

}



import java.awt.*;
import javax.swing.event.*;

public class Block extends Point
{
  private boolean alive = true;
  //zapped if pac closer than this
  private double zapRange = size;
  //limits on how far a block can move
  protected int xLimit;
  protected int yLimit;

  public Block(int x, int y, int s, Color c, int xL, int yL)
  {
    super(x,y,s,c);
    xLimit = xL;
    yLimit = yL;
  }

  public void up()    { super.up();    boundCheck();}
  public void down()  { super.down();  boundCheck(); }
  public void left()  { super.left();  boundCheck(); }
  public void right() { super.right(); boundCheck(); }
```

```java
   private void boundCheck()
   {
     if (x > xLimit) x = x - xLimit;
     else if (x < size) x = xLimit - size;
     if (y > yLimit) y = y - yLimit;
     else if (y < size) y = yLimit - size;
   }

   public void tryKill(Pac p)
   {
     double d;   // distance apart
     d = Math.sqrt((y-p.y)*(y-p.y)+(x-p.x)*(x-p.x));
     if (d < zapRange) alive = false;
   }

   public boolean isAlive() { return alive; }

   public void show(Graphics g)
   {
     if (alive)
     {
       //draw the Block
       g.setColor(col);
       g.fillRect (x, y, size, size);
     }

   }

}


import javax.swing.*;
import java.awt.*;
import java.awt.event.*;

public class PacMan extends JFrame
{

  DrawPanel drawArea = new DrawPanel();
  int winWidth;
  int winHeight;
  int winBorder; //a buffer to ensure that objects
                 //don't go outside the window

  Pac pc;
  int numBlocks = 5;
  Block[] blockArmy = new Block[numBlocks];

  public PacMan()
  {

    setTitle("PacMan");

    for(int i = 0; i < numBlocks; i++)
```

```
          {
            int x = (int) (winWidth*Math.random());
            int y = (int) (winHeight*Math.random());
            blockArmy[i] = new Block(x,y,15,Color.black,
                                     winWidth,winHeight);
          }

          addKeyListener(new KeyAdapter()
          {
            public void keyPressed(KeyEvent e)
            {
              int key = e.getKeyCode();
              if (key ==  KeyEvent.VK_UP) pc.up();
              if (key ==  KeyEvent.VK_DOWN) pc.down();
              if (key ==  KeyEvent.VK_LEFT) pc.left();
              if (key ==  KeyEvent.VK_RIGHT) pc.right();

              for(int i=0; i<numBlocks; i++)
                blockArmy[i].tryKill(pc);

              if (finished()) endGame();

              repaint();
            }
          });

          Timer t = new Timer(100, new ActionListener()
          {
            public void actionPerformed(ActionEvent e)
            {
              for(int i=0; i< numBlocks; i++)
                if (blockArmy[i].isAlive())
                {
                  double r = Math.random();
                  if (r < 0.25) blockArmy[i].left();
                  else if (r < 0.5) blockArmy[i].right();
                  else if (r < 0.75) blockArmy[i].up();
                  else blockArmy[i].down();
                  blockArmy[i].tryKill(pc);
                }
              repaint();
            }
          });
          t.start();

          getContentPane().add(drawArea);
          drawArea.setBackground(new Color(200,200,255));
          setDefaultCloseOperation(JFrame.EXIT_ON_CLOSE);
          pack();
        }

        private void endGame()
        {
          JOptionPane.showMessageDialog(this, "Well done, you won!");
```

```
      System.exit(0);
   }

   private boolean finished()
   {
      boolean won = true;
      for(int i=0; i<numBlocks; i++)
         if (blockArmy[i].isAlive() == true) return false;
      return won;
   }

   class DrawPanel extends JPanel
   {

      public DrawPanel()
      {
         winWidth = 600;
         winHeight = 600;
         winBorder = 10;
         setPreferredSize
                  (new Dimension(winWidth+winBorder,
                                 winHeight+winBorder));

         pc = new Pac(winWidth/2, winHeight/2, 18, Color.blue);
      }

      protected void paintComponent (Graphics g)
      {
         super.paintComponent (g);

         pc.show(g);   //draw PacMan

         //draw the Blocks
         for (int i = 0; i < numBlocks; i++)
            blockArmy[i].show(g);
      }
   }

   public static void main(String[] args)
   {
      PacMan pm = new PacMan();
      pm.setVisible(true);
   }

}
```

8.6 Drawing mathematical graphs

Although Essential Grapher draws 'mathematical' graphs quite adequately, you may (if you are at all like us) be curious about how to write your own graphing programs. Our aim in this section, therefore, is to draw a graph of a given mathematical function from first principles, without any assistance from our essential package (see Figure 8.6).

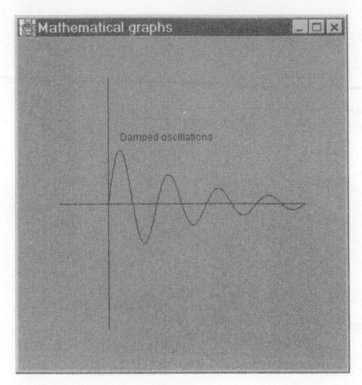

Figure 8.6 The graph of $e^{-0.1x}\sin x$

You will no doubt readily appreciate that drawing even fairly simple mathematical graphs poses a non-trivial challenge, because you have to think in terms of absolute pixel coordinates. How would you, for example, go about drawing the graph of $y = x^2$ from $x = 0$ to $x = 10$?

If we define *world coordinates* as the familiar x-y cartesian coordinate system that we all used at school, then a point with world coordinates (x, y) has to be transformed into a pixel somewhere on the panel on which we are drawing. An additional irritation is that vertical pixel coordinates increase as you move down the screen, contrary to world y coordinates.

What we need is a class with a set of methods which will *transform* our more natural world coordinates into absolute pixel coordinates. These methods are contained in the `MyWorld` class listed below:

```java
public class MyWorld
//transforms world coordinates into pixel coordinates
{
    private double xmin;
    private double xmax;
    private double ymin;
    private double ymax;
    private int xrange;
    private int yrange;
    private int topborder;
    private int leftborder;
    public MyWorld( double xleft, double xright, double ydown,
                    double yup, int width, int height )
    {
        xmin = xleft; xmax = xright; ymin = ydown; ymax = yup;
```

```
        xrange = width; yrange = height;
        topborder = 50; leftborder = 50;
    }
    public int xp( double xworld )
    {
        return (int) Math.round(leftborder + xrange * (xworld - xmin)
                              / (xmax - xmin));
    }
    public int yp( double yworld )
    {
        return (int) Math.round(topborder + yrange * (yworld - ymax)
                              / (ymin - ymax));
    }
}
```

Note:

- The constructor for the MyWorld class creates a 'viewing object' or 'view' in world coordinates, running from xleft to xright along the *x*-axis and from ydown to yup along the *y*-axis. The last two parameters width and height are the dimensions of the view in pixels.
- The two methods xp and yp respectively transform their *x* and *y* world coordinate arguments into absolute horizontal and vertical pixels, which are returned. The yp method also inverts the vertical axis.

The following program MyGraph uses MyWorld to draw the graph of the damped oscillations $y = e^{-0.1x} \sin x$ for *x* from 0 to 8π in steps of $\pi/40$. It also draws the *x*- and *y*-axes.

```
import javax.swing.*;
import java.awt.*;
import java.awt.event.*;

public class MyGraph extends JFrame
{

    DrawPanel drawArea = new DrawPanel();
        int winWidth;
        int winHeight;

    public MyGraph()
    {
        setTitle("Mathematical graphs");
        getContentPane().add(drawArea);
        drawArea.setBackground(new Color(0,255,0));
        setDefaultCloseOperation(JFrame.EXIT_ON_CLOSE);
        pack();
    }

    class DrawPanel extends JPanel
    {

        public DrawPanel()
```

```
        {
          winWidth = 400;
          winHeight = 400;

          setPreferredSize (new Dimension(winWidth,winHeight));
        }

        protected void paintComponent (Graphics g)
        {
          super.paintComponent (g);

          double xmin = -2*Math.PI;
          double xmax = 8*Math.PI;
          double ymin = -2;
          double ymax = 2;
          double x, y, xold, yold;
          MyWorld w2p = new MyWorld( xmin, xmax, ymin, ymax, 300, 300 );

          g.drawString( "Damped oscillations", w2p.xp(Math.PI/2),
                                                w2p.yp(ymax/2) );
          g.drawLine( w2p.xp(xmin), w2p.yp(0),
                      w2p.xp(xmax), w2p.yp(0) ); // x-axis
          g.drawLine( w2p.xp(0), w2p.yp(ymin),
                      w2p.xp(0), w2p.yp(ymax) ); // y-axis

          xold = 0; yold = 0;
          for (x = 0; x < 8*Math.PI; x = x+Math.PI/40)
          {
            y = Math.exp( -0.1*x) * Math.sin(x);
            g.drawLine( w2p.xp(xold), w2p.yp(yold),
                        w2p.xp(x), w2p.yp(y) );
            xold = x;
            yold = y;
          }
        }
    }

    public static void main(String[] args)
    {
        MyGraph d = new MyGraph();
        d.setVisible(true);
    }

}
```

Note:

- MyGraph creates a MyWorld viewing object w2p (for 'world to pixel') with appropriate ranges of world coordinates.

- The actual graph is drawn in the paintComponent method using the drawLine method of the Graphics class. The drawLine method has four arguments, x1, y1, x2 and y2, and draws a line between the points (x1, y1) and (x2, y2). These arguments are updated repeatedly in the for loop to draw the graph.

Try Exercise 8.12.

8.7   Fractals

The popularization of fractals in recent years has led to a wealth of coffee table books with the most beautiful and fascinating pictures. Two such fractals are the *Julia* and *Mandelbrot* sets.

The Julia set

In this section we give a simple program for drawing the Julia set of the complex polynomial

$$z^2 - \mu, \tag{8.1}$$

where z is a complex variable, $z = x + iy$, and μ is a complex constant (parameter), $\mu = a + ib$.
   A working definition of the Julia set of this family of polynomials is as follows:

- Take a region of the complex plane.
- For *every point* z_0 in this region calculate the *iterated function sequence* (IFS) of the polynomial (8.1):

$$z_1 = z_0^2 - \mu,$$
$$z_2 = z_1^2 - \mu,$$
$$\dots$$
$$z_n = z_{n-1}^2 - \mu$$

- If an n can be found such that $z_n^2 > R$, where R is the radius of a (large) disk in the complex plane, z_0 is said to have *escaped*.
- The set of all points z_0 in the region of interest which do *not* escape is the Julia set of the polynomial.

One way to compute the IFS requires the real and imaginary parts of the polynomial $z^2 - \mu$, which are $x^2 - y^2 - a$, and $2xy - b$ respectively.
   The code below draws the Julia set of $z^2 - 1.25$, so $a = 1.25$ and $b = 0$. Ideally R should be as large as possible, but we will take it as 10, since this gives quite a reasonable picture. You can experiment with larger values if you like! If z_0 has not escaped by the time n has reached the value of maxIts (40), we will assume that it will never escape. The program checks each pixel in the world coordinate range $-2 \le x \le 2$, $-1 \le y \le 1$, to see if it escapes (applying the reverse of the transformation used in MyWorld to change world coordinates to absolute coordinates). If the pixel escapes it is lit up in a different colour, depending on how quickly it escapes. The Julia set is then the set of pixels shaded in the background colour. (Strictly speaking, the Julia set is the *boundary* of the region in the background colour, and the region itself is the *filled* Julia set.) Note that the program does not use the MyWorld class. It may take a few seconds before you see anything.

```
import javax.swing.*;
import java.awt.*;
import java.awt.event.*;
```

```java
public class JuliaSet extends JFrame
{

    DrawPanel drawArea = new DrawPanel();
    int winWidth;
    int winHeight;

    public JuliaSet()
    {
        setTitle("Julia Set");
        getContentPane().add(drawArea);
        drawArea.setBackground(new Color(0,255,0));
        setDefaultCloseOperation(JFrame.EXIT_ON_CLOSE);
        pack();
    }

    class DrawPanel extends JPanel
    {
        public DrawPanel()
        {
            winWidth = 800;
            winHeight = 600;

            setPreferredSize (new Dimension(winWidth,winHeight));
        }

        protected void paintComponent (Graphics g)
        {
            super.paintComponent (g);

            int maxIts = 40;          // max number of iterations
            double r = 10;            // infinity
            double  a, b;             // real and imag parts of mu
            double xmin, xmax, ymin, ymax; // range of world coords
            double x, y, x0, y0, newX, newY; // world coords
            int n;                    // iteration counter
            int xp, yp;               // pixel coords
            int maxX, maxY;           // pixel range
            int R, G, B;              // RGB parameters
            int topBorder = 50;       // dont draw on the menubar!
            xmin = -2;
            xmax = 2;
            ymin = -1;
            ymax = 1;
            maxX = 790;
            maxY = 500;
            a = 1.25;
            b = 0;

            for (xp = 0; xp <= maxX; xp++)
```

```
        for (yp = 0; yp <= maxY; yp++)
        {
          x0 = (xmax - xmin) * xp / maxX + xmin;
          y0 = (ymin - ymax) * yp / maxY + ymax;
          x = x0;
          y = y0;
          n = 0;

          while (n < maxIts && x*x + y*y <= r)
          {
            n++;
            newX = x*x - y*y - a;
            newY = 2*x*y - b;
            x = newX;
            y = newY;

            if (x*x + y*y > r)
            {
              n = n %7 + 1;
              B = n % 2;
              if (n <=3)
                R = 0;
              else
                R = 1;
              if (n == 2 | n == 3 | n == 6 | n == 7)
                G = 1;
              else
                G = 0;
              g.setColor( new Color(255*R, 255*G, 255*B) );
              g.drawLine( xp, yp+topBorder, xp, yp+topBorder );
            }
            else
            {
              // black inside the Set
              g.setColor(Color.black);
              g.drawLine( xp, yp+topBorder, xp, yp+topBorder );
            }
          }
        }
    }

    public static void main(String[] args)
    {
      JuliaSet d = new JuliaSet();
      d.setVisible(true);
    }

}
```

Note:

- The complicated relationship between the iteration counter n for an escaped pixel and the values of R, G and B in the setColor methods of the Graphics class transforms n into a selection of the original 'bright VGA' colours.
- The boundary of the filled Julia set has the self-replicating property characteristic of fractals. Change the program (by adjusting xmin, xmax, etc.) to 'zoom' in on one of the 'spires' sticking out of the main body of the set. A little patience will be richly rewarded.

Try Exercise 8.13.

The Mandelbrot set

The *Mandelbrot set* was discovered by Benoit Mandelbrot, and has been described as the most complicated object known to man. It is related to the Julia set, and is drawn in much the same way, although it is more difficult to think about.

The Julia set above is for the polynomial $z^2 - \mu$, with $\mu = 1.1$. If you run the program for a different value of the parameter μ, the set will look different. The Mandelbrot set is concerned with μ, and is drawn in the *parameter* space of the polynomial. The Mandelbrot set is in fact the set of all values of μ for which the *origin* does not escape.

Recall that $\mu = a + ib$. For all possible values of a and b now (as opposed to x and y for the Julia set) we compute the IFS of $z^2 - \mu$, starting at $z = 0$ each time. If z_n (the nth iterate) for a particular μ does not escape it belongs to the Mandelbrot set. The program is very similar to the one for the Julia set:

```java
import javax.swing.*;
import java.awt.*;
import java.awt.event.*;

public class MandelbrotSet extends JFrame
{

  DrawPanel drawArea = new DrawPanel();
  int winWidth;
  int winHeight;

  public MandelbrotSet()
  {
    setTitle("Mandelbrot Set");
    getContentPane().add(drawArea);
    drawArea.setBackground(new Color(0,255,0));
    setDefaultCloseOperation(JFrame.EXIT_ON_CLOSE);
    pack();
  }

  class DrawPanel extends JPanel
  {

    public DrawPanel()
    {
    winWidth = 700;
```

```
    winHeight = 700;

    setPreferredSize (new Dimension(winWidth,winHeight));
}

protected void paintComponent (Graphics g)
{
  super.paintComponent (g);
  int maxIts = 40;        // max number of iterations
  double r = 10;          // infinity
  double  a, b;           // real and imag parts of mu
  double xmin, xmax, ymin, ymax; // range of world coords
  double x, y, newX, newY; // world coords
  int n;
  int xp, yp;             // pixel coords
  int maxX, maxY;         // pixel range
  int R, G, B;            // RGB parameters
  int topBorder = 50;     // dont draw on the menubar!
  xmin = -0.5;
  xmax = 1.5;
  ymin = -1;
  ymax = 1;
  maxX = 500;
  maxY = 500;

  for (xp = 0; xp <= maxX; xp++)
    for (yp = 0; yp <= maxY; yp++)
    {
      a = (xmax - xmin) * xp / maxX + xmin;
      b = (ymin - ymax) * yp / maxY + ymax;
      x = 0;
      y = 0;
      n = 0;

      while (n < maxIts && x*x + y*y <= r)
      {
        n++;
        newX = x*x - y*y - a;
        newY = 2*x*y - b;
        x = newX;
        y = newY;
      }

      if (x*x + y*y > r)
      {
        n = n %7 + 1;
        B = n % 2;
        if (n <=3)
            R = 0;
```

```
            else
                R = 1;
            if (n == 2 | n == 3 | n == 6 | n == 7)
                G = 1;
            else
                G = 0;
            g.setColor( new Color(255*R, 255*G, 255*B) );
            g.drawLine( xp, yp+topBorder, xp, yp+topBorder );
          }
          else {
            // black inside the Set
            g.setColor(Color.black);
            g.drawLine( xp, yp+topBorder, xp, yp+topBorder );
          }
        }
      }
    }

    public static void main(String[] args)
    {
      MandelbrotSet d = new MandelbrotSet();
      d.setVisible(true);
    }

}
```

The Mandelbrot set is a 'fuzzy' fractal. If you enlarge one of the little 'snowmen' on its boundary (coastline) you will see a figure which is similar but not *identical* (zooming on the Julia set coastline reveals identical replicas of the Julia set). In fact the structures on the boundaries of the Mandelbrot set resemble Julia sets. It is as if the coastline of the Mandelbrot set is made by stitching together microscopic copies of the Julia sets which it represents.

Zooming in on the 'sea' outside the Mandelbrot set may be rewarding too. You may find islands there that no-one else has ever seen.

Try Exercise 8.14.

Summary

- GUIs can be implemented in Java using either the AWT or Swing.
- GUI programs are *event-driven*. An *event* is any user action on the interface, such as pushing a button.
- The Swing class that implements an independent window on the screen is called JFrame.
- There are three main types of components: top-level containers (e.g. JFrame), intermediate containers (e.g. JPanel) and atomic components (e.g. JButton).
- To program an interface to respond to user events, we have to write *listeners* for the relevant components.
- Components can be arranged using layout managers. Commonly used layout managers include: BorderLayout, FlowLayout and GridLayout.
- Painting (drawing) may be done on an extended JPanel object, which must override the paintComponent method to do the actual painting.
- Various shapes may be drawn with methods of the Graphics class.
- Our MyWorld class may be used to draw mathematical graphs by transforming natural world coordinates into absolute pixel coordinates.

Exercises

8.1   Change the FirstGUI application from Section 8.2 so that the window has a title (use the setTitle method of the JFrame class). When you have this working, notice that if you minimize your window, the title is also shown at the bottom of the screen.

8.2   The on-line Swing tutorial is a very useful resource. In this exercise you are required to look in the Swing tutorial for certain information on components. In your browser go to Sun's Java web page:

```
http://java.sun.com
```

Click on **Java Tutorial** and then on **Creating a GUI with JFC/Swing**. Somewhere in the tutorial, you will find a section on 'A Visual Index to the Swing Components' (you will have to browse around a bit and we encourage you to read along the way). Using this resource, find answers to the following questions:

(a)   List three types of Swing buttons (give the Swing class name of each).
(b)   What is the main difference between a JComboBox and a JList (from the end user's perspective)?
(c)   What is the purpose of a JTextField?

8.3   Add a JTextField component to SimpleFrame from Section 8.2. Use the Swing tutorial or the Java API to find out how to do this.

8.4   Add a JComboBox component to SimpleFrame from Section 8.2 (use any three strings as options). Use the Swing tutorial or the Java API to find out how to do this.

8.5   Add a **Quit** button to class SimpleFrame. Program it so that it exits the program (note: the command System.exit(0) will exit a program).

8.6   Write two classes called FirstWindow and SecondWindow, both extending JFrame. Add a JButton component to FirstWindow called open and add any component to SecondWindow. Write code so that if the user clicks on the open button of FirstWindow, it will display SecondWindow.

8.7   Write a program that uses the GridLayout manager to place six buttons on a panel, in three rows of two buttons each. Give each button a label with a different length. (Read up how to use the GridLayout in the Java Swing tutorial or Java API.)

8.8   Your friend has just starting programming graphical user interfaces in Java. He is struggling and has come to you for help. His program looks like this:

```java
import javax.swing.*;
import java.awt.*;
public class MyFrame extends JFrame {
   private JButton button = new JButton ("Quit");
   private JLabel label = new JLabel("Welcome!");
   public MyFrame() {
      Container back = getContentPane();
      back.add(label);
      back.add(button);
      pack();
   }
   public static void main (String [] args) {
      MyFrame frame = new MyFrame();
      frame.setVisible(true);
   } // main method
} // SimpleAWT class
```

The problem he is having is that when he runs the program, only the button displays and not the label.

(a) Explain why this is happening.

(b) How will you change the program, so that both components display?

8.9 Add an empty border to the background panel of SimpleFrame and see what impact it has on the layout of the window.

8.10 Modify the ColourChooser application, so that it includes a button called "Reset" which sets all the sliders to position 0 (colour black).

8.11 Add three JTextField components to the ColourChooser application. These text fields should be positioned between the labels and sliders and should allow the user to type in a numeric value (between 0 and 255). In response to the user typing a value and pressing enter, the relevant slider should update its position and the colour should change. You must also change the program so that the values in the text fields will be updated when the user changes the position of the sliders. The reset button from Exercise 8.10 will also have to be changed to update the values in the text fields.

8.12 Extend MyGraph of Section 8.6 to draw the graph of a more general damped oscillation,

$$y(x) = y_0 e^{-kx} \sin \omega x,$$

with suitably labelled JTextField components in the panel to enable you to change the values of y_0, k and ω.

8.13 Modify the JuliaSet class of Section 8.7 to the Julia set of $z^2 - \mu$, for $\mu = -0.27334 + 0.007421i$. You may need to use a slightly smaller region than the one in the JuliaSet program for the best effect.

8.14 Modify the MandelbrotSet class of Section 8.7 to zoom in on some parts of the coastline of the Mandelbrot set, e.g. the region $0.04 \le a \le 0.06$, $0.98 \le b \le 1$, where $\mu = a + ib$.

9
Input/output

Objectives

By the end of this chapter, you should be able to do the following:

- read data into a program through command line parameters;
- read in data from the keyboard or a file and write data to a file without using the `essential` package;
- extract particular data from a common delimited text file by tokenizing the input;
- create a stream to an Internet web site and read HTML code.

9.1 Introduction

Usually a program needs some form of input to do the job and produces some form of output. There are a number of ways of obtaining data as input to a running program. Some of these ways include:

- input on startup of the program through the command line parameters (this is explained in the next section);
- input from the keyboard while the program is running using `System.in` (or an intermediary class such as the `Keyboard` class, which uses `System.in`);
- input via a graphical user interface (from a text field, for example);
- input from a file on disk.

Similarly, a running program can produce output in various ways, such as:

- displaying results onto the screen, at the command prompt, using `System.out`;
- displaying data through a graphical user interface;
- writing data to a file on disk.

In this chapter we will look at some of the interesting detail of how input and output work.

9.2 Input through command line parameters

Input from command line parameters is sometimes a useful and easy way of obtaining a small amount of input from the user. Have you ever wondered what the `String[]` argument of the `main` method is used for? The following program illustrates how it can be used:

```
public class CommandLine
{
  public static void main(String[] args)
  {
    System.out.println("First argument: " + args[0]);
    System.out.println("Second argument: " + args[1]);
  }
}
```

Compile `CommandLine.java` and run it using the following command:

```
java CommandLine doodle 49
```

The output of the program is:

```
First argument: doodle
Second argument: 49
```

Can you see what is happening? Java stores any data following the file name of the `java` command in an array of `Strings`. This array is passed to the `main` method as the first and only argument in the argument list. For this reason we usually use the name `args` for the formal parameter of the `main` method to indicate that the array stores arguments. The first command line argument (in this case `doodle`), is stored as the first element of the array, at position 0; the second at position 1, and so on. This is done automatically by the Java interpreter. Any number of arguments can be provided—the size of the `args` array will change accordingly.

Note that all command line arguments are stored as `Strings`, so if one of the arguments is a number, it will have to be converted from a `String` to an appropriate number type.

Now do Exercises 9.1 to 9.3.

9.3 Input from the keyboard without the `essential` package

In Chapter 1, Section 1.4, we showed you a program that performed user input from the keyboard without using the `essential.Keyboard` class. In this chapter we will explain the details. Here is a similar program that simply reads in a string from the keyboard and echos it back to the screen:

```
import java.io.*;
public class TestInput
{
  public static void main(String args[]) throws IOException
  {
    BufferedReader din = new BufferedReader(
                      new InputStreamReader(System.in));
    System.out.print("Enter a String: ");
    String s = din.readLine();
    System.out.println("you entered: " + s);
  }
}
```

Note that we import `java.io`, which is Java's standard package for performing input and output. The `essential` package is not needed, so is not imported. Also note the `throws IOException` clause in the header of the `main` method. This is an indication that an error could occur with the input/output inside the `main` method. We say that an exception *could be* thrown. This clause is required for the program to compile. Exceptions will be explained in detail in Chapter 10.

In the following sections, we will explain:

* the notion of streams;
* the `System` class, with the `in`, `out` and `err` data members;
* the `InputStreamReader` and `BufferedReader` classes;

9.4   Streams

A *stream* is the name given to a flow of data in or out of a program. If we want to obtain data from somewhere outside our program (such as the keyboard, or a file), we need to have an *input stream* corresponding to that input device. In the same way, if we want to write to external devices (such as the screen or a file), our program must define *output streams* corresponding to those output devices. A program can have multiple input and output streams to different devices, as illustrated in Figure 9.1.

For your convenience, some streams are defined as part of the standard Java, such as `System.in` (which is a stream linked to the keyboard), `System.out` (which is a stream linked to the screen) and `System.err` (the standard error output stream, also linked to the screen). As we shall see, the output stream, `System.out`, can be re-directed to a file. Figure 9.2 shows these three standard streams.

Output redirection

You can send the output from any program to a file using the output redirection symbol (>). Consider the following program, for example:

```
public class TimesTables
{
    public static void main(String args[])
```

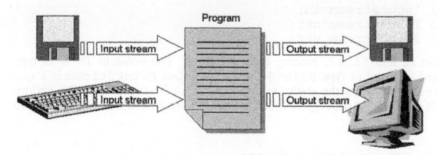

Figure 9.1 Streams passing data into and out of a program to external devices

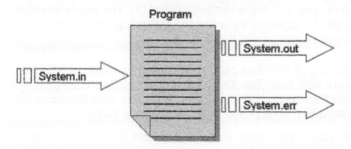

Figure 9.2 Three standard Java streams

```
   {
      for(int i = 2; i <= 12; i++)
      {
         for(int j = 1; j <= 12; j++)
           System.out.println(i + " X " + j + " = " + i*j);
         System.out.println("----------------------");
      }
   }
}
```

The output is a long list of multiplication tables, which scrolls past in the output window. To retain the output, you can redirect it to a file as follows:

```
java TimesTables > times.txt
```

This sends all the `System.out` output to the file `times.txt`, instead of to the output window. If the file `times.txt` does not exist, it is automatically created. If the file already exists, it is overwritten. Any `System.err` statements will still be printed to the screen and not redirected to the file. We could therefore print information or error messages or prompts to the user using `err` instead of `out`. For example:

```
System.err.println("Enter number of times tables to print:");
...
System.err.println("Times tables complete");
```

Now do Exercise 9.4.

The System *class*

The `System` class is defined in the `java.lang` package, which is automatically imported by Java. It contains various useful members and methods (including the `exit` method). The streams `in`, `out` and `err` are defined in System, as follows:

```
public static final InputStream in;
public static final PrintStream out;
public static final PrintStream err;
```

All three are declared as `static` and `final`, making them constants. The constant `in` is of type `InputStream`, while `out` and `err` are of type `PrintStream`. The class `PrintStream` is a specialized class of `OutputStream`, which has the ability to print data in a convenient way. The various `print` and `println` methods for different data types, which we are so accustomed to using, are housed in the `PrintStream` class.

The InputStream *and* InputStreamReader *classes*

We know that `System.in` is linked to the keyboard, and the type of `in` is `InputStream`. If you look inside the `InputStream` class in the API, you will see a method, `read()`. You might therefore expect that input from the keyboard could simply be captured by using the following statement:

```
System.in.read();
```

The problem is that the `read()` method of the `InputStream` class reads in only a single byte of data. This is not very useful, as we would rather work with text. The `InputStreamReader` class provides a convenient bridge from byte streams to character streams, i.e. it reads in bytes and converts them into characters. We can create an `InputStreamReader` object from `System.in`, as follows:

```
InputStreamReader input = new InputStreamReader(System.in);
```

We can now use the variable `input` to read in characters.

The `BufferedReader` *class*

Input and output operations are slow, because they involve access to external devices. When we use an `InputStreamReader` object, text is read in character by character and therefore requires many accesses to the keyboard. A more efficient way of reading data is to wait until sufficient characters have been typed before reading them in as a chunk. Such a 'waiting area' is called a *buffer*. The `BufferedReader` class buffers input in this way and provides useful methods for reading in text a line at a time. We can create a `BufferedReader` object from `System.in` as follows:

```
InputStreamReader input = new InputStreamReader(System.in);
BufferedReader bInput = new BufferedReader(input);
```

Alternatively, we can put the two statements together, in the more compact form:

```
BufferedReader bInput = new BufferedReader(
                    new InputStreamReader(System.in)) ;
```

The variable `bInput` now refers to the keyboard and is a `BufferedReader` object, so we can read in whole lines of text as follows:

```
String line = bInput.readLine() ;
```

Note: the `readLine` method of `BufferedReader` is distinct from `Keyboard.readLine`. (If you look inside the `Keyboard` class you will see that `Keyboard.readLine` uses `BufferedReader`'s `readLine`.)

The detail of the `TestInput` program from Section 9.3 should now be clear to you.

Now do Exercises 9.5 to 9.6.

Reading in numbers

The `Keyboard` class provides useful methods for reading in numbers, such as `readInt` and `readDouble`. If we are not using the `Keyboard` class, we are limited to the methods provided in the `BufferedReader` class, namely `read` and `readLine`, which read in individual characters and text respectively. To read in numeric values from the keyboard, we will have to translate the `String` input into numbers. A convenient way of converting a `String` into an int, is to use the `Integer.parseInt` method. To convert a `String` to a double, use the `Double.parseDouble` method. Here are some examples:

```
String s1 = "-245";
String s2 = "-0.345";
String s3 = "5E-8";
int n1 = Integer.parseInt(s1);
double n2 = Double.parseDouble(s2);
double n3 = Double.parseDouble(s3),
```

Now do Exercise 9.7.

9.5 File input/output

Information held in variables and objects vanish when the program ends. In contrast, data stored in files is *persistent*, meaning that it is saved to disk for future reference. In this section we will not only look at how to save data to a file, but also how to read data from files into our programs. Although we have performed some of these operations before (using the `essential.FileIO` class), in this chapter we will look at how it is done without the `essential` package.

Types of files

Information can be stored in a file either in a character form (called a *text file*) or in a binary form (*binary file*). Storing data in a binary form is faster and more compact than storing it in a text form. The disadvantage of binary files is that the contents cannot be viewed easily with a text editor, as can be done with text files.

Files can be accessed

- *sequentially*, where data must be accessed item by item from the beginning to the end, or
- *randomly*, where items are accessed by specifying their location in the file.

We will be concentrating on text files, accessed sequentially. For help on random access files and binary files, see the Java Tutorial, in particular the Lesson on **I/O: Reading and Writing**. In Section 10.5 we show an example program that reads in data from a binary file.

File handling

Java has a class called `File` for handling file objects. The following program shows how some of the methods of `File` can be used:

```java
import java.io.*;
public class FileHandling
{
  public static void main(String[] args)
  {
    File f1 = new File("test.txt");
    if (f1.exists())
      System.out.println("test.txt exists");
    else
      System.out.println("test.txt does not exist");
    File f2 = new File("exercises\\temp\\Test.class");
    if (f2.exists())
    {
      f2.delete();
      System.out.println("Test.class deleted");
    }
  }
}
```

Assume that a file `test.txt` exists in the current directory and that a subfolder `exercises\temp` also exists which contains a file called `Test.class`. The output would then be:

```
test.txt exists
Test.class deleted
```

Note the following about the program above:

- To create a `File` object, we specify the file name as a string.
- To test if a file exists in the current directory, we use the `exists` method, which returns a `boolean`.
- We can specify a file name including a path, as in the case of `f2`. To specify a backslash (\) within a string, we use a double backslash (\\), otherwise the single backslash is interpreted as the beginning of a special character ('\n', for example).
- To delete a file on disk, use the `delete` method (use with caution, it cannot be undone!).

A further useful method of the `File` class is the method `isDirectory`, which is used to find out if the given file is a directory or not. If a file is a directory, the `list` method returns the names of files that occur in that directory, as an array of `Strings`.

Now do Exercise 9.8.

Reading in from a text file

The following program reads in text from any file specified by the user. The text is read in line by line and printed to the screen.

```java
import java.io.*;
public class FileInput
{
  public static void main(String[] args) throws IOException
  {
    BufferedReader kb_in = new BufferedReader(
                        new InputStreamReader(System.in));
    System.out.print("Enter the name of the file to be read: ");
    String filename = kb_in.readLine();
    BufferedReader file_in = new BufferedReader(
                        new FileReader(filename));
    System.out.println("Contents of file:");
    String line = file_in.readLine();
    while(line != null)
    {
      System.out.println(line);
      line = file_in.readLine();
    }
  }
}
```

Run the program, enter the name of any text file (a .java file, for example) and see what happens. Note the following about the program:

- In the program we declare two BufferedReader objects. The first one (kb_in) is linked to the keyboard. The second one (file_in) is linked to the file specified by the user.
- Multiple lines are read in from the file in a while loop. When the end of the file is reached, readLine will return the value null.
- Before the program ends, the file is closed, indicating to the operating system that it is no longer in use by our program.

Now do Exercise 9.9.

Writing to files

The class PrintWriter provides a convenient way of writing to text files. All the print and println methods we are accustomed to using with System.out can be used with a PrintWriter object. The following program writes three simple lines to a file called new.txt:

```java
import java.io.*;
public class FileOutput
{
  public static void main(String[] args) throws IOException
  {
    PrintWriter pout = new PrintWriter(new FileWriter("new.txt"));
    pout.println("Line 1");
    pout.println("Line 2");
    pout.println("------");
```

```
      pout.close();
   }
}
```

If the file `new.txt` does not exist, it will be created automatically by the program. If `new.txt` does exist before running the program, the contents will be overwritten. Note that we close the file before the program terminates.

Now do Exercise 9.10.

9.6 Manipulating data

You may sometimes have data files which are not in the required format for your program or which contain redundant data. In these cases you will need to manipulate the data to suit your needs.

Say, for example, you are doing research into the effects of wind and rain on levels of pollution. You obtain weather data from a weather station. They send you separate files for each month of the year that you requested. The format of one of the files is shown in Table 9.1.

We need some way of splitting up the data into individual values and ignoring the values we are not interested in. We can do this through a process called *tokenizing*.

Tokenizing strings

Data from text files is often stored in a *common delimited* format. This means that the data values are separated by some *delimiter*. The delimiter could be a space or spaces (as in the case of the weather data file), or a comma or semi-colon—any character which is repeated between data values and which does not occur inside the data values (such as a full stop). We call the data values *tokens* and the process of extracting the individual tokens, *tokenizing*.

Java provides a useful class called `StringTokenizer` for extracting tokens from a string which is common delimited. The following program reads in data from `jan99.txt` and creates a second file called `jan99_new.txt`, which contains only the date, rainfall and wind values:

```
import java.io.*;
import java.util.*;

public class WeatherData
{
  public static void main(String[] args) throws IOException
  {
    BufferedReader file_in = new BufferedReader(
                    new FileReader("jan99.txt"));
    PrintWriter file_out = new PrintWriter(
                    new FileWriter("jan99_new.txt"));

    String line = file_in.readLine();  // ignore the first line
    line = file_in.readLine();
    while(line != null)
```

Table 9.1 Sample weather station data. File `jan99.txt`

date	tempMax	tempMin	rain	humid	wind
1	25.3	12.04	0	48	26
2	27.6	13.2	0	63	35
3	18.5	10.7	26.5	100	43
...					

```
      {
        StringTokenizer st = new StringTokenizer(line);
        file_out.print(st.nextToken());  // write date field
        st.nextToken();    // ignore tempMax
        st.nextToken();    // ignore tempMin
        file_out.print(" " + st.nextToken()); // write rain field
        st.nextToken();    // ignore humid
        file_out.println(" " + st.nextToken()); // write wind value
        line = file_in.readLine();  // read next line from input file
      }
      file_in.close();
      file_out.close();
    }
}
```

In the program we do the following:

- create a `BufferedReader` object (`file_in`) for reading in from `jan99.txt`.
- create a `PrintWriter` object (`file_out`) for writing to `jan99_new.txt`.
- read in the first line of text from `jan99.txt`, which contains the names of the columns. We ignore this line by simply reading in a second line of text.
- Inside the loop we create a `StringTokenizer` object, called `st`. With `st` we can retrieve tokens one by one using the `nextToken` method. We only write the first token (the day), the fourth token (the rain value) and the sixth token (the wind value). The other values are ignored by calling `nextToken` and not doing anything with the return value.
- Once all the lines have been processed, both files are closed.

In the program above we used the default form of the `StringTokenizer`, which assumes that the delimiter is *white space* (i.e. spaces, tabs, etc). If a file is delimited by a different character, it must be specified as the second argument to the `StringTokenizer` constructor, for example:

```
StringTokenizer st = new
        StringTokenizer(line, ",");   // use comma as delimiter
```

Now do Exercise 9.11.

9.7 Streams and the Internet

Streams need not be limited to files. We can create streams which connect to web sites on the Internet, using the URL class. The following program creates a stream to the web site of the Department of Computer Science at the University of Cape Town. Through this stream, the HTML code of the web site is read, line by line, and printed to the screen (Note: you will have to be linked to the Internet for this program to work):

```
import java.io.*;
import java.net.*;
public class TestURL
{
    public static void main(String[] args) throws Exception
    {
        URL s = new URL("http://www.cs.uct.ac.za");
        BufferedReader s1 = new BufferedReader(
                    new InputStreamReader(s.openStream()));
```

```
      String line = s1.readLine();
      while (line != null)
      {
        System.out.println(line);
        line = s1.readLine();
      }
    }
}
```

Run the program and see what happens. If you understand HTML code, the output should make sense to you. If the program takes very long to run or you get an 'Operation timed out' error, then you may want to change the URL in the program above to a site geographically close to you.

In this program we import `java.net`, which is the Java package for networking. We also say `throws Exception`, rather than `throws IOException`, since there are other types of exceptions that can occur. This will be explained in the next chapter.

Now do Exercise 9.12.

Summary

- Input can be sent to a Java program through *command line parameters*, which are sent to the main method as an array of `Strings`.
- A *stream* is the name given to a flow of data in to or out of a program.
- `System.in` is a predefined input stream that is linked to the keyboard.
- `System.out` and `System.err` are predefined output steams that are linked to the screen.
- Output sent to `System.out` can be redirected to a file using the output redirection symbol (`>`).
- The `InputStreamReader` class reads in bytes and converts them into characters. The `BufferedReader` class buffers input and provides useful methods for reading in text a line at a time.
- To convert a string to a numeric value we can use `Integer.parseInt` for integers and `Double.parseDouble` for real numbers.
- The class `File` can be used for handling file objects on disk.
- To read in data from a text file we use the `FileReader` class and buffer the input using the `BufferedReader` class.
- To write data to a text file we use the `FileWriter` class. The `PrintWriter` class provides convenient `print` and `println` methods for writing output and can be used with `FileWriter`.
- Data values can be extracted from common delimited files using the `StringTokenizer` class.
- We can create streams to Internet web sites and input HTML code into our program.

Exercises

9.1 Try running the `CommandLine` program from Section 9.2 without any arguments, i.e. with the command:

```
java CommandLine
```

What error is generated? Can you explain why this particular error is generated?

9.2   Look at the following program:

```
public class CommandLine
{
  public static void main(String args[])
  {
    System.out.println("The sum of the arguments is: " +
                        (args[0] + args[1] + args[2]));
  }
}
```

What will be the output from the following run?

```
java CommandLine 1 2 3
```

Explain your answer above and change the program so that it correctly adds the numbers (Hint: If you do not know how to convert a String into an integer, look ahead at the section on **Reading in numbers** in Section 9.4).

9.3   Write a program that takes any number of numeric command line arguments and prints out the sum.

9.4   Write a program which prints out the integers from 35 to 125, each with their corresponding Unicode character. Redirect the output to a file called unicode.txt. Check the output by looking inside unicode.txt.

9.5   Do Exercise 1.3 from Chapter 1, this time without using the essential package.

9.6   Write a program that asks the user to input any character. Your program should print out the unicode value of that character. Write it without using the essential package. (Hint: use the method read, which reads in a single character, instead of using readLine. Notice that read conveniently returns an int, representing the integer value of the character.)

9.7   Change the TimesTables program from Section 9.4, so that the user is asked for the range of times tables to be printed out. For example, if the user requests times tables from 5 to 11, the program should print out seven times tables.

9.8   Write a program called DirJava, which lists all .java files in a given folder. The user should specify the folder on the command line. If no command line argument is given, the program should list all .java files in the current directory. Hints:

- The current directory is referred to by the dot operator, so to create a File object representing the current directory, use new File(".").
- Use the endsWith method of the String class to test the types of files.

9.9   Write a program that prints out the averages between numbers stored in corresponding lines in two separate files. For example, if file1 contains the values:

```
10
5
20.5
8
```

and file2 contains the values:

```
20
5
20.75
6
```

your program should print out:

```
15
5
20.75
7
```

You can assume that both files have the same number of values. Create sample files to test your program.

9.10 In Section 9.4 we wrote a program called `TimesTables` that printed out a list of multiplication tables. Change the program so that it automatically writes the output to the file `times.txt` without the user having to redirect the output to a file.

9.11 Write a program called `PrintDown` that reads in a file of numbers all on the same line and outputs a file with the numbers on separate lines. Write your program so that the input file is the first command line argument and the output file the second argument. For example, if a file `num.txt` looks like this:

```
3.3  17  86.5  -87
```

then the command

```
java PrintDown num.txt out.txt
```

will create a file called out.txt, which looks like this:

```
3.3
17
86.5
-87
```

9.12 Write a program called `DownloadWeb` that asks the user for the URL of any web site. The program should then write the HTML code of that site to a file called `download.html`. Run your program on a sample site and check it by opening `download.html` in a web browser. (Note: only the text will be downloaded, not any images.)

10
Exceptions

10.1 Introduction

Programs that you write should be *robust*. This means that when something unexpected happens, your program should do something sensible (i.e. not crash or produce senseless results).

An *exception* is an indication that something unexpected has happened (at run-time), and the program cannot continue running merrily—there has to be code somewhere which explains what to do. Many kinds of errors can cause exceptions, ranging from programming bugs or invalid user input to a hard drive crash. It is the programmer's responsibility to *expect the unexpected* and write code to handle unexpected events.

10.2 Exceptions in Java

Consider the following program:

```
import java.io.*;
public class Square
{
    public static void main (String args []) throws Exception
    {
        BufferedReader in = new BufferedReader(
                    new InputStreamReader(System.in));
        System.out.print("Enter a number: ");
        String s = in.readLine();
```

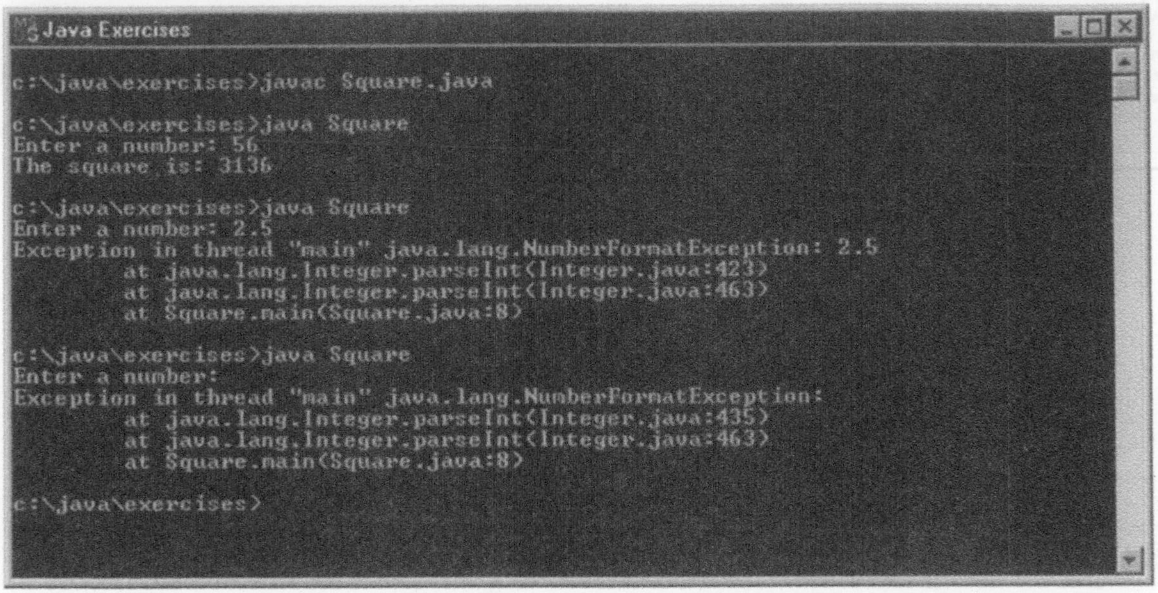

Figure 10.1 Three sample runs of Square.java showing one valid input and two invalid inputs

```
    int num = Integer.parseInt(s);
    System.out.println("The square is: " + (num*num));
    }
}
```

Figure 10.1 shows three sample runs of the program. In the first run the user entered a valid integer (56), in the second run the user entered an invalid integer (2.5) and in the third run the user entered nothing. In both the second and third runs an exception was generated and the program terminated without the final println being executed.

In this way exceptions can cause abnormal termination of a program. Java's default operation when an exception occurs is to write such a four line (or longer) error message and terminate the program. In this chapter we will see how to handle exceptions by intercepting this default operation.

Exception classes

Consider the Integer.parseInt method again. In the Java API the parseInt method header looks like this:

```
public static int parseInt(String s) throws NumberFormatException
```

The throws NumberFormatException clause is an indication that something *may* go wrong in that method, i.e. it is possible that an exception will occur. If you click on **NumberFormatException**, you will see that it is a class (see Figure 10.2).

All exceptions are instances of classes derived from java.lang.Exception. Notice that NumberFormatException inherits from IllegalArgumentException, which inherits from RuntimeException, which inherits from Exception. If you click on **java.lang.Exception** and look under **Direct Known Subclasses**, you will get a feeling for how *many* different types of exceptions there are in Java. The names of exception classes also serve as descriptions of the type of exception they represent. Try to figure out what kind of errors some of the Exception subclasses represent, based on their names.

Now do Exercise 10.1.

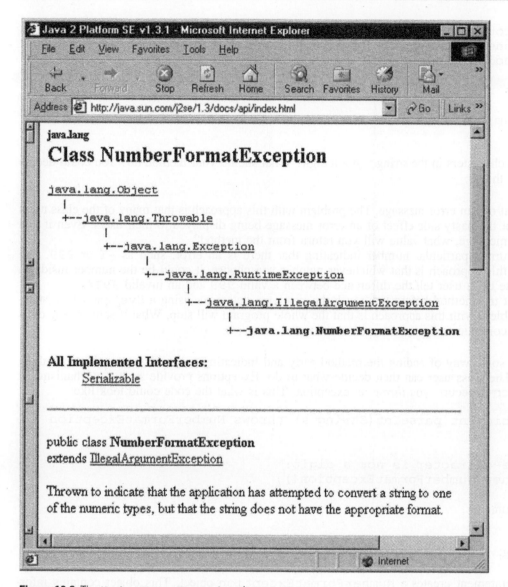

Figure 10.2 The NumberFormatException class

10.3 Throwing exceptions

Imagine that you are working for Sun Microsystems and have been asked to write the Integer.parseInt method. You put on the class provider hat to remind yourself that this method will be used by programmers writing many different kinds of applications. The method outline could look something like this:

```
public static int parseInt(String s)
{
    int num = 0;   // the number to be returned

    /* check if the first character is a minus sign
       and store this as a boolean */
```

```
    /* go through String s backwards char by char to check that
       each one is a digit.  Multiply each digit by power
       (depending on position) and add to num */

    /* change num to be negative if necessary */

    return num;
}
```

What if one of the characters in the string is not a digit? What should your method do? You could decide to do a number of things:

- You could print out an error message. The problem with this approach is that many of the class users might not want the nasty side effect of an error message being displayed to their users. Even if you print an error message, what value will you return from the method?
- You could return a particular number indicating that there is an error, such as -1 or 999. The problem with this approach is that whichever number you choose, it could be the number inside s. How would the class user tell the difference between a valid 999 and an invalid 999?
- You could exit the method before you reach the return statement, using a System.exit statement. The problem with this approach is that the whole program will stop. What if some of the class users want to continue and maybe try other values?

What you want is some way of ending the method early and indicating to the class user that something has gone wrong. The class user can then decide what to do. Exceptions provide such a mechanism. At the place that the error occurs, you *throw* an exception. This is what the code could look like:

```
public static int parseInt(String s) throws NumberFormatException
{
    ...
    // if the character is not a digit:
      throw new NumberFormatException();
    ...
    return num;
}
```

Note the following:

- The throw statement creates a NumberFormatException object. This object contains information about the exception, including its type and the state of the program when the error occurred. The class user can query this exception object if necessary.
- When the throw statement is executed, the method is terminated early. Exceptions therefore provide a way of 'jumping' out of the method. The remaining statements (such as the return statement) are not reached if the exception is thrown.
- The throws NumberFormatException clause of the method header is a warning to class users that this particular kind of error could occur.

In summary, when we write classes to be used by others (or ourselves), we should anticipate possible errors and generate exceptions. In this way, the class user can decide what to do when an exception occurs (exit the program, fix the error, or continue without doing anything). The appropriate way of handling an exception will be different, depending on the nature of the program calling the method. Therefore, the responsibility of deciding what to do in the event of an error rests with the programmer using the method, not the programmer writing the method.

Now do Exercise 10.2.

When to specify the throws *clause in a method header*

Compile the following two classes as separate files and see what happens:

```java
import java.io.*;
public class TestInput
{
  public static void main(String args[])
  {
    FileReader f = new FileReader("test.txt");
  }
}

public class TestParseInt
{
  public static void main(String args[])
  {
    int num = Integer.parseInt("35");
  }
}
```

The result of the compilations is shown in Figure 10.3. The first class (TestInput) generates an error, while the second class compiles without any errors. Look at the detail of the error carefully. The compiler is stating that the FileNotFoundException must be 'caught or declared to be thrown'. This means that we must either handle (i.e. catch) the exception, or specify that we are not handling the exception. This is known as Java's *catch or specify* requirement.

Here is an analogy to explain the *catch or specify* requirement: Say something goes wrong at home, such as the drain blocking. Household rules specify that if anybody finds the drain blocked, they must either unblock the drain (i.e. *handle* the problem), or tell somebody else about it. Johnny finds out that the drain has blocked. He decides to 'pass the buck', so he *throws* up his hands and tells Sue that the drain is blocked and he is doing nothing about it. Sue, likewise, decides to 'pass the buck'. So she throws up her hands and tells Greg that the drain is blocked and she is doing nothing about it. Greg needs to

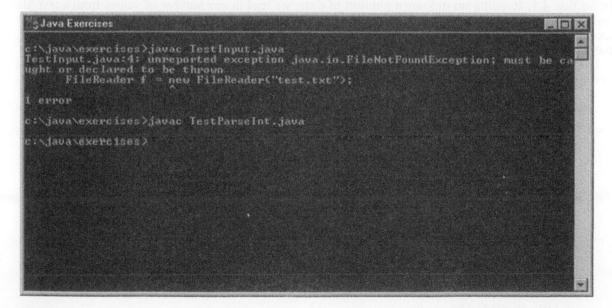

Figure 10.3 The class TestInput does not compile, whereas the class TestParseInt does

wash his clothes, so he decides to handle the problem. He takes the problem in hand (*catches* it) and unblocks the drain. Since he has fixed the problem, he does not have to tell anybody else about it.

For TestInput to compile correctly, we need to add a throws clause to the header as follows:

```
public class TestInput
{
    public static void main(String[] args)
                    throws FileNotFoundException
    {
        ...
```

You may be wondering why the second program (TestParseInt) did not give a similar error. We have used the parseInt method, which throws NumberFormatException, so why do we not have to specify the NumberFormatException in the throws clause of the main method? The reason for this is that Java has different types of exceptions. There is a class of exceptions that do not have to obey the *catch or specify* requirement. These are known as *runtime exceptions*. You may recall that NumberFormatException inherits from IllegalArgumentException, which inherits from RuntimeException. All runtime exception classes are subclasses of this RuntimeException class. These are exceptions that can occur anywhere in a program and so the cost of checking for them by the compiler exceeds the benefit of forced checking. The rest of the exceptions (non-runtime exceptions) are called *checked exceptions* and these must all be caught or specified, i.e. they are 'checked' by the Java compiler.

Now do Exercises 10.3 to 10.4.

10.4 Handling exceptions

Up till now we have been leaving it up to Java to handle all exceptions. Java's default way of handling exceptions is to print out a rather technical message and abort the program. In this section we will look at how to handle exceptions by catching them.

Example: finding averages

In Section 4.1, **Reading an unknown amount of data**, we read in any number of values from a text file and computed the average. The method (called average) was defined inside EssentialMath and it took the name of the file as an argument. We will now define a similar method, also called average, but with no arguments, that reads in a single line of values from the keyboard instead.

Here is the EssentialMath class containing the new average method and a class FindAverage that uses it:

```
import java.io.*;
import java.util.*;   // for StringTokenizer

public class EssentialMath
{
    ...
    public static double average() throws IOException
    {
        System.out.println("Enter numbers on the same line:");
        BufferedReader br = new BufferedReader(
                        new InputStreamReader(System.in));
        String s = br.readLine();
        StringTokenizer st = new StringTokenizer(s);
        double sum = 0;
        int numValues = 0;
```

```
    while (st.hasMoreTokens())
    {
      String n = st.nextToken();
      double num = Double.parseDouble(n);
      sum += num;
      numValues++;
    }  // while
    double avg = sum/numValues;
    return avg;
  }
}

public class FindAverage
{
  public static void main(String args[]) throws IOException
  {
    System.out.println("AVERAGE CALCULATOR");
    double avg = EssentialMath.average();
    System.out.println("The average is: " + avg);
    System.out.println("------ The End ------");
  }
}
```

The method average calls two methods that can throw exceptions.

- First the readLine method of BufferedReader, which throws an IOException and
- second the Double.parseDouble method that throws a NumberFormatException.

Notice that we specify the IOException in the throws clause of the method, but not the NumberFormatException. As explained earlier, this is because IOException is a checked exception, whereas NumberFormatException is a runtime exception. Also notice that we have to specify the IOException in the throws clause of the main method as well. This is because the main method uses EssentialMath.average which may throw an IOException. In this way, a checked exception must be specified all the way down the *calling chain*.

Catching an exception

When you run the program, it expects some numbers as input. If you type in an invalid number, an exception will be generated by the parseDouble method. This will result in a printed error message similar to those shown in Figure 10.1. We would like to *catch* this exception and, instead of aborting the program, ignore any invalid numbers and simply continue. Here is our modified average method that catches the NumberFormatException exception:

```
    . . .
    double sum = 0;
    int numValues = 0;
    int numErrors = 0;  // number of invalid numbers entered
    while (st.hasMoreTokens())
    {
      String n = st.nextToken();
      try
      {                // beginning of try block
        double num = Double.parseDouble(n);
        sum += num;
        numValues++;
```

```
       } catch(NumberFormatException e) {
         numErrors++;
         System.out.println("Invalid number at position " +
                          (numValues+numErrors) + " ignored.");
       }
     } // while
     double avg = sum/numValues;
     return avg;
```

With our modified program, the following input:

```
 50.5    5,5    -50.5    9    @@
```

would generate this output:

```
Invalid number at position 2 ignored.
Invalid number at position 5 ignored.
The average is: 3.0
------ The End ------
```

We now explain what we have done. To catch an exception, we wrap the code which can generate an exception in a *try block*. A `try` block is just a `try` statement followed by block markers enclosing the code which could generate an exception. We handle the exception using a `catch` statement, which follows the `try` block. Here is the basic structure of a `try-catch` statement:

```
   try
{
   // statements that could generate an exception
} catch (ExceptionClass e) {
   // code that handles the exception
}
```

The `catch` statement looks like a method declaration with a single formal argument. The argument type indicates which exception is being caught. The parameter e refers to the exception object created when the exception was thrown. If you look at the `Exception` class in the Java API, you will see which methods you can call using the e parameter.

The `try` and `catch` statements belong together and there can be no code between the end of the `try` and the beginning of the `catch`. To emphasize this, we usually put the `catch` statement on the same line as the end of the `try` block.

In particular, in our modified `average` method, we do the following:

- We wrap three statements inside the `try` block. The first statement is where the exception could be thrown. If an exception occurs, the program jumps to the `catch` clause and the remaining two statements inside the `try` block are *not executed*. The statements inside the `catch` block are executed and the program continues by looping back to the beginning of the `while` loop. If an exception is not thrown, all the statements inside the `try` block are executed and the statements inside the `catch` block are ignored.
- We keep track of the number of invalid numbers, so that we can report back to the user which entries were ignored.
- If NumberFormatException was a checked exception, we could remove it from the throws clause of both the `average` method and the `main` method, since it is no longer thrown by the method.

Now do Exercises 10.5 to 10.6.

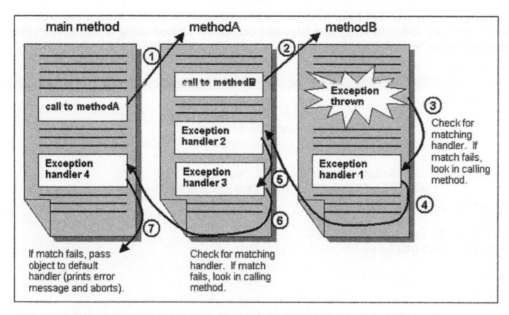

Figure 10.4 When an exception is thrown, Java searches for a matching handler all the way up the calling chain

What happens when an exception is thrown

The code inside a catch block is called an *exception handler*. The job of the exception handler is to recover from the problem so that the program can either try another tack or simply continue. Since each catch statement has an associated exception type (as indicated by the formal parameter), each exception handler only handles exceptions of that type.

You can have multiple catch clauses after a single try block, as follows:

```
try
{
    // many statements which can cause different types of exceptions
} catch (ExceptionType1 e) {
    // code to handle ExceptionType1
} catch (ExceptionType2 e) {
    // code to handle ExceptonType2
}
```

When an exception is thrown somewhere in a method, the exception object is matched against any exception handlers in that method, i.e. it is checked against each of the catch clauses below the try block. If there is a match, the code inside that catch block is executed and the program continues from after the try-catch code. If there is no match, the object is passed to the calling method and the process is continued in this way up the calling chain. Figure 10.4 shows an unhandled exception being passed back along the calling chain.

10.5 Exceptions and file input

Many things can go wrong when we read from files, so we dedicate a section to the use of exceptions with files.

To illustrate the full complexity of reading from files, we will work with a binary file. The file we will be working with is called trc_v1.data and it contains the first volume of South Africa's TRC (Truth and Reconciliation Commission) report. It is a long report, containing thousands of lines of text (if you are interested in reading more about the TRC, go to the site www.truth.org.za).

To run the following program, you will have to download the file `trc_v1.data` from our website. Remember that binary files are different from text files and cannot be viewed using a text editor. The following program reads in the first 11 lines from the file.

```java
import java.io.*;

public class ReadBinary
{
  public static void main(String[] args) throws
          FileNotFoundException, EOFException, IOException
  {
    DataInputStream in = new DataInputStream(
                new FileInputStream("trc_v1.data"));
    for(int i=0; i<=10; i++)
    {
      String s = in.readUTF();
      System.out.println(s);
    }
    in.close();
  }
}
```

Notice that the methods used for reading in data from binary files are different from those we use for reading in from text files. The `main` method above uses two methods that could throw exceptions:

- The `FileInputStream` constructor could throw a `FileNotFoundException`.
- The `readUTF` method of `DataInputStream` could throw an `EOFException` if the input stream reaches the end of the file, or it could throw an `IOException` if any other I/O error occurs.

All three of these exceptions are checked exceptions, so must be specified in the `throws` clause of the method.

Groups of exceptions

You will recall that all exceptions in Java are subclasses of `java.lang.Exception`. If you look in the API, you will see that both `FileNotFoundException` and `EOFException` are subclasses of `IOException`. In the `main` method of `ReadBinary` we could therefore shorten the `throws` clause to:

> `... throws IOException`

This compiles because `IOException` is a more general form of exception and so 'covers' all the specialized exception subclasses. In the same way, we could use:

> `... throws Exception`

to specify *all* types of exceptions. Although this may seem simpler, we do not recommend this approach. It is better programming practice to specify individual exceptions in the `throws` clause so that it is clear which exceptions could be thrown by the method.

Forcing the exceptions

Before we change the code to handle the exceptions, we must make sure that we can create conditions under which the exceptions will be generated. We will be generating the `FileNotFoundException` and the `EOFException`. First try running the program with `trc_v1.data` in the current directory. You should see the first few lines of the report (starting with `"Volume ONE Chapter ONE"`). To generate the `FileNotFoundException`, do the following:

- Move `trc_v1.data` into a different directory. (Alternatively, you can temporarily rename the file to some other name, such as `trc.data`.)
- Run the program (it is not necessary to re-compile, because the program has not changed).
- The `FileNotFoundException` should be generated.

Move `trc_v1.data` back to the current directory (or rename it back to `trc_v1.data` if you renamed the file) and run the program to see that it is working correctly again.

To generate the `EOFException`, do the following:

- First make sure that the program is working correctly and reading from `trc_v1.data`.
- Make a copy of `trc_v1.data`, called `backup.data`.
- Open `trc_v1.data` in a text file editor. You will either see nothing, or some strange characters. Simply push **Enter** and save the file. In this way you have corrupted the binary data in the file.
- Run the program again. The `EOFException` should be generated.

Copy `backup.data` to `trc_v1.data` to restore the file. Run the program to see that it is working correctly again.

Catching `FileNotFoundException` *and* `EOFException`

Here is a first attempt at catching both exceptions. In each case we simply print a message and exit the program.

```java
import java.io.*;

public class ReadBinary
{
  public static void main(String[] args) throws IOException
  {
    try
    {
      DataInputStream in = new DataInputStream(
                new FileInputStream("trc_v1.data"));
      for(int i=0; i<=10; i++)
      {
        String s = in.readUTF();
        System.out.println(s);
      }
      in.close();
    }catch(FileNotFoundException e) {
      System.out.println("Could not find file trc_v1.data");
      System.exit(0);
    }catch(EOFException e) {
      System.out.println("Reached end of file trc_v1.data");
      System.exit(0);
    }
  }
}
```

Notice the following:

- Since we are catching both the `FileNotFoundException` and the `EOFException`, we take them out of the `throws` clause.
- We have one `try` clause and two `catch` clauses. When an exception is thrown somewhere in the `try` block, Java will try to match the exception object with each `catch` clause from top to bottom.

Only one of the catch blocks will be executed. If it does not match either of the handlers, then the exception will be thrown on to the Java interpreter.

Looping while file not found

When the file trc_v1.data is not found in the current directory, we would like to give the user a chance to move the file to the correct place before the program gives up and aborts. Here is our modified program:

```java
import java.io.*;
import essential.*;

public class ReadBinary
{
  public static void main(String[] args) throws IOException
  {
    boolean fileFound = false;
    do
    {
      try
      {
        DataInputStream in = new DataInputStream(
                  new FileInputStream("trc_v1.data"));
        fileFound = true;
        for(int i=0; i<=10; i++)
        {
          String s = in.readUTF();
          System.out.println(s);
        }
        in.close();
      }catch(FileNotFoundException e) {
        System.out.println("Could not find file trc_v1.data");
        System.out.println(
            "Please make sure the file is in the current directory");
        System.out.println(
            "Press enter when ready, or X to quit ...");
        String s = Keyboard.readLine();
        if ((s.equals("X") || s.equals("x"))) System.exit(0);
      }catch(EOFException e) {
        System.out.println("Reached end of file trc_v1.data");
        System.exit(0);
      } // try-catch
    }while(!fileFound); // do loop
  }
}
```

Note the following:

- We enclose the entire try block in a do loop.
- We define a boolean variable (fileFound) to use in the condition of the do loop.
- fileFound is set to true just after the statement where the FileNotFoundException could be thrown. This statement will only be reached if the file is in fact found.

- If the file is not found, we print a suitable message and give the user time to move the file to the current directory or to quit the program. If the user chooses to quit, the program terminates, otherwise the loop will repeat.

Now do Exercise 10.7.

The finally *statement*

There is an optional clause which ends off a try-catch statement, called the *finally block*. Statements inside the finally block are executed regardless of what happens in the try block, i.e. if an exception is thrown or not. In our ReadBinary program above, the in.close() statement will only be reached if an exception is not thrown. This is an example of a statement that should go in a finally block, because we would want the file to be closed if it has been opened. Here is the code:

```
DataInputStream in = null;
try
{
  in = new DataInputStream(
          new FileInputStream("trc_v1.data"));
  fileFound = true;
  for(int i=0; i<=10; i++)
  {
    String s = in.readUTF();
    System.out.println(s);
  }
}catch(FileNotFoundException e) {
  ...
}catch(EOFException e) {
  ...
}finally {
  if (in != null)
    in.close();
}
```

Notice that we have moved the declaration of the variable in to outside the scope of the try statement. This is so that the variable will be accessible from inside the finally block, which is outside the scope of the try statement.

Summary

- Programs that you write should be *robust*. It is your responsibility, as a programmer, to *expect the unexpected* and write code to handle unexpected events.
- An *exception* is an indication that something unexpected has happened at run-time.
- It is the class user's responsibility to decide what to do when an exception is generated.
- To catch an exception, we wrap the code that can generate an exception in a try block and follow it with a catch statement matching the exception we want to catch. The code inside a catch block is called an *exception handler*.
- Java's default operation when an exception occurs is to write an error message and terminate the program. This can be intercepted by writing exception handlers for particular exceptions.
- All exceptions in Java are instances of classes derived from java.lang.Exception.
- Java's *catch or specify* requirement states that all *checked* exceptions that can be thrown within a method must be caught or declared to be thrown.

- When an exception is thrown in a method, the exception is matched against any existing exception handlers in that method and, failing that, in methods further up the calling chain.
- The `finally` block is used for any cleanup code that would be repeated in both the `try` and `catch` clauses.

Exercises

10.1 For each of the following methods, find out what exceptions they throw:

(a) The `FileReader(String)` constructor of `java.io.FileReader`.
(b) The `charAt(int)` method of `java.lang.String`.
(c) The `compareTo(String)` method of `java.lang.String`.
(d) The `URL(String)` constructor of `java.net.URL`.
(e) The `openStream` method of `java.net.URL`.

10.2 Download the source code of the `essential.Matrix` class from our website. In the first constructor, two exceptions are thrown. Look at the first exception and explain in English under which conditions this exception will be thrown.

10.3 Run the following program and note down which exception is generated:

```
public class TestCompare
{
  public static void main(String args[])
  {
    String s1 = "hello";
    String s2 = "HELLO";
    s2 = null;
    System.out.println(s1.compareTo(s2));
  }
}
```

Why did we not have to specify this particular exception in a `throws` clause in the header of `main`?

10.4 Consider the following program before answering the questions below:

```
import java.net.*;
public class Google
{
  public static void main(String[] args)
  {
    URL s = new URL("http://www.google.com");
  }
}
```

Does the program compile successfully? If not, what error message does it generate and how will you need to change the program so that it does compile successfully?

10.5 Take the code from Exercise 10.4 and modify it to catch the `MalformedURLException` instead of specifying it in the `throws` clause. You should print out a suitable error message if the exception is thrown. Experiment with different URLs to find one that throws the exception.

10.6 The following program uses the essential.Matrix class (see Chapter 12):

```
import essential.*;

public class UseMatrix
{
  public static void main(String[] args) throws MatrixException
  {
    Matrix m1 = new Matrix(2,3);
    m1.setElementAt(1,1,4);
    m1.setElementAt(2,2,1);
    m1.setElementAt(3,3,0.5);
    System.out.println(m1);
  }
}
```

Run the program and see if you can figure out where the exception is being thrown. Change the program to catch the exception and print out a sensible message.

10.7 Modify the ReadBinary class from Section 10.5, **Looping while file not found**, so that it counts the number of words in trc_v1.data rather than printing out the first few lines. The only output from the program (except for messages in the event of an error) should be the number of words in the report. Hints:

- Unlike the readLine method of BufferedReader, the readUTF method does not return null when the end of file is reached. Instead, an EOFException is thrown.
- To count the number of words in any string, you can use a StringTokenizer object.

Part III
Some applications

11
Simulation

Objectives

By the end of this chapter you should be able to

- create a random number generator using the Random class;
- simulate a variety of real-life situations using random numbers, such as the spin of a coin, bacteria division, radioactive decay and traffic flow.

Simulation is an area of application where computers have come into their own. A simulation is a *computer experiment* which mirrors some aspect of the real world that appears to be based on random processes, or is too complicated to understand properly. (Whether events can be really random is actually a philosophical or theological question.) Some examples are: radio-active decay, rolling dice, bacteria division and traffic flow. The essence of a simulation program is that the programmer is unable to predict beforehand exactly what the outcome of the program will be, which is true to the event being simulated. For example, when you spin a coin, you do not know for sure what the result will be.

11.1 Random number generation

The Math.random *method*

Random events are easily simulated in a Java program with the method Math.random, which we have briefly encountered already. Math.random returns a *uniformly distributed pseudo-random number r* in the range $0 \leq r < 1$. (A conventional computer cannot at the moment generate truly random numbers, but they can be practically unpredictable.) Math.random can return 2^{53} different values all with equal probability.

The first call to Math.random in a program creates a 'random number generator'—essentially a complicated algorithm for producing a sequence of pseudo-random numbers. The sequence has to have a starting point, which is called the *seed* of the generator. The seed when Math.random is called for the first time is the current system time in milliseconds, returned behind the scenes by System.currentTimeMillis.

Seeding the random number generator

There are times when you want a program to generate the *same* sequence of random numbers every time it runs, for example, in order to debug it properly (it's often difficult enough to debug a program without the numbers changing every time you run it!).

Another example could be a complex simulation model of an ecosystem. You may want to recreate a particular random rainfall pattern for example, to investigate its effect on the rest of the system.

`Math.random` cannot be 'seeded' to reproduce a particular sequence. However, it in fact makes use of the more general `Random` class in the `java.util` package, which can be seeded in a program.

The `Random` *class*

The following program gets the current system time, and demonstrates how to use the `Random` class to generate two identical sequences of random numbers from the time:

```
import java.util.*;
public class RandomStuff
{
    public static void main(String[ ] args)
    {
        long seed = System.currentTimeMillis();
        Random myRand = new Random( seed );

        System.out.println( "seed: " + seed + "\n" );

        for (int i = 1; i <= 5; i++)
            System.out.println( myRand.nextDouble() );

        System.out.println( "------------------" );
        myRand.setSeed( seed );

        for (int i = 1; i <= 5; i++)
            System.out.println( myRand.nextDouble() );

    }
}
```

Output:

```
seed: 1005653282150

0.9451874437521086
0.27869488750867966
0.6909704295658767
0.5730443218764234
0.9997579275602388
------------------
0.9451874437521086
0.27869488750867966
0.6909704295658767
0.5730443218764234
0.9997579275602388
```

Note:

- The statement

  ```
  Random myRand = new Random( seed );
  ```

  creates a random number generator object myRand, seeded with the argument in the constructor call. The seed must be long.
  If the constructor is called without an argument the current system time is used to seed the generator. The point about using the constructor with an argument is that you can use the same seed to generate an identical sequence later on.
- The method nextDouble of the Random class generates the next random number in the sequence.
- The method setSeed sets the seed of the generator. If the seed has been used before, the same sequence will be generated.

Normal (Gaussian) random numbers

The method nextGaussian of the Java API class Random generates *Gaussian* or *normal* random numbers (as opposed to *uniform*) with a mean of 0 and a standard deviation of 1.
Try Exercises 11.1 and 11.2.

11.2 Spinning coins

When a fair (unbiased) coin is spun, the probability of getting heads or tails is 0.5 (50%). Since a value returned by Math.random is equally likely to anywhere in the interval [0, 1) we can represent heads, say, with a value less than 0.5, and tails otherwise.

Suppose an experiment calls for a coin to be spun 50 times, and the results recorded. In real life you may need to repeat such an experiment a number of times; this is where computer simulation is handy. The following code simulates spinning a coin 50 times:

```
double r;    // random number

for (int i = 1; i <= 50; i++)
{
    r = Math.random();
    if (r < 0.5)
        System.out.print( "H" );
    else
        System.out.print( "T" );
}
```

Here is the output from two sample runs:

```
HHHHTTTTHTTTTHHHTTHHTTTTHTHTHHTTHTTTHHTHHHHHHTHHTH
HTHTHHHHHHTHHHHHHHTTTHTHTTHHHTTHHTTHTTTTHTTHHTTHHTT
```

Note that it should be impossible in principle to tell from the output alone whether the experiment was simulated or real (if the random number generator is sufficiently random).

Can you see why it would be wrong to code the if part of the coin simulation like this:

```
if (Math.random() < 0.5)
    System.out.print( "H" );
```

```
if (Math.random() >= 0.5)
    System.out.print( "T" );
```

The basic principle is that `Math.random` should be called only *once* for each 'event' being simulated. Here the single event is spinning a coin, but `Math.random` is called twice. Furthermore, since two different random numbers are generated, it is quite possible that *both* logical expressions will be true, in which case H and T will both be displayed for the same coin!

To avoid this error it is safer to assign the value returned by `Math.random` to a variable, (r above), and to use this variable in the `if` statement.

Try Exercises 11.3 and 11.4

11.3   Rolling dice

When a fair dice is rolled, the number uppermost is equally likely to be any integer from 1 to 6. We saw in **Rolling dice** (Chapter 2) how to use `Math.random` to simulate this process. The following code generates 10 random integers in the range 1–6:

```
for (i = 1; i <= 10; i++)
{
    numberOnDice = (int) Math.floor(6*Math.random())+1;
    System.out.print( numberOnDice + " " );
}
```

Here are the results of two such simulations:

```
4 5 1 6 5 3 2 3 3 3
2 3 3 1 4 4 1 2 1 5
```

We can do statistics on our simulated experiment, just as if it were a real one. For example, we could estimate the mean and standard deviation of the number obtained when the dice is rolled 100 times.

Try Exercises 11.5 to 11.7.

11.4   Bacteria division

If a fair coin is spun, or a fair dice is rolled, the different events (e.g. getting 'heads', or a 6) happen with equal likelihood. Suppose, however, that a certain type of bacteria divides (into two) in a given time interval with a probability of 0.75 (75%), and that if it does not divide, it dies. Since a value generated by `Math.random` is equally likely to be anywhere between 0 and 1, the chances of it being *less than* 0.75 are precisely 75%. We can therefore simulate this situation as follows:

```
r = Math.random();
if (r < 0.75)
    System.out.println( "I am now we" );
else
    System.out.println( "I am no more" );
```

Again, the basic principle is that one random number should be generated for each event being simulated. The single event here is the bacterium's life history over the time interval.

Try Exercises 11.8 to 11.10.

11.5   Radioactive decay

Radioactive Carbon 11 has a decay-rate of $k = 0.0338$ per minute, i.e. a particular C^{11} atom has a 3.38% chance of decaying in any one minute. Suppose we have 100 such atoms. The following structure plan indicates how we could simulate their decay:

1. Start with $n = 100$ atoms
2. Repeat, say, for 100 minutes
   - generate n random numbers to decide how many atoms decay in that minute
   - reduce n by the number of atoms decaying in that minute
   - print (and/or plot) n (the number of undecayed atoms remaining).

The following program defines a class `Reactor`, creates an object `carbon11` of that class, decays `carbon11` for 100 minutes, and prints and plots the number of undecayed atoms each minute:

```
import essential.*;

public class Reactor
{
    private int initialAtoms;
    private double decayRate;
    private int atoms[];   // number of atoms at each minute

    public Reactor( int iA, double dR )
    { initialAtoms = iA; decayRate = dR; }

    public int decay(int numAtoms)
    {
        int numberDecaying = 0;
        for (int atom = 1; atom <= numAtoms; atom++)
        {
            if (Math.random() < decayRate)
                numberDecaying++;
        }
        return numberDecaying;
    }

    public void decayFor( int simulationTime )
    {
        atoms = new int[simulationTime+1];
        int numberDecaying;
        atoms[0] = initialAtoms;

        for (int minutes = 1; minutes <= simulationTime; minutes++)
        {
            int prevAtoms = atoms[minutes-1];
            numberDecaying = decay(prevAtoms);
            atoms[minutes] = prevAtoms - numberDecaying;
        }
    }


    public void plotValues(boolean plotTheoretical)
    {
        Graph reactorDraw = new Graph();
        reactorDraw.setPointShape(new
```

```
                    CirclePoint(PointShape.UNFILLED));
                reactorDraw.setDrawingStyle(Graphable.PLOTPOINTS);
                reactorDraw.setAxes(0, atoms.length-1, 0, initialAtoms);
                for(int i = 0; i < atoms.length; i++ )
                    reactorDraw.addPoint(i,atoms[i]);
                if (plotTheoretical)
                {
                    // put in code to create an ExponentialGraph:
                    ExponentialGraph theoryG =
                        new ExponentialGraph(initialAtoms, -decayRate);

                }
            }

            public void printValues()
            {
                for(int i = 0; i < atoms.length; i++ )
                    System.out.println(i + "   " + atoms[i]);
            }

            public static void main(String[] args)
            {
                Reactor carbon11 = new Reactor(100, 0.0338);
                carbon11.decayFor(100);
                carbon11.printValues();
                carbon11.plotValues(true);
            }

        }
```

Figure 11.1 shows the graphical output of the simulation. Superimposed on the simulation results is the theoretical formula, $R(t) = R_0 e^{-kt}$ (exponential decay), where $R(t)$ is the number of undecayed atoms remaining at time t, R_0 is the initial value of R, and k is the decay rate.

Estimation of half-life

The *half-life* of a radioactive element is defined as the time taken for half of the atoms in a sample of the element to decay. (Because the decay is exponential the half-life is the same whatever the size of the sample.) It's a nice problem to estimate the half-life by simulation: let the atoms decay until only half are left, record the time taken for this to happen, repeat the process a large number of times to find the average half-life. See if you can write a method halfLife for the Reactor class to do this before looking at the answer below.

```
        public double halfLife(int numberOfSimulations)
        {
            double sum = 0;     // running total for half-life
            int half;           // half-life
            int remainingAtoms;

            for (int i = 1; i <= numberOfSimulations; i++)
            {
                remainingAtoms = initialAtoms;
```

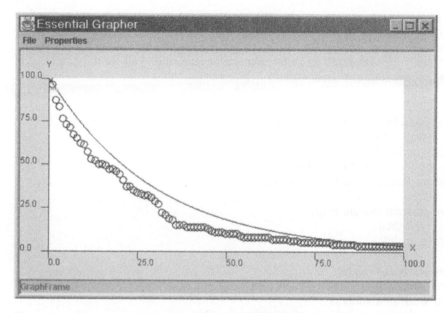

Figure 11.1 Radioactive decay of Carbon 11 – simulated and theoretical

```
            half = 0;
            while (remainingAtoms > 0.5*initialAtoms)
            {
                int numberDecaying = decay(remainingAtoms);
                remainingAtoms -= numberDecaying;
                half++;
            }
            sum += half;
        }
        return sum/numberOfSimulations;
}
```

Here's the result of 1000 simulations:

```
    20.468
```

The formula for the half-life is $\log(2)/k$, i.e. 20.507.
  Try Exercise 11.11.

11.6 A random walk

A drunken sailor has to negotiate a jetty to get to his ship. The jetty is 50 paces long and 20 wide. A colleague places him in the middle of the jetty at the quay-end, pointing toward the ship. Suppose at every step he has a 40% chance of lurching toward the ship, but a 20% chance of lurching to the left or right (he manages to be always facing the ship). If he reaches the ship-end of the jetty, he is hauled aboard by waiting mates.

  The problem is to simulate his progress along the jetty, and to estimate his chances of getting to the ship without falling into the sea. To do this correctly, we must simulate one *random walk* along the jetty, find out whether or not he reaches the ship, and then repeat this simulation 1000 times, say. The proportion of simulations that end with the sailor safely in the ship will be an estimate of his chances of making it to the ship. For a given walk we assume that if he has not either reached the ship or fallen into the sea after, say, 10 000 steps, he dies of thirst on the jetty.

To represent the jetty, we set up co-ordinates so that the x-axis runs along the middle of the jetty with the origin at the quay-end. x and y are measured in steps. The sailor starts his walk at the origin each time. Here is a structure plan for simulating n such walks:

1. Initialize variables, including number of walks n
2. Repeat n simulated walks down the jetty:
    Start at the quay-end of the jetty
    While still on the jetty and still alive repeat:
        Get a random number R for the next step
        If $R < 0.4$ then
            Move forward (to the ship)
        Else if $R < 0.7$ then
            Move port (left)
        Else
            Move starboard (right)
    If he got to the ship then
        Count that walk as a success
3. Compute and print estimated probability of reaching the ship.

Note: if the random number R is less than 0.4 he moves forward, if it is between 0.4 and 0.7 he moves left, and if it is greater than 0.7 he moves right.

The following program generalizes the problem by allowing you to specify the probability of walking straight in the `Sailor` constructor. The width and length of the jetty, and the maximum number of steps after which the sailor dies of thirst, are the same for all `Sailor` objects, so are declared as constants.

```java
public class Sailor
{
    public static int JETTY_WIDTH = 20;
    public static int JETTY_LENGTH = 50;
    public static int MAX_STEPS = 10000; //after which he dies of thirst
    private double probOfWalkingStraight;

    public Sailor(double prob)
    {
        probOfWalkingStraight = prob;
    }

    /* randomWalk():  returns true if the sailor reached the ship */
    public boolean randomWalk()
    {
      int x = 0, y = 0;
      int steps = 0;
        while ((x <= JETTY_LENGTH) && (Math.abs(y) <= (JETTY_WIDTH/2))
                && (steps < MAX_STEPS))
        {
          steps++;              //that's another step
          double randomNum = Math.random(); //random number for that step
          if (randomNum < probOfWalkingStraight) //which way did he go?
            x = x + 1;        //maybe forward ...
```

```
            else if (randomNum < 1 - (1 - probOfWalkingStraight)/2)
                y = y + 1;        //... or to port ...
            else
                y = y - 1;        //... or to starboard
        }  // end of while
        if (x > JETTY_LENGTH)
            return true;   //he actually made it this time!
        else
            return false;
    }

    /* randomWalk(int n): n = the number of times to walk
     * returns the probability of reaching the ship (as a percentage)
     */
    public double randomWalk(int n)
    {
        int numSuccesses = 0;
        for(int i=0; i<n; i++)
        {
            if(randomWalk()) numSuccesses++;
        }
        return ((double)numSuccesses / n) * 100;
    }

    public static void main(String[] args)
    {
        Sailor drunkDan = new Sailor(0.4);
        System.out.println
                ("Probability of drunk Dan reaching ship (1000 walks): "
                + drunkDan.randomWalk(1000) + "%");
        Sailor soberSam = new Sailor(0.8);
        System.out.println
                ("Probability of sober Sam reaching ship (1000 walks): "
                + soberSam.randomWalk(1000) + "%");
        System.out.println("************** WIDER JETTY ***************");
        Sailor.JETTY_WIDTH = 40;
        System.out.println
                ("Probability of drunk Dan reaching ship (1000 walks): "
                + drunkDan.randomWalk(1000) + "%");
        System.out.println
                ("Probability of sober Sam reaching ship (1000 walks): "
                + soberSam.randomWalk(1000) + "%");


    }
}
```

Note: if p is the probability of walking straight, then $(1 - p)/2$ is the probability of going left or right. Therefore, if the random number R is less than p the sailor goes straight. If R is greater than p but less than $1 - (1 - p)/2$ he goes left, otherwise he goes right.

Some results:

```
    Probability of drunk Dan reaching ship (1000 walks): 59.8%
    Probability of sober Sam reaching ship (1000 walks): 99.7%
```

```
*************** WIDER JETTY ****************
Probability of drunk Dan reaching ship (1000 walks): 96.6%
Probability of sober Sam reaching ship (1000 walks): 100.0%
```

11.7 Traffic flow

A major application of simulation is in modelling the traffic flow in large cities, in order to test different traffic light patterns before inflicting them on the real traffic. In this example we look at a very small part of the problem: how to simulate the flow of a single line of traffic through one set of traffic lights. We make the following assumptions (you can make additional or different ones if like):

1. Traffic travels straight, without turning.
2. The probability of a car arriving at the lights in a particular second is independent of what happened during the previous second. This is called a *Poisson process*. This probability (call it p) may be estimated by watching cars at the intersection and monitoring their arrival pattern. In this simulation we take $p = 0.3$.
3. When the lights are green, assume the cars move through at a steady rate of, say, eight every ten seconds.
4. In the simulation, we will take the basic time period to be ten seconds, so we want a display showing the length of the queue of traffic (if any) at the lights every ten seconds.
5. We will set the lights red or green for variable multiples of ten seconds.

The situation is modelled with a class Traffic. The method carsArriveFor runs the simulation for a number of 10-second periods. During each 10 seconds it generates the random arrival of cars. At the end of each such period, it calls method go or stop depending on whether the lights are green or red (no orange is available at this stage!).

The method go uses a 'timer' (greenTimer) which it increments and checks how long the lights have been green for. When the time is up, it changes the colour of the lights (and resets greenTimer). It also lets up to eight cars through.

The method stop is similar, except that it doesn't let any cars through (traffic is remarkably well-behaved!).

Both methods call displayQueue to print a row of asterisks representing the cars waiting at the lights at the end of each 10-second period.

```java
import java.text.*;
public class Traffic
{
    private int cars = 0;    //number of cars in queue
    private int greenFor;    //period lights are green
    int greenTimer = 0; //timer for green lights
    private String lights = "R";    //colour of lights
    private double probOfCar;    //probability of a car arriving
    private int redFor; // period lights are red
    int redTimer = 0; //timer for red lights

    public Traffic( double p, int gF, int rF )
    {
        probOfCar = p;
        greenFor = gF;
        redFor = rF;
    }
```

```java
public void displayQueue()
{

    System.out.print ( " " + lights + "   " );
    for (int i = 1; i <= cars; i++)  // display * for each car
        System.out.print( "*" );

    System.out.println();              // new line

}

public void go()
{
    greenTimer++;         //advance green timer
    cars -= 8;            // let 8 cars through

    if (cars < 0)         // ... there may have been < 8
        cars = 0;

    displayQueue();

    if (greenTimer == greenFor)  // check if lights need to change
    {
        lights = "R";
        greenTimer = 0;
    }

}

public void stop()
{
    redTimer++;           //advance red timer
    displayQueue();

    if (redTimer == redFor)  // check if lights need to change
    {
        lights = "G";
        redTimer = 0;
    }

}

public void carsArriveFor( int numberOfPeriods )
{

    //for each 10-sec period:
    for (int period = 1; period <= numberOfPeriods; period++)
    {

        for (int second = 1; second <= 10; second++)
```

```
                 if (Math.random() < probOfCar)
                      cars++;   //cars arriving in 10 seconds

             DecimalFormat df = new DecimalFormat( "00" );
             System.out.print( df.format(period) );

             if (lights.equals("G"))
                 go();
             else
                 stop();

         }
    }

    public static void main(String [] args)
    {
         Traffic mainRd = new Traffic( 0.3, 2, 4 );
         mainRd.carsArriveFor( 24 );
    }

}
```

If the lights are red for 40 seconds (redFor = 4) and green for 20 seconds (greenFor = 2), typical output for 240 seconds (numberOfPeriods = 24) is as follows:

```
01 R   ****
02 R   *********
03 R   ***********
04 R   ***************
05 G   *********
06 G   ******
07 R   ********
08 R   *************
09 R   ***************
10 R   ********************
11 G   ***************
12 G   ***********
13 R   **************
14 R   ****************
15 R   *****************
16 R   *********************
17 G   ***************
18 G   **********
19 R   **************
20 R   ******************
21 R   ********************
22 R   *********************
23 G   *****************
24 G   *************
```

From this particular run it seems that a traffic jam is building up, although more and longer runs are needed to see if this is really so. In that case, one can experiment with different periods for red and green lights in order to get an acceptable traffic pattern before setting the real lights to that cycle. Of course, we can get closer to reality by considering two-way traffic, and allowing cars to turn in both directions, and occasionally to break down, but this program gives the basic ideas.

Try Exercise 11.12.

Summary

- A simulation is a computer program written to mimic a real-life situation which is apparently based on chance.
- The pseudo-random number generator `Math.random` returns uniformly distributed random numbers in the range [0, 1), and is the basis of most of the simulations discussed in this chapter.
- The Java API class `Random` has methods for generating uniformly and normally distributed random numbers, and for setting the seed of the random sequence.
- Each independent event being simulated requires one and only one random number.

Exercises

11.1   (a)   Write a program to generate 100 normal random numbers and compute their mean and standard deviation. **Hint:** use the methods `mean` and `std` you wrote previously for the `EssentialMath` class.

     (b)   Repeat with 1000 random numbers. The mean and standard deviation should be closer to 0 and 1 this time.

11.2   If r is a normal random number with mean 0 and standard deviation 1 (as generated by `Random.nextGaussian`), it can be transformed into a random number X with mean μ and standard deviation σ by the relation

$$X = \sigma r + \mu.$$

In an experiment a Geiger counter is used to count the radio-active emissions of cobalt 60 over a 10-second period. After a large number of such readings are taken, the count rate is estimated to be normally distributed with a mean of 460 and a standard deviation of 20.

     (a)   Simulate such an experiment 200 times by generating 200 random numbers with a mean of 460 and a standard deviation of 20. Estimate the mean and standard deviation of the random numbers generated.

     (b)   Repeat a few times to note how the mean and standard deviation changes each time.

11.3   Write a program which simulates spinning a coin a large number of times and estimates the probability of getting heads.

11.4   Generate some strings of 80 random alphabetic letters (lowercase only). For fun, see how many real words, if any, you can find in the strings.

11.5   Write a program which uses simulation to estimate the mean and standard deviation of the number obtained by rolling a dice.

11.6   In a game of Bingo the numbers 1 to 99 are drawn at random from a bag. Write a program to simulate the draw of the numbers (each number can be drawn only once), printing them out in the order in which they are drawn.

11.7   A random number generator can be used to estimate π as follows (such a method is called a *Monte Carlo* method). Write a program which generates random points in a square with sides of length 2, say, and which counts what proportion of these points falls inside the circle of unit radius that fits exactly into the square. This proportion will be the ratio of the area of the circle to that of the square. Hence estimate π. (This is not a very efficient method, as you will see from the number of points required to get even a rough approximation.)

11.8 One of us (BDH) is indebted to a colleague, Gordon Kass, for suggesting this problem. Dribblefire Jets Inc. make two types of aeroplane, the two-engined DFII, and the four-engined DFIV. The engines are terrible and fail with probability 0.5 on a standard flight (the engines fail independently of each other). The manufacturers claim that the planes can fly if at least half of their engines are working, i.e. the DFII will crash only if both its engines fail, while the DFIV will crash if all four, or if any three engines fail.

You have been commissioned by the Civil Aviation Board to ascertain which of the two models is less likely to crash. Since parachutes are expensive, the cheapest (and safest!) way to do this is to simulate a large number of flights of each model. For example, two calls of Math.random could represent one standard DFII flight: if both random numbers are less than 0.5, that flight crashes, otherwise it doesn't. Write a program which simulates a large number of flights of both models, and estimates the probability of a crash in each case. If you can run enough simulations, you may get a surprising result. (Incidentally, the probability of n engines failing on a given flight is given by the binomial distribution, but you do not need to use this fact in the simulation.)

11.9 The aim of this exercise is to simulate bacteria growth.
Suppose that a certain type of bacteria divides or dies according to the following assumptions:

(a) during a fixed time interval, called a *generation*, a single bacterium divides into two identical replicas with probability p;
(b) if it does not divide during that interval, it dies;
(c) the offspring (called daughters) will divide or die during the next generation, independently of the past history (there may well be no offspring, in which case the colony becomes extinct).

Start with a single individual and write a program which simulates a number of generations. Take $p = 0.75$. The number of generations which you can simulate will depend on your computer system. Carry out a large number (e.g. 100) of such simulations. The probability of ultimate extinction, $p(E)$, may be estimated as the proportion of simulations that end in extinction. You can also estimate the mean size of the nth generation from a large number of simulations. Compare your estimate with the theoretical mean of $(2p)^n$.

Statistical theory shows that the expected value of the extinction probability $p(E)$ is the smaller of 1, and $(1 - p)/p$. So for $p = 0.75$, $p(E)$ is expected to be 1/3. But for $p \leq 0.5$, $p(E)$ is expected to be 1, which means that extinction is certain (a rather unexpected result). You can use your program to test this theory by running it for different values of p, and estimating $p(E)$ in each case.

11.10 Two players, A and B, play a game called *Eights*. They take it in turns to choose a number 1, 2 or 3, which may not be the same as the last number chosen (so if A starts with 2, B may only choose 1 or 3 at the next move). A starts, and may choose any of the three numbers for the first move. After each move, the number chosen is added to a common running total. If the total reaches 8 exactly, the player whose turn it was wins the game. If a player causes the total to go over 8, the other player wins. For example, suppose A starts with 1 (total 1), B chooses 2 (total 3), A chooses 1 (total 4) and B chooses 2 (total 6). A would like to play 2 now, to win, but he can't because B cunningly played it on the last move, so A chooses 1 (total 7). This is even smarter, because B is forced to play 2 or 3, making the total go over 8 and thereby losing.

Write a program to simulate each player's chances of winning, if they always play at random.

11.11 This exercise tackles the simulation of radioactive decay from a different point of view to the one we used in Section 11.5. It is profoundly satisfying to simulate a problem in two such different ways and come up with the same result!

Radioactive Carbon 11 has a decay-rate k of 0.0338 per minute.

Suppose we start with 100 such atoms. We would like to simulate their fate over a period of 100 minutes, say. We want to end up with a graph showing how many atoms remain undecayed after 1, 2, ..., 100 minutes.

We need to simulate when each of the 100 atoms decays. This can be done, for each atom, by generating a random number r for each of the 100 minutes, until either $r > k$ (that atom decays), or the 100 minutes is up. If the atom decayed at time $t < 100$, increment the frequency distribution $f(t)$ by 1. $f(t)$ will be the number of atoms decaying at time t minutes.

Now convert the number $f(t)$ decaying each minute to the number $R(t)$ *remaining* each minute. If there are n atoms to start with, after one minute, the number $R(1)$ remaining will be $n - f(1)$, since $f(1)$ is the number decaying during the first minute. The number $R(2)$ remaining after two minutes will be $n - f(1) - f(2)$. In general, the number remaining after t minutes will be

$$R(t) = n - \sum_{x=1}^{t} f(x).$$

Write a program to compute $R(t)$ and plot it against t. Superimpose on the graph the theoretical result,

$$R(t) = 100 \exp^{-kt}.$$

Typical results are shown in Figure 11.1.

11.12 The aim of this exercise is to simulate the service of customers in a supermarket checkout queue, in order to see how long the average customer spends at the till (i.e. being checked out, and paying).

Observations at a standard till have shown that:

- Customers have between 1 and 70 items in their trolleys or baskets.
- Cashiers take between 2 and 2.5 seconds to ring up each item.
- Payment takes between 15 and 20 seconds.
- There is a chance of 1 in 100 that any particular item is unmarked. If a customer has one *or more* unmarked items then an extra 30 seconds must be added to the payment time, i.e. an extra 30 seconds no matter how many are unmarked.

Write a program which simulates a large number of such customers, and which finds the average time in service (i.e. the time for all a customer's items to be rung up, and for payment to be made).

Assume that values are uniformly (evenly) distributed in the ranges given above.

12

Modelling with matrices

Objectives

By the end of this chapter you should be able to

- use the Matrix class in our essential package;
- write programs using matrices to solve problems in a number of application areas, such as networks, population dynamics, Markov processes and linear equations.

12.1 Using the Matrix class

You will have appreciated in Chapter 6 that matrix multiplication in Java is quite complicated. Since many interesting scientific and engineering applications involve matrix multiplication we have included a Matrix class in the essential package which makes this operation (among other things) much easier.

If we have two square matrices **A** and **B**, where

$$\mathbf{A} = \begin{bmatrix} 1 & 2 \\ 3 & 4 \end{bmatrix}$$

and

$$\mathbf{B} = \begin{bmatrix} 5 & 6 \\ 0 & -1 \end{bmatrix}$$

their product **C** = **AB** is given by

$$\mathbf{C} = \begin{bmatrix} 5 & 4 \\ 15 & 14 \end{bmatrix}.$$

The following program shows you how to use the Matrix class to multiply these two matrices:

```
import essential.*;

public class MatrixMultiply
{
    public static void main(String args[]) throws MatrixException
```

```
        {
            int rows = 2;
            int cols = 2;

            Matrix C = new Matrix(rows, cols);

            // set up 2-D array as usual
            double [][] a = {{1, 2}, {3, 4}};

            // construct Matrix object from the 2-D array
            Matrix A = new Matrix(a);

            double [][] b = {{5, 6}, {0, -1}};
            Matrix B = new Matrix(b);

            C = A.multiply(B);

            System.out.println( "A x B: \n" + C );
        }
    }
```

Output:

```
        A x B:
        [    5     4    ]
        [   15    14    ]
```

Note:

- The 2-D arrays a and b are set up as described in Chapter 6 to represent the two matrices **A** and **B**. They are then used as arguments for the Matrix constructor to create two Matrix objects A and B.
- An alternative Matrix constructor takes the number of rows and columns as arguments and sets up a Matrix object with all elements initially zero (e.g. C).
- The elements of a and b could be read from the keyboard using the Keyboard class, or from a text file, using the FileIO class (see Section 12.2).
- Matrix objects may be printed directly with System.out.println, because the class Matrix has a toString method.
- The throws MatrixException clause is required, because the Matrix methods may throw this exception.
- Matrices of any size may be multiplied in this way, as long as their dimensions are correct: **A** can be multiplied by **B** (in that order) if the number of *columns* of **A** is the same as the number of *rows* of **B**.

In particular, one of the matrices may be a column vector (a Matrix object with two rows, each with one column). The following program multiplies the matrix **A** above by the vector **x**, where

$$x = \begin{bmatrix} 2 \\ 3 \end{bmatrix}.$$

```
        import essential.*;

        public class MatrixByVector
        {
            public static void main(String args[]) throws MatrixException
            {
```

```
double [] [] a = {{1, 2}, {3, 4}};
Matrix A = new Matrix(a);

double [] [] x = {{2}, {3}};
x[0][0] = 2;
x[1][0] = 3;

Matrix X = new Matrix(x);
Matrix V = A.multiply(X);

System.out.println( "A x X: \n" + V);
        }
    }
```

Output:

```
A x X:
[    8   ]
[   18   ]
```

The identity matrix

The *identity* matrix **I** is a square matrix with 1's on the 'main' diagonal and 0's everywhere else. For example, the 3×3 identity matrix looks like this:

$$\begin{bmatrix} 1 & 0 & 0 \\ 0 & 1 & 0 \\ 0 & 0 & 1 \end{bmatrix}.$$

A property of **I** is that

$$\mathbf{AI} = \mathbf{IA} = \mathbf{A},$$

where **A** is any square matrix the same size as **I**. The Matrix class has a `static` method `identityMatrix` which creates an identity matrix of given size, e.g.

```
Matrix I3 = Matrix.identityMatrix(3);
```

Try Exercise 12.1.

12.2 Networks

In our first application of matrix multiplication we consider a problem which at first glance seems to have nothing to do with this.

A spy ring

Suppose five spies in an espionage ring have the code names Alex, Boris, Cyril, Denisov and Eric (whom we can label A, B, C, D and E respectively). The hallmark of a good spy network is that no agent is able to contact all the others. The arrangement for this particular group is:

- Alex can contact only Cyril;
- Boris can contact only Alex or Eric;
- Denisov can contact only Cyril;
- Eric can contact only Cyril or Denisov.

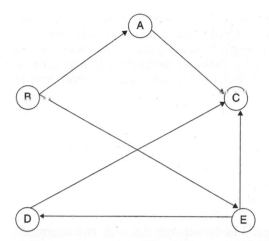

Figure 12.1 The network represented by the matrix **A**

(Cyril can't contact anyone in the ring: he takes information out of the ring to the spymaster. Similarly, Boris brings information in from the spymaster: no-one in the ring can contact him.) The need for good spies to know a bit of matrix theory becomes apparent when we spot that the possible paths of communication between the spies can be represented by a 5 × 5 matrix, with the rows and columns representing the transmitting and receiving agents respectively, thus:

	A	B	C	D	E
A	0	0	1	0	0
B	1	0	0	0	1
C	0	0	0	0	0
D	0	0	1	0	0
E	0	0	1	1	0

We will call this matrix **A**. It represents a *directed network* with the spies at the *nodes*, and with *arcs* all of length 1, where a network is a collection of points called nodes. The nodes are joined by lines called arcs. In a directed network, movement (e.g. of information) is only possible along the arcs in one direction (see Figure 12.1).

The matrix **A** is known as an *adjacency* matrix, with a 1 in row i and column j if there is an arc from node i to node j, or a 0 in that position if there is no arc between those two nodes. The diagonal elements of **A** (i.e. a_{11}, a_{22}, etc.) are all zero because good spies do not talk to themselves (since they might then talk in their sleep and give themselves away). Each 1 in **A** therefore represents a single path of length 1 arc in the network.

Now let's multiply the adjacency matrix **A** by itself, to get what is called $\mathbf{A}^2$:

$$\begin{bmatrix} 0 & 0 & 1 & 0 & 0 \\ \mathbf{1} & \mathbf{0} & \mathbf{0} & \mathbf{0} & \mathbf{1} \\ 0 & 0 & 0 & 0 & 0 \\ 0 & 0 & 1 & 0 & 0 \\ 0 & 0 & 1 & 1 & 0 \end{bmatrix} \times \begin{bmatrix} 0 & 0 & \mathbf{1} & 0 & 0 \\ 1 & 0 & \mathbf{0} & 0 & 1 \\ 0 & 0 & \mathbf{0} & 0 & 0 \\ 0 & 0 & \mathbf{1} & 0 & 0 \\ 0 & 0 & \mathbf{1} & 1 & 0 \end{bmatrix} = \begin{bmatrix} 0 & 0 & 0 & 0 & 0 \\ 0 & 0 & 2 & 1 & 0 \\ 0 & 0 & 0 & 0 & 0 \\ 0 & 0 & 0 & 0 & 0 \\ 0 & 0 & 1 & 0 & 0 \end{bmatrix}.$$

Row 2 and column 3 have been emboldened in the two versions of **A** above to help interpret $\mathbf{A}^2$. The element 2 in $\mathbf{A}^2$ (row 2, column 3) results when row 2 of **A** is multiplied term by term with column 3, and the products added. This gives us the scalar product

$$1 \times 1 + 0 \times 0 + 0 \times 0 + 0 \times 1 + 1 \times 1 = 2.$$

The first non-zero term arises because there is a path from node 2 to node 1, which we will denote by (2–1), followed by a path (1–3), giving a composite path (2–1–3) of length 2, i.e. from Boris to Cyril via Alex. The second non-zero term arises because there is a path (2–5) followed by a path (5–3), giving a second composite path (2–5–3) of length 2, i.e. from Boris to Cyril again, but via Eric this time. It is clear that the entries in $\mathbf{A}^2$ represent the number of paths of length 2 between the various nodes in the network (on the strict understanding that all arcs are of length 1). There are therefore only four paths of length 2: two from Boris to Cyril, as we have seen, one from Boris to Denisov, and one from Eric to Cyril.

If we now multiply the matrix $\mathbf{A}^2$ by $\mathbf{A}$ again, to form the third power of $\mathbf{A}$, we get the rather dull matrix

$$\mathbf{A}^3 = \begin{bmatrix} 0 & 0 & 0 & 0 & 0 \\ 0 & 0 & 1 & 0 & 0 \\ 0 & 0 & 0 & 0 & 0 \\ 0 & 0 & 0 & 0 & 0 \\ 0 & 0 & 0 & 0 & 0 \end{bmatrix}.$$

The single 1 in $\mathbf{A}^3$ tells us that there is only one path of length 3 in the network (i.e. with two intermediaries) and that it is from Boris to Cyril. Drawing the network, or alternatively examining the appropriate row and column in $\mathbf{A}^2$ and $\mathbf{A}$ that give rise to this single entry in $\mathbf{A}^3$, reveals that the actual route is Boris-Eric-Denisov-Cyril.

If we now compute $\mathbf{A}^4$, we will find that every element is zero (such a matrix is called the *null matrix*), signifying that there are no paths of length 4 in the network, which can be verified by inspection. All higher powers of $\mathbf{A}$ will also obviously be null, since if there are no paths of length 4, there can hardly be any that are longer!

In general, then, the element in row i and column j of the kth power of an adjacency matrix is equal to the number of paths consisting of k arcs linking nodes i and j.

Coming back to our spy network, since the elements of $\mathbf{A}$ are the number of paths of length 1, and the elements of $\mathbf{A}^2$ are the number of paths of length 2, etc., then clearly the sum of all these powers of $\mathbf{A}$ will tell us how many paths of any length there are altogether between the various nodes. We can therefore define a *reachability* matrix $\mathbf{R}$ for this 5×5 network:

$$\mathbf{R} = \mathbf{A} + \mathbf{A}^2 + \mathbf{A}^3 + \mathbf{A}^4.$$

$\mathbf{R}$ is also a 5×5 matrix, and its elements give the total number of paths of communication between the agents. Doing the calculation gives us

$$\mathbf{R} = \begin{bmatrix} 0 & 0 & 1 & 0 & 0 \\ 1 & 0 & 3 & 1 & 1 \\ 0 & 0 & 0 & 0 & 0 \\ 0 & 0 & 1 & 0 & 0 \\ 0 & 0 & 2 & 1 & 0 \end{bmatrix}.$$

So we can read off from the reachability matrix $\mathbf{R}$ the fact that there are, for example, three different paths between Boris and Cyril, but only two between Eric and Cyril (the actual lengths of these paths will have been calculated in finding the powers of $\mathbf{A}$). The name 'reachability' is used because the non-zero elements of $\mathbf{R}$ indicate who may contact whom, directly or indirectly, or for a general distance network, which nodes can be reached from each node.

The reachability matrix

In general, the reachability matrix $\mathbf{R}$ of a $n \times n$ network may be defined as the sum of the first $(n-1)$ powers of its associated adjacency matrix $\mathbf{A}$. You may be wondering why we can stop at the $(n-1)$th power of $\mathbf{A}$. The elements of $\mathbf{A}^{(n-1)}$ will be the number of paths that have $(n-1)$ arcs, i.e. that connect n nodes (since each arc connects two nodes). Since there are no further nodes that can be reached, it is not necessary to raise $\mathbf{A}$ to the nth power.

The following program sets up the adjacency matrix of our spy ring and computes the reachability matrix R.

```
import essential.*;

public class Reachable
{
    public static void main(String args[]) throws MatrixException
    {
        Matrix A = Matrix.readMatrix("adjacent.txt"); // adjacency
                                                      // matrix
        int numberOfNodes = A.getRowCount(); // A is square
        Matrix R;
        Matrix B;

        R = A.copy();
        B = A.copy();           // initialize B to A

        for (int n = 1; n <= numberOfNodes-2; n++)
        {
            B = B.multiply(A);
            R = R.add(B);
        }

        System.out.println( "Reachability matrix:\n" + R );
    }
}
```

Note:

- The getRowCount method of the Matrix class returns the number of rows in the adjacency matrix (which must be a square matrix).
- The copy method creates a copy of the calling matrix, which is A in this example.
- The readMatrix method without a parameter enables you to input a matrix from the keyboard— you are prompted for the dimensions of the matrix, and then for each row.
- The program uses the matrix B to store the intermediate powers of A, adding them to R each time. It uses a static method readMatrix of the essential.Matrix class to create and read the adjacency matrix from a text file. The first line of the text file must contain the dimensions of the matrix. For example, the adjacency matrix for our spy ring is saved in the text file adjacent.txt as follows:

```
5x5
0 0 1 0 0
1 0 0 0 1
0 0 0 0 0
0 0 1 0 0
0 0 1 1 0
```

- The number of additions required in the for loop is $n - 2$. For example if $n = 5$,

$$\mathbf{R} = \mathbf{A} + \mathbf{A}^2 + \mathbf{A}^3 + \mathbf{A}^4,$$

giving three additions.

It may help to go through the `for` loop by hand to convince yourself that it works correctly. Keep track of the contents of B and R in terms of the adjacency matrix A.

12.3 Leslie matrices: population growth

Another very interesting and useful application of matrices is in population dynamics.

Suppose we want to model the growth of a population of rabbits, in the sense that given their number at some moment, we would like to estimate the size of the population in a few years' time. One approach is to divide the rabbit population up into a number of age classes, where the members of each age class are one time unit older than the members of the previous class, the time unit being whatever is convenient for the population being studied (days, months, etc.). (The word 'class' is used here in the usual English sense, not in the Java sense!) We used the idea of age classes in the RabbitColony example of Chapter 3; in that example, however, unlike this one, rabbits did not die.

If X_i is the size of the ith age class, we define a *survival factor* P_i as the proportion of the ith class that survive to the $(i+1)$th age class, i.e. the proportion that 'graduate'. F_i is defined as the *mean fertility* of the ith class. This is the mean number of newborn individuals expected to be produced during one time interval by each member of the ith class at the beginning of the interval (only females count in biological modelling, since there are always enough males to go round!).

Suppose for our modified rabbit model we have three age classes, with X_1, X_2 and X_3 members respectively. We will call them young, middle-aged and old-aged for convenience. We will take our time unit as one month, so X_1 is the number that were born during the current month, and which will be considered as youngsters at the end of the month. X_2 is the number of middle-aged rabbits at the end of the month, and X_3 the number of oldsters. Suppose the youngsters cannot reproduce, so that $F_1 = 0$. Suppose the fertility rate for middle-aged rabbits is 9, so $F_2 = 9$, while for oldsters $F_3 = 12$. The probability of survival from youth to middle-age is one third, so $P_1 = 1/3$, while no less than half the middle-aged rabbits live to become oldsters, so $P_2 = 0.5$ (we are assuming for the sake of illustration that all old-aged rabbits die at the end of the month—this can be corrected easily). With this information we can quite easily compute the changing population structure month by month, as long as we have the population breakdown to start with.

If we now denote the current month by t, and next month by $(t + 1)$, we can refer to this month's youngsters as $X_1(t)$, and to next month's as $X_1(t+1)$, with similar notation for the other two age classes. We can then write a scheme for updating the population from month t to month $(t + 1)$ as follows:

$$X_1(t + 1) = F_2 X_2(t) + F_3 X_3(t),$$

$$X_2(t + 1) = P_1 X_1(t),$$

$$X_3(t + 1) = P_2 X_2(t).$$

We now define a population vector $\mathbf{X}(t)$, with three components, $X_1(t)$, $X_2(t)$, and $X_3(t)$, representing the three age classes of the rabbit population in month t. The above three equations can then be rewritten as

$$\begin{bmatrix} X_1 \\ X_2 \\ X_3 \end{bmatrix}_{(t+1)} = \begin{bmatrix} 0 & F_2 & F_3 \\ P_1 & 0 & 0 \\ 0 & P_2 & 0 \end{bmatrix} \times \begin{bmatrix} X_1 \\ X_2 \\ X_3 \end{bmatrix}_t$$

where the subscript at the bottom of the vectors indicates the month. We can write this even more concisely as the matrix equation

$$\mathbf{X}(t + 1) = \mathbf{L}\,\mathbf{X}(t), \tag{12.1}$$

where $\mathbf{L}$ is the matrix

$$\begin{bmatrix} 0 & 9 & 12 \\ 1/3 & 0 & 0 \\ 0 & 1/2 & 0 \end{bmatrix}$$

in this particular case. **L** is called a *Leslie matrix*. A population model can always be written in the form of Equation (12.1) if the concepts of age classes, fertility, and survival factors, as outlined above, are used.

Now that we have established a matrix representation for our model, we can easily write a program using matrix multiplication and repeated application of Equation (12.1):

$$\mathbf{X}(t + 2) = \mathbf{L}\,\mathbf{X}(t + 1),$$

$$\mathbf{X}(t + 3) = \mathbf{L}\,\mathbf{X}(t + 2), \text{ etc.}$$

However, we need only a single `Matrix` object X to represent the population vector **X** in the program below, because repeated matrix multiplication by the Leslie matrix L will continually update it:

```
X = L.multiply(X)
```

The class `Leslie` defined below sets up and handles a general Leslie matrix, so you can use it for any application of Leslie matrices. It is followed by a brief description.

```
import essential.*;

public class Leslie
{
    private int size;
    private Matrix L;      //Leslie matrix
    private Matrix X;      //Population vector

    public Leslie( double [] f, double [] p )
                            throws MatrixException
    {
        size = f.length;
        L = new Matrix(size, size);
        X = new Matrix(size, 1);

        //construct Leslie matrix:
        //first row for fertilities
        //be careful of subscripts for f!
        for (int i = 1; i <= size; i++)
            L.setElementAt(1, i, f[i-1]);

        //now the survivals below the main diagonal:
        //be careful of subscripts for p!
        for (int i = 2; i <= size; i++)
            L.setElementAt(i, i-1, p[i-2]);
    }

    public double getAgeClass(int row) throws MatrixException
    {
        return X.getElementAt(row,1);
    }

    public double getTotal() throws MatrixException
    {
        double totalPopulation = 0;

        for (int i = 1; i <= size; i++)
```

```java
                        totalPopulation += X.getElementAt(i, 1);

        return totalPopulation;
    }

    public void setAgeClass(int row, double val)
                                    throws MatrixException
    {
        X.setElementAt(row, 1, val);
    }


    public void update() throws MatrixException
    // updates population vector by one time unit
    {
        X = L.multiply(X);
    }

    public static void main(String args[])
                                    throws MatrixException
    {
        int numberOfClasses = 3;
        double [] f = new double[numberOfClasses];
        double [] p = new double[numberOfClasses];

        //assign (or read) fertilities:
        f[0] = 0;
        f[1] = 9;
        f[2] = 12;
        //assign (or read) survivals:
        p[0] = 1.0/3;
        p[1] = 1./2;
        p[2] = 0;

        Leslie rabbits = new Leslie(f, p);
        //start with one oldie only
        rabbits.setAgeClass(numberOfClasses, 1);
        System.out.println( "Month Young Middle Old Total" );

        for (int month = 1; month <= 24; month++)
        {
            System.out.print( month + "    " );
            rabbits.update();    //update population by one month

            //print each age class
            for (int i = 1; i <= numberOfClasses; i++)
                System.out.print( rabbits.getAgeClass(i) + "    " );

            System.out.println( rabbits.getTotal() );
        }
    }
}
```

Note:

- The class `Leslie` has two data members which are objects of the `Matrix` class: L represents the Leslie matrix, and X represents the population vector.
- The constructor of the `Leslie` class constructs the Leslie matrix L from data (fertility rates and survival factors) supplied by the user in `main`, using the `Matrix` method `setElementAt`. Care needs to be taken over the subscripts: the arrays p and f start with subscripts of zero, whereas the `setElementAt` and `getElementAt` methods use row and column values starting at 1.
- An instance `rabbits` of `Leslie` is created in `main`.
- The `Leslie` method `setAgeClass` uses the `Matrix` method `setElementAt` to set the initial value of the population vector X.
- The `Leslie` method `update` implements Equation (12.1).
- The `Leslie` method `getAgeClass` uses the `Matrix` method `getElementAt` to return the size of a particular age class (i.e. an element of X).
- The `Leslie` method `getTotal` returns the total population size at any time by summing the elements of X.

The program above starts with a single old (female) rabbit in the population, so $X_1 = X_2 = 0$, and $X_3 = 1$. Here is the output:

Month	Young	Middle	Old	Total
1	12.0	0.0	0.0	12.0
2	0.0	4.0	0.0	4.0
3	36.0	0.0	2.0	38.0
4	24.0	12.0	0.0	36.0
5	108.0	8.0	6.0	122.0
6	144.0	36.0	4.0	184.0
7	372.0	48.0	18.0	438.0
8	648.0	124.0	24.0	796.0
9	1404.0	216.0	62.0	1682.0
10	2688.0	468.0	108.0	3264.0
11	5508.0	896.0	234.0	6638.0
12	10872.0	1836.0	448.0	13156.0
13	21900.0	3624.0	918.0	26442.0
14	43632.0	7300.0	1812.0	52744.0
15	87444.0	14544.0	3650.0	105638.0
16	174696.0	29148.0	7272.0	211116.0
17	349596.0	58232.0	14574.0	422402.0
18	698976.0	116532.0	29116.0	844624.0
19	1398180.0	232992.0	58266.0	1689438.0
20	2796120.0	466060.0	116496.0	3378676.0
21	5592492.0	932040.0	233030.0	6757562.0
22	1.118472E7	1864164.0	466020.0	1.3514904E7
23	2.2369716E7	3728240.0	932082.0	2.7030038E7
24	4.4739144E7	7456572.0	1864120.0	5.4059836E7

It so happens that there are no 'fractional' rabbits in this example. If there are any, they should be kept, and not rounded (and certainly not truncated). Fractions occur in general because the fertility rates and survival probabilities are averages.

If you look carefully at the output you may spot that after some months the total population doubles every month. This factor is called the *growth factor*, and is a property of the particular Leslie matrix being used (if you know about such things, it's the *dominant eigenvalue* of the matrix). The growth factor is 2 in this example, but if the values in the Leslie matrix are changed, the long-term growth factor changes too (try it and see).

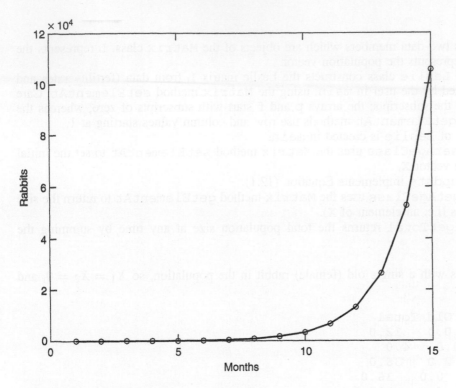

Figure 12.2 Total rabbit population over 15 months

Figure 12.2 shows how the total rabbit population grows over the first 15 months. The graph demonstrates *exponential* growth. If you plot the population over the full 24-month period, you will see that the graph gets much steeper. This is a feature of exponential growth.

You probably didn't spot that the numbers in the three age classes tend to a limiting ratio of 24:4:1. This can be demonstrated very clearly if you run the model with an initial population structure having this limiting ratio. The limiting ratio is called the *stable age distribution* of the population, and again it is a property of the Leslie matrix (in fact, it is the *eigenvector* belonging to the dominant eigenvalue of the matrix). Different population matrices lead to different stable age distributions.

The interesting point about this is that a given Leslie matrix always eventually gets a population into the *same* stable age distribution, which increases eventually by the *same* growth factor each month, *no matter what the initial population breakdown is*. For example, if you run the above model with any other initial population, it will always eventually get into a stable age distribution of 24:4:1 with a growth factor of 2 (try it and see).

12.4 Markov processes

Often a process that we wish to model may be represented by a number of possible *discrete* (i.e. discontinuous) states that describe the outcome of the process. For example, if we are spinning a coin, then the outcome is adequately represented by the two states 'heads' and 'tails' (and nothing in between). If the process is random, as it is with spinning coins, there is a certain probability of being in any of the states at a given moment, and also a probability of changing from one state to another. If the probability of moving from one state to another depends on the present state only, and not on any previous state, the process is called a *Markov chain*. The progress of the drunken sailor in Chapter 11 is an example of such a process. Markov chains are used widely in such diverse fields as biology and business decision making, to name just two areas.

A random walk

This example is a variation on the random walk simulation of Chapter 11. A street has six intersections. A short-sighted student wanders down the street. His home is at intersection 1, and his favourite internet cafe at intersection 6. At each intersection other than his home or the cafe he moves in the direction of the cafe with probability 2/3, and in the direction of his home with probability 1/3. In other words, he is twice as likely to move towards the cafe as towards his home. He never wanders down a side street. If he reaches his home or the cafe, he disappears into them, never to re-appear (when he disappears we say in Markov jargon that he has been *absorbed*).

We would like to know: what are the chances of him ending up at home or in the cafe, if he starts at a given corner (other than home or the cafe, obviously)? He can clearly be in one of six states, with respect to his random walk, which can be labelled by the intersection number, where state 1 means *Home* and state 6 means *Cafe*. We can represent the probabilities of being in these states by a six-component *state vector* $\mathbf{X}(t)$, where $X_i(t)$ is the probability of him being at intersection i at moment t. The components of $\mathbf{X}(t)$ must sum to 1, since he has to be in one of these states.

We can express this Markov process with the following *transition probability matrix*, $\mathbf{P}$, where the rows represent the next state (i.e. corner), and the columns represent the present state:

	Home	2	3	4	5	Cafe
Home	1	1/3	0	0	0	0
2	0	0	1/3	0	0	0
3	0	2/3	0	1/3	0	0
4	0	0	2/3	0	1/3	0
5	0	0	0	2/3	0	0
Cafe	0	0	0	0	2/3	1

The entries for *Home-Home* and *Cafe-Cafe* are both 1 because he stays there with certainty.

Using the probability matrix $\mathbf{P}$ we can work out his chances of being, say, at intersection 3 at moment $(t + 1)$ as

$$X_3(t + 1) = 2/3 X_2(t) + 1/3 X_4(t).$$

To get to 3, he must have been at either 2 or 4, and his chances of moving from there are 2/3 and 1/3 respectively.

Mathematically, this is identical to the Leslie matrix problem. We can therefore form the new state vector from the old one each time with a matrix equation:

$$\mathbf{X}(t + 1) = \mathbf{P}\,\mathbf{X}(t).$$

If we suppose the student starts at intersection 2, the initial probabilities will be (0, 1, 0, 0, 0, 0). Our Leslie matrix program may be easily adapted to generate future states of a Markov process:

```
import essential.*;
import java.text.*;

public class Markov
{
    private int size;
    private Matrix P;    //Transition probability matrix
    private Matrix X;    //State vector

    public Markov( int s, double [] subdiag, double [] diag,
                double[] superdiag ) throws MatrixException
    {
        size = s;
```

```
        P = new Matrix(size, size);  // all elements zero
        X = new Matrix(size, 1);

        //construct transition matrix:
        //be careful of subscripts ...

        for (int i = 1; i <= size; i++)
            //diag's first subscript is zero!
            P.setElementAt(i,i,diag[i-1]);

        for (int i = 2; i <= size; i++)
        {
            P.setElementAt(i,i-1,subdiag[i-2]);
            P.setElementAt(i-1,i,superdiag[i-2]);
        }
    }

    public double getState(int row) throws MatrixException
    {
        return X.getElementAt(row,1);
    }

    public void setState(int row, double val) throws MatrixException
    {
        X.setElementAt(row, 1, val);
    }

    public void update() throws MatrixException
    // updates state vector by one time unit
    {
        X = P.multiply(X);
    }

    public static void main(String args[]) throws MatrixException
    {
        int numberOfStates = 6;
        DecimalFormat dfTime = new DecimalFormat("00");
        DecimalFormat dfState = new DecimalFormat("0.0000");

        //initialize (or read) sub-diagonal
        double [] subdiag = {0, 2./3, 2./3, 2./3, 2./3};
        //initialize (or read) diagonal:
        double [] diag = {1, 0, 0, 0, 0, 1};
        //initialize (or read) super-diagonal
        double [] superdiag = {1./3, 1./3, 1./3, 1./3, 0};

        Markov walker = new Markov(numberOfStates, subdiag, diag,
                                   superdiag);
        walker.setState(2, 1); //start at Intersection 2
        System.out.println
        ( "time  Home         2       3       4       5       Cafe" );
```

```
for (int time = 1; time <= 50; time++)
{
    System.out.print( dfTime.format(time) + "    " );
    walker.update();      //update population by one month

    //print each age class
    for (int i = 1; i <= numberOfStates; i++)
        System.out.print( dfState.format(walker.getState(i))
                            + "    " );

    System.out.println();
}
}
}
```

Note:

- Our student is not allowed to skip intersections. Therefore the transition matrix **P** can only have non-zero elements on the main diagonal and on the two diagonals immediately above and below it: the sub- and super-diagonals. Not so?
  The user can therefore specify these three diagonals as Markov constructor arguments.

Output:

time	Home	2	3	4	5	Cafe
01	0.3333	0.0000	0.6667	0.0000	0.0000	0.0000
02	0.3333	0.2222	0.0000	0.4444	0.0000	0.0000
03	0.4074	0.0000	0.2963	0.0000	0.2963	0.0000
04	0.4074	0.0988	0.0000	0.2963	0.0000	0.1975
05	0.4403	0.0000	0.1646	0.0000	0.1975	0.1975
06	0.4403	0.0549	0.0000	0.1756	0.0000	0.3292
07	0.4586	0.0000	0.0951	0.0000	0.1171	0.3292
08	0.4586	0.0317	0.0000	0.1024	0.0000	0.4073
09	0.4692	0.0000	0.0553	0.0000	0.0683	0.4073
10	0.4692	0.0184	0.0000	0.0596	0.0000	0.4528
...						
20	0.4829	0.0012	0.0000	0.0040	0.0000	0.5119
...						
30	0.4838	0.0001	0.0000	0.0003	0.0000	0.5158
...						
40	0.4839	0.0000	0.0000	0.0000	0.0000	0.5161
...						
50	0.4839	0.0000	0.0000	0.0000	0.0000	0.5161

By running the program for long enough, we soon find the limiting probabilities: he ends up at home about 48% of the time, and at the cafe about 52% of the time. Perhaps this is a little surprising; from the transition probabilities, we might have expected him to get to the cafe rather more easily. It just goes to show that you should never trust your intuition when it comes to statistics!

Note that the Markov chain approach is *not* a simulation: one gets the *theoretical* probabilities each time (this can all be done mathematically, without a computer). But it is interesting to confirm the limiting probabilities by *simulating* the student's progress, using a random number generator.

Try Exercises 12.2 to 12.4.

12.5   Linear equations

A problem that often arises in scientific applications is the solution of a system of linear equations, e.g.

$$2x + 2y + 2z = 0 \tag{12.2}$$

$$3x + 2y + 2z = 1 \tag{12.3}$$

$$3x + 2y + 3z = 1. \tag{12.4}$$

If we define the matrix **A** as

$$\mathbf{A} = \begin{bmatrix} 2 & 2 & 2 \\ 3 & 2 & 2 \\ 3 & 2 & 3 \end{bmatrix},$$

and the vectors **x** and **b** as

$$\mathbf{x} = \begin{bmatrix} x \\ y \\ z \end{bmatrix}, \qquad \mathbf{b} = \begin{bmatrix} 0 \\ 1 \\ 1 \end{bmatrix},$$

we can write the above system of three equations in matrix form as

$$\begin{bmatrix} 2 & 2 & 2 \\ 3 & 2 & 2 \\ 3 & 2 & 3 \end{bmatrix} \begin{bmatrix} x \\ y \\ z \end{bmatrix} = \begin{bmatrix} 0 \\ 1 \\ 1 \end{bmatrix},$$

or even more concisely as the single matrix equation

$$\mathbf{Ax} = \mathbf{b}. \tag{12.5}$$

The solution may then be written as

$$\mathbf{x} = \mathbf{A}^{-1}\mathbf{b}, \tag{12.6}$$

where $\mathbf{A}^{-1}$ is the *matrix inverse* of **A** (i.e. the matrix which when multiplied by **A** gives the identity matrix **I**).

The essential.Matrix class has a method invert() which inverts a square matrix. It is demonstrated in the following program which inverts a matrix A of random elements. The inverse (Ainv) is then multiplied by the original matrix. The result, which should be the identity matrix, is printed:

```java
import essential.*;

public class InvertTester
{
    public static void main(String args[]) throws MatrixException
    {
        int n = 3;
        double [][] a = new double[n][n];

        for (int i = 0; i < n; i++)
            for (int j = 0; j < n; j++)
                a[i][j] = Math.random();

        Matrix A = new Matrix(a);
        Matrix Ainv = A.invert();

        System.out.println(Ainv.multiply(A));
    }
}
```

Output:

```
[    1.0000000000000004   3.3306690738754696E-16   4.440892098500626E-16    ]
[   -4.440892098500626E-16   0.9999999999999998   -8.881784197001252E-16   ]
[    0    0    1.0000000000000002 ]
```

Note how rounding error creeps into all the elements. If you did the calculations 'by hand' they would all be 1's or 0's exactly.

The following program, LinearSolver, solves a general system of linear equations. It reads the coefficients of **A** and **b** from the text files A.txt and B.txt and uses Equation (12.6) to find the solution, which is printed.

```
import essential.*;

public class LinearSolver
{
    public static void main(String args[]) throws MatrixException
    {
        Matrix A = Matrix.readMatrix( "A.dat" ); //coefficient matrix
        Matrix b = Matrix.readMatrix( "B.dat" ); //right-hand side
        Matrix Ainv = A.invert();
        Matrix X = A.invert().multiply(b);

        System.out.println( "Ainv:\n" + Ainv );       //for interest
        System.out.println( "Solution:\n" + X );

        Matrix R = A.multiply(X).subtract(b);
        System.out.println( "Residual:\n" + R );
    }
}
```

The text file A.txt for the matrix **A** of the system (12.2)–(12.4) is

```
3x3
2 2 2
3 2 2
3 2 3
```

while the text file B.txt for the vector **b** is

```
3x1
0
1
1
```

The output from LinearSolver includes the following:

```
Ainv:
[   -1    1    0    ]
[   1.5  0    -1    ]
[   0    -1   1     ]

Solution:
[    1    ]
[   -1    ]
[    0    ]
```

In terms of our notation, this means that the solution is $x = 1, y = -1, z = 0$.

Limitations of the `invert` method of `Matrix`

The `invert` method of `Matrix` uses the most basic *Gauss reduction* to invert a matrix. If you are familiar with Gauss reduction, you will be aware that things can go wrong, as described below in the terminology of Gauss reduction. The first problem mentioned can be dealt with by the current version of `invert`. You are invited to develop `invert` further yourself, if you are interested, in order to handle the remaining problems.

- The pivot element could be zero. This happens quite easily when the coefficients are all integers. This is fairly straightforward to handle, since rows of the system can be interchanged without changing the solution. The method `invert` looks down the column under the pivot element. If it cannot find a non-zero pivot it throws an exception. If it does find a non-zero pivot in a particular row, it swops that row with the pivot row and continues.

  You can check how `invert` handles a zero pivot element by replacing the coefficient of x in Equation (12.2) by zero. This gives a zero pivot element immediately.
- A row of zeros could appear right across the augmented matrix, in which case a non-zero pivot element cannot be found. In this case the system of equations is indeterminate (under-determined), and an exception should be thrown to this effect.
- A row of the array could be filled with zeros, except for the extreme right-hand element. In this case the equations are inconsistent and no solution can be found. An exception should also be thrown in this case.

Try Exercise 12.5.

The residual

When solving a system of linear equations it is useful to check your solution by computing the *residual* **r**, defined as

$$\mathbf{r} = \mathbf{Ax} - \mathbf{b}.$$

Theoretically, the residual should be zero, since the expression **Ax** is supposed to equal **b**, according to Equation(12.5). The residual is easily computed in `LinearSolver`, by simply adding the line

```
Matrix R = A.multiply(X).subtract(b);
```

Note that the `Matrix` methods `multiply` and `subtract` can be 'cascaded' in a single statement. This is because the method `multiply` returns a `Matrix` object which is then used as the object for calling `subtract`. The following is a typical residual for a 3×3 system with random elements:

```
[    -1.6653345369377348E-16  ]
[    -1.1102230246251565E-16  ]
[    -2.220446049250313E-16   ]
```

Since all the elements of the residual are very small we can be confident that we do indeed have the correct solution.

Unfortunately, even getting a very small residual does not necessarily guarantee that the solution is meaningful, as we shall see in the next section.

Try Exercise 12.6.

Ill-conditioned systems

Sometimes the coefficients of a system of equations are the results of an experiment, and may be subject to error. We need in that case to know how sensitive the solution is to the experimental errors. As an example, consider the system

$$10x + 7y + 8z + 7w = 32$$
$$7x + 5y + 6z + 5w = 23$$
$$8x + 6y + 10z + 9w = 33$$
$$7x + 5y + 9z + 10w = 31$$

Use `LinearSolver` (you need only put the values of the matrices **A** and **b** in text files and change the names in the program) to show that the solution is

```
[    0.9999999999999432   ]
[    0.9999999999999432   ]
[    1.0000000000000284   ]
[    1.0000000000000142   ]
```

The residual is very small, and all seems well:

```
[   -6.394884621840902E-13  ]
[   -4.405364961712621E-13  ]
[   -3.836930773104541E-13  ]
[   -2.8421709430404007E-13 ]
```

However, if we change the right-hand side constants to 32.1, 22.9, 32.9 and 31.1 respectively, the 'solution' is now

```
[    6.000000000000199    ]
[   -7.200000000000273    ]
[    2.900000000000625    ]
[   -0.10000000000002274     ]
```

Once again, the residual is very small.

A system like this is called *ill-conditioned*, meaning that a small change in the coefficients leads to a large change in the solution. It is possible to anticipate ill conditioning to some extent. Recall that the solution of the system is

$$\mathbf{x} = \mathbf{A}^{-1}\mathbf{b}.$$

Errors in **b** are likely to be magnified in **x** when $\mathbf{A}^{-1}$ has large entries. Ill conditioning should therefore be suspected whenever $\mathbf{A}^{-1}$ has entries that are much larger than 1. This is definitely the case here; the largest entry in $\mathbf{A}^{-1}$ is 68.

Some authors suggest the rule of thumb that a matrix is ill-conditioned if its *determinant* is small compared to the entries in the matrix. In this case the determinant of **A** is 1 which is about an order of magnitude smaller than most of its entries. If you know how to compute a determinant it would be useful to add such a method to `Matrix`.

Try Exercises 12.7 and 12.8.

Summary

- Matrix multiplication, which is easily implemented with the `Matrix` class, has a large number of applications.
- The reachability matrix of a network may be computed from powers of the adjacency matrix of the network.
- Leslie matrices are used to model the dynamics of populations which may be grouped into age classes.
- Markov processes are modelled with transition probability matrices.
- Systems of linear equations may be solved using the `invert` method of the `Matrix` class.

Exercises

12.1 Write a short program to verify that a square matrix **A** multiplied by the identity matrix **I** gives **A**, by generating a 3×3 matrix **A** with random elements and multiplying it with the identity.

12.2 Compute the limiting probabilities for the student in Section 12.4 when he starts at each of the remaining intersections in turn, and confirm that the closer he starts to the cafe", the more likely he is to end up there.

Compute $\mathbf{P}^{50}$ separately in a `for` loop. Can you see the limiting probabilities in the first row?

12.3 Suppose that his home or the cafe are no longer absorbing states for our student in Section 12.4. Instead, if he is at home, he remains there with probability 1/3 but moves towards the cafe with probability 2/3. If he is in the cafe, he stays there with probability 2/3, but moves towards his home with probability 1/3.

Change the entries of the transition matrix P in Markov to handle this situation. Run the amended program for all possible initial states (home, intersection 1, ..., cafe), and confirm that in *all cases* the limiting probabilities of him being in any of the states are

$$0.0159 \quad 0.0318 \quad 0.0635 \quad 0.1270 \quad 0.2539 \quad 0.5079$$

12.4 Write a program to simulate the progress of the short-sighted student in Section 12.4. Start him at a given intersection, and generate a random number to decide whether he moves toward the internet cafe or home, according to the probabilities in the transition matrix. For each simulated walk, record whether he ends up at home or in the cafe. Repeat a large number of times. The proportion of walks that end up in either place should approach the limiting probabilities computed using the Markov model described in Section 12.4. **Hint:** if the random number is less than 2/3 he moves toward the cafe (unless he is already at home or in the cafe, in which case that random walk ends), otherwise he moves toward home.

12.5 The *transpose* of an $n \times m$ matrix is the $m \times n$ matrix that results when the rows and columns of the original matrix are interchanged, i.e. a_{ij} is replaced by a_{ji}. If you have found your way around the Matrix class why not try writing a method for it which returns the transpose of a matrix passed as an argument?

12.6 Use LinearSolver (Section 12.5) to set up and solve a 3×3 system of linear equations with random coefficients. Verify that you have a correct solution by computing the residual.

12.7 Solve the equations

$$2x - y + z = 4$$
$$x + y + z = 3$$
$$3x - y - z = 1$$

using LinearSolver. Check your solution by computing the residual. Do you suspect ill conditioning (where small changes in the coefficients cause large changes in the solution), and why, or why not?

12.8 This problem, suggested by R.V. Andree, demonstrates ill conditioning. Use LinearSolver to show that the solution of the system

$$x + 5.000y = 17.0$$
$$1.5x + 7.501y = 25.503$$

is $x = 2$, $y = 3$. Compute the residual.

Now change the term on the right-hand side of the second equation to 25.501, a change of about one part in 12000, and find the new solution and the residual. The solution is completely different. Also try changing this term to 25.502, 25.504, etc. If the coefficients are subject to experimental errors, the solution is clearly meaningless. Do the entries in $\mathbf{A}^{-1}$ confirm ill conditioning?

Another way to anticipate ill conditioning is to perform a *sensitivity analysis* on the coefficients: change them all in turn by the same small percentage, and observe what effect this has on the solution.

13

Introduction to numerical methods

Objectives

After studying this chapter you should be able to write programs to

- solve equations in one unknown;
- evaluate definite integrals;
- solve systems of ordinary differential equations;
- solve parabolic partial differential equations.

A major use of computers in science and engineering is in finding numerical solutions to mathematical problems which have no analytical solutions (i.e. solutions which may be written down in terms of polynomials and standard mathematical functions). In this chapter we look briefly at some areas where *numerical methods* have been highly developed, e.g. solving non-linear equations, evaluating integrals, and solving differential equations.

13.1 Equations

In this section we consider how to solve equations in one unknown, numerically. The usual way of expressing the problem is to say that we want to solve the equation $f(x) = 0$, i.e. we want to find its *root* (or roots). This process is also described as finding the *zeros* of $f(x)$. There is no general analytical method for finding roots for an arbitrary $f(x)$.

Newton's method

Newton's method (also called the Newton-Raphson method) is perhaps the easiest numerical method to implement for solving equations. It was introduced as a special case for finding square roots in Chapter 2. Newton's method is an *iterative* procedure, meaning that it repeatedly attempts to improve an estimate of the root. If x_k is an approximation to the root, we can relate it to the next approximation x_{k+1} using the right-angle triangle in Figure 13.1:

$$f'(x_k) = \frac{f(x_k) - 0}{x_k - x_{k+1}},$$

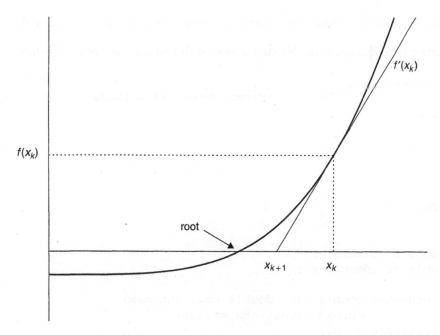

Figure 13.1 Newton's method

where $f'(x)$ is df/dx. Solving for x_{k+1} gives

$$x_{k+1} = x_k - \frac{f(x_k)}{f'(x_k)}.$$

A structure plan to implement Newton's method is:

1. Given a starting value x_0 and required relative error e:
2. While relative error $|(x_k - x_{k-1})/x_k| \geq e$ repeat up to, say, $k = 20$:
   $x_{k+1} = x_k - f(x_k)/f'(x_k)$
   Print x_{k+1} and $f(x_{k+1})$.

Note:

- It is necessary to limit the number of repeats in step 2 since the process may not converge.
- The relative error $|(x_k - x_{k-1})/x_k|$ is usually used when testing for convergence.
  A condition on the absolute error $|x_k - x_{k-1}|$ may be satisfied too soon if the root is much smaller than expected.

A Function *class*

We could rush ahead and design a class to implement Newton's method to solve a particular equation. Try it if you like. It would include methods to return $f(x)$ and $f'(x)$. However, the limitations of our particular solution become apparent as soon as we try to solve a different equation: the methods returning $f(x)$ and its derivative have to be redefined, and the whole class needs to be recompiled. This makes it unsuitable to include our class in a package of numerical methods for general use. In fact, this problem crops up again and again when coding numerical methods. We want a package of classes to handle various numerical procedures where the user can specify a particular function or set of functions without having to rewrite and recompile code which should really be hidden from the average class user.

We get around this difficulty in Java by making use of abstract classes, which were introduced in Chapter 7.

Here is an abstract class `Function`. It implements Newton's method to find the roots of an equation, which has yet to be defined:

```java
/* An abstract class Function to implement various numerical methods:
   Newton's method to find roots
   ...
*/

import java.util.*;

public abstract class Function
{

    public abstract double f (double x);
    public abstract double df (double x);

    public double getRootNewton(double est, double tol, int max)
                            throws EquationException{
      double rootErrorTolerance = tol;
      int maxIterations = max;
      //the actual number of iterations it took to converge:
      int numIterations = 0;
      boolean converged = false;     //whether Newton converged or not
      double currentEstimate = est; //est is initial guess
      double root = est;            //final value of the root
      double prevEstimate = est;
      double relativeError;

      System.out.println("**Finding a root using Newton-Raphson method**");
      System.out.println();
      System.out.println("Iteration\t\tRoot estimate\t\t\t\tFunction value");
      System.out.println(numIterations + "\t\t\t\t" + currentEstimate +
                            "\t\t\t" + f(currentEstimate));

      while ((numIterations < maxIterations) &&  !converged)
      {
        numIterations++;
        prevEstimate = currentEstimate;

        //Newton's algorithm:
        currentEstimate = prevEstimate -
                          (f(prevEstimate)/df(prevEstimate));

        root = currentEstimate;
        System.out.println(numIterations + "\t\t\t\t" + currentEstimate +
                            "\t\t\t" + f(currentEstimate));
        relativeError = Math.abs((currentEstimate -
                        prevEstimate)/currentEstimate);
        converged = relativeError <= rootErrorTolerance;
      }
```

```
      if (converged)
      {
        System.out.println("Method converged");
        return root;
      }
      else
      {
        throw new EquationException
                ("Could not find root: method did not converge");
      }
    }
}
```

Note:

- A general function $f(x)$ and its derivative are implemented as abstract methods:

  ```
          public abstract double f (double x);
          public abstract double df (double x);
  ```

  These can be regarded as placeholders, waiting for the details to be filled in later. We can then write a perfectly general method getRootNewton to implement our structure plan for Newton's method.
- If convergence does not occur in getRootNewton an exception is thrown. This is described in detail below.
- Our class Function can now be compiled and hidden away in a package, if necessary (see Chapter 3: **Making your own package**).

  Let's use Function now to solve the equation $x^3 + x - 3 = 0$. Two further classes are required.

1. We need to extend Function with a class which implements methods to return $f(x)$ and its derivative, $3x^2 + 1$:

   ```
                class CubicEquation extends Function
                {
                    public double f(double x)
                    {
                            return x*x*x + x - 3;
                    }

                    public double df(double x)
                    {
                            return 3*x*x + 1;
                    }
                }
   ```

2. Finally, we need a class to instantiate a CubicEquation object and to call the object's relevant methods:

   ```
          import essential.*;

          public class CubicTester
          {
              public static void main(String[] args)throws Exception
   ```

```
        {
            CubicEquation cubic = new CubicEquation();
            System.out.print( "Estimate of root: " );
            double myGuess = Keyboard.readDouble();
            System.out.println();
            System.out.println("Root = "
                        + cubic.getRootNewton(myGuess, 1e-8, 20));
        }
    }
```

Here is the output for an initial estimate of 1 and a relative error of 10^{-8}:

```
    Estimate of root: 1.0
    **Finding a root using Newton-Raphson method**

    Iteration         Root estimate                    Function value
    0                 1.0              -1.0
    1                 1.25                  0.203125
    2                 1.2142857142857142               0.004737609329445558
    3                 1.213412175782825                2.779086666571118E-6
    4                 1.2134116627624065               9.583445148564351E-13
    5                 1.2134116627622296               -4.440892098500626E-16
    Method converged
    Root = 1.2134116627622296
```

Note that the Function method getRootNewton returns the final root after printing all the intermediate iterations x_k and function values $f(x_k)$.

Defining a new exception

Newton's method unfortunately does not always converge. In this case, we need to let the class user know that we could not find a root given the initial estimate. This is clearly a good case for throwing an exception—we cannot return an answer, so we throw an exception to indicate that something has gone wrong.

But, what type of exception should we throw? Recall from Chapter 10 that there are many different exception classes that are all subclasses of the class Exception. The name of each exception class is an indication of the type of exception (for example, FileNotFoundException). We should do the same in this case—define an exception class with a name that describes the kind of exception. We will call it EquationException. Here is the class:

```
    public class EquationException extends Exception
    {
        public EquationException()
        {
            super("No detailed information supplied");
        }
        public EquationException(String s) {
            super(s);
        }
    }
```

When we define a new exception class, we are required to do the following:

- The class must extend `Exception` (or a subclass of `Exception`).
- We must provide two constructors:

  1. a default constructor, which can either be blank, or call the superclass constructor as we have done above;
  2. a parameterized constructor which takes a single `String` argument and passes this to the superclass constructor.

Notice at the end of the `getRootNewton` method in `Function`, if the iterations do not converge we throw an `EquationException` by creating an exception object and supplying it with a string describing the problem in more detail.

If Newton's method fails to find a root, the Bisection method, discussed below, can be used.
Try Exercises 13.1 to 13.4.

Complex roots

If you are not familiar with complex numbers you can safely skip this short section.

A nice spin-off of Newton's method is that it can be used to find complex roots, but only if the starting guess is complex. Our `essential` package has a `Complex` class for creating and manipulating complex numbers. It is used here (with explanation below) to find a complex root of $x^2 + x + 1 = 0$.

```java
import essential.*;

public class FunctionComplex
{

    public Complex f (Complex x)
    {
        return x.multiply(x).add(x).add(1); // x^2 + x + 1
    }

    public Complex df (Complex x)
    {
        Complex a;
        a = Complex.multiply(2, x);   // 2x
        return a.add(1);              // 2x + 1
    }

    public void getRootNewton(double tol, int max)
    {
        double rootErrorTolerance = tol;
        int maxIterations = max;
        //the actual number of iterations it took to converge:
        int numIterations = 0;
        boolean converged = false;     //whether Newton converged or not
        double relativeError;

        Complex rootEstimate = Complex.read();
        System.out.println( rootEstimate );
        Complex prevEstimate = new Complex(rootEstimate);
```

```
      while((numIterations <= maxIterations) && !converged)
      {
        numIterations++;
        prevEstimate = rootEstimate;
        //x = x - f(x)/df(x):
        rootEstimate = rootEstimate.subtract(f(rootEstimate)
                        .divide(df(rootEstimate)));
        System.out.println(rootEstimate );
        relativeError = Complex.abs(rootEstimate.subtract(prevEstimate))
                        /Complex.abs(rootEstimate);
        converged = relativeError <= rootErrorTolerance;
      }
    }

    public static void main( String[] args )
    {
      FunctionComplex fc = new FunctionComplex();
      fc.getRootNewton(1e-4, 20);
    }
}
```

Using a complex starting value of $1 + i$ for x gives the following output:

```
Enter real part
1.0
Enter imaginary part
1.0
-----------
1.0 + 1.0i
0.07692307692307687 + 0.6153846153846154i
-0.5155925155925156 + 0.6320166320016632i
-0.4931668689796128 + 0.9089862093763263i
-0.49968450674714165 + 0.8670173059345632i
-0.4999996392488419 + 0.8660259139020026i
-0.4999999999997875 + 0.8660254037845138i
```

Since complex roots occur in complex conjugate pairs, the other root is $-0.5 - 0.866i$.
  Note:

- The Complex class has methods add to update a Complex value by a Complex value or a double value. Both these forms are used in the method f of FunctionComplex above. See the documentation of the essential package for more details.
- Suppose we have two complex numbers z_1 and z_2,

$$z_1 = x_1 + iy_1,$$

$$z_2 = z_2 + iy_2,$$

where x_1, x_2 and y_1, y_2 are their real and imaginary parts respectively. The product z_1z_2 is defined so that the real part of the product is $x_1x_2 - y_1y_2$, while the imaginary part of the product is $y_1x_2 + x_1y_2$. The Complex class has a multiply method which returns the product of two Complex objects. This form is used in the method f of FunctionComplex to calculate x^2.
There is also a static version of multiply which is used to calculate $2x$ in the method df of FunctionComplex.

- The quotient z_1/z_2 of two complex numbers has a real part of $(x_1x_2 + y_1y_2)/(x_2^2 + y_2^2)$ and an imaginary part of $(y_1x_2 - x_1y_2)/(x_2^2 + y_2^2)$.
  The `Complex` method `divide` is used to calculate $f(x)/f'(x)$ in the `getRootNewton` method of `FunctionComplex`.

The Bisection method

The Bisection method is an alternative to Newton's method for solving equations.

Consider again the problem of solving the equation $f(x) = 0$, where

$$f(x) = x^3 + x - 3.$$

We attempt to find by inspection, or trial-and-error, two values of x, call them x_L and x_R, such that $f(x_L)$ and $f(x_R)$ have different signs, i.e. $f(x_L)f(x_R) < 0$. If we can find two such values, the root must lie somewhere in the interval between them, since $f(x)$ changes sign on this interval (see Figure 13.2). In this example, $x_L = 1$ and $x_R = 2$ will do, since $f(1) = -1$ and $f(2) = 7$. In the Bisection method, we estimate the root by x_M, where x_M is the midpoint of the interval $[x_L, x_R]$, i.e.

$$x_M = (x_L + x_R)/2. \tag{13.1}$$

Then if $f(x_M)$ has the same sign as $f(x_L)$, as drawn in the figure, the root clearly lies between x_M and x_R. We must then redefine the left-hand end of the interval as having the value of x_M, i.e. we let the new value of x_L be x_M. Otherwise, if $f(x_M)$ and $f(x_L)$ have *different* signs, we let the new value of x_R be x_M, since the root must lie between x_L and x_M in that case. Having redefined x_L or x_R, as the case may be, we bisect the new interval again according to Equation (13.1) and repeat the process until the distance between x_L and x_R is as small as we please.

The neat thing about this method is that, *before* starting, we can calculate how many bisections are needed to obtain a certain accuracy, given initial values of x_L and x_R. Suppose we start with $x_L = a$, and $x_R = b$. After the first bisection the worst possible error (E_1) in x_M is $E_1 = |a - b|/2$, since we are estimating the root as being at the midpoint of the interval $[a, b]$. The worst that can happen is that the root is actually at x_L or x_R, in which case the error is E_1. Carrying on like this, after n bisections the

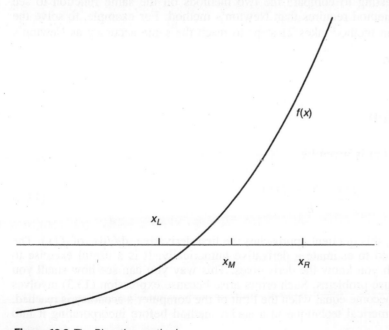

Figure 13.2 The Bisection method

worst possible error E_n is given by $E_n = |a - b|/2^n$. If we want to be sure that this is less than some specified error E, we must see to it that n satisfies the inequality $|a - b|/2^n < E$, i.e.

$$n > \frac{\log(|a - b|/E)}{\log(2)} \tag{13.2}$$

Since n is the number of bisections, it must be an integer. The smallest integer n that *exceeds* the right-hand side of Inequality (13.2) will do as the maximum number of bisections required to guarantee the given accuracy E.

The following scheme may be used to program the Bisection method. It will work for any function $f(x)$ that changes sign (in either direction) between the two values a and b, which must be found beforehand by the user.

    1. Given a, b and E
    2. Initialize x_L and x_R
    3. Compute maximum bisections n from Inequality (13.2)
    4. Repeat n times:
        Compute x_M according to Equation (13.1)
        If $f(x_L)f(x_M) > 0$ then
          Let $x_L = x_M$
        otherwise
          Let $x_R = x_M$
    5. The root is x_M.

We have assumed that the procedure will not find the root exactly; the chances of this happening with real variables are infinitesimal.

The main advantage of the Bisection method is that it is *guaranteed to find a root* if you can find two starting values for x_L and x_R between which the function changes sign. You can also compute in advance the number of bisections needed to attain a given accuracy. Compared to Newton's method it is inefficient. Successive bisections do not necessarily move closer to the root, as usually happens with Newton's method. In fact, it is interesting to compare the two methods on the same function to see how many more steps the Bisection method requires than Newton's method. For example, to solve the equation $x^3 + x - 3 = 0$, the Bisection method takes 21 steps to reach the same accuracy as Newton's in five steps.

Try Exercises 13.5 to Exercises 13.6.

13.2 Numerical differentiation

The *Newton quotient* for a function $f(x)$ is given by

$$\frac{f(x + h) - f(x)}{h}, \tag{13.3}$$

where h is 'small'. As h tends to zero, this quotient approaches the first derivative, df/dx, of $f(x)$. The Newton quotient may therefore be used to estimate a derivative numerically. It is a useful exercise to do this with a few functions for which you know the derivatives. This way you can see how small you can make h before rounding errors cause problems. Such errors arise because expression (13.3) involves subtracting two terms that eventually become equal when the limit of the computer's accuracy is reached. We will first experiment with this numerical technique in a `main` method before incorporating it into the `Function` class.

As an example, the following program uses the Newton quotient to estimate $f'(x)$ for $f(x) = x^2$ at $x = 2$, for smaller and smaller values of h (the exact answer is 4).

```java
import java.text.*;

public class NumericalDerivative
{
    public static void main(String[] args)
    {
        double h = 1;
        double x = 2;
        double newtonQuotient;
        DecimalFormat df = new DecimalFormat("0.###########E0");

        for (int i = 1; i <= 20; i++)
        {
            newtonQuotient = (f(x+h)-f(x))/h;
            System.out.println( df.format(h) + "  " +
                                df.format(newtonQuotient));
            h = h/10;
        }

    }

    public static double f( double x )
    {
        return x*x;
    }
}
```

Note the use of the symbol E in the `DecimalFormat` pattern to format output in scientific notation. Output:

```
1E0   5E0
1E-1  4.1E0
1E-2  4.01E0
1E-3  4.001E0
1E-4  4.000100000008E0
1E-5  4.000010000027E0
1E-6  4.000001000648E0
1E-7  4.000000091153E0
1E-8  3.99999997569E0
1E-9  4.000000330961E0
1E-10 4.000000330961E0
1E-11 4.000000330961E0
1E-12 4.000355602329E0
1E-13 3.996802888651E0
1E-14 4.085620730621E0
1E-15 3.552713678801E0
1E-16 0E0
1E-17 0E0
1E-18 0E0
1E-19 0E0
```

The results show that the best h for this particular problem is about 10^{-8}. But for h smaller than this the estimate gradually becomes less accurate.

Generally, the best h for a given problem can only be found by trial and error. Finding it can be a non-trivial exercise. This problem does not arise with numerical integration, because numbers are *added* to find the area, not subtracted.

We now add numerical differentiation to the `Function` class as follows:

- replace the abstract method `df` with a method `df` to return the Newton quotient as defined above;
- define a data member `h` for the step-length, with a method `setH` to specify the value of `h`.

Here is our modified `Function` class:

```
public abstract class Function
{
    private double h;

    public abstract double f (double x);

    public double df (double x)
    {
        double newtonQuotient = (f(x+h)-f(x))/h;
        return newtonQuotient;
    }

    public void setH (double h) {
        this.h = h;
    }
    ...
```

Note that if you want to use the analytical derivative you can always override `df` in any subclass of `Function`.

13.3 Integration

Although most 'respectable' mathematical functions can be differentiated analytically, the same cannot be said for integration. There are no general rules for integrating, as there are for differentiating. For example, the indefinite integral of a function as simple as e^{-x^2} cannot be found analytically. We therefore need numerical methods for evaluating integrals.

This is actually quite easy, and depends on the fact that the definite integral of a function $f(x)$ between the limits $x = a$ and $x = b$ is equal to the area under $f(x)$ bounded by the x-axis and the two vertical lines $x = a$ and $x = b$. So all numerical methods for integrating simply involve more or less ingenious ways of estimating the area under $f(x)$.

The Trapezoidal rule

The Trapezoidal (or Trapezium) rule is fairly simple to program. The area under $f(x)$ is divided into vertical panels each of width h, called the *step-length*. If there are n such panels, then $nh = b - a$, i.e. $n = (b - a)/h$. If we join the points where successive panels cut $f(x)$, we can estimate the area under $f(x)$ as the sum of the area of the resulting trapezia (see Figure 13.3). If we call this approximation to the integral S, then

$$S = \frac{h}{2}\left[f(a) + f(b) + 2\sum_{i=1}^{n-1} f(x_i) \right],$$

(13.4)

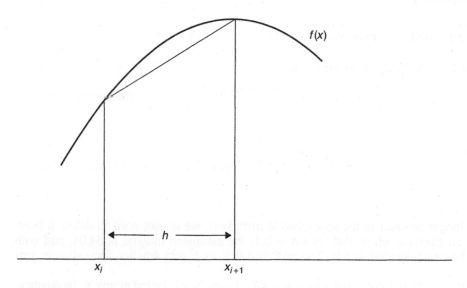

Figure 13.3 The Trapezoidal rule

where $x_i = a + ih$. Equation (13.4) is the Trapezoidal rule, and provides an estimate for the integral

$$\int_a^b f(x)\mathrm{d}x.$$

We implement the Trapezoidal rule as a method of the Function class. The integrand is then the abstract method f to be provided by a concrete subclass.

```java
public double getIntegralTrapezoidal(double a, double b, double h)
{
    double sum = 0;
    int n = (int) Math.round((b-a)/h);

    for (int i = 1; i <= n-1; i++)
        sum += f(a + i*h);

    sum = h/2*(f(a) + f(b) + 2*sum);
    return sum;
}
```

Note:

- The limits of integration a and b and the step-length h are passed to the getIntegral method.
- The user must choose h in such a way that the number of steps n will be an integer—a check for this could be built in.

Suppose we want to integrate $f(x) = x^3$ between the limits 0 and 4. Here's how to do it with the method f implemented in an anonymous class object (see Section 8.2):

```java
public class TrapTester
{
    public static void main(String[] args)
```

```
    {
        Function cubic = new Function()
        {
            public double f(double x)
            {
                return x*x*x;
            }
        };
        System.out.println("Integral = "
                            + cubic.getIntegralTrapezoidal(0,4,0.01));
    }
}
```

Note that since df is no longer abstract in the superclass Function, we do not need to define it here.

Run TrapTester as an exercise. Show that with $h = 0.1$, the estimated integral is 64.04, and with $h = 0.01$ it is 64.0004 (the exact integral is 64). You will find that as h gets smaller, the estimate gets more accurate.

This example assumes that $f(x)$ is a continuous function which may be evaluated at any x. In practice, the function could be defined at discrete points supplied as results of an experiment. For example, the speed $v(t)$ of an object might be measured every so many seconds, and one might want to estimate the distance travelled as the area under the speed-time graph. In this case, getIntegralTrapezoidal would have to be changed by replacing f with a vector of function values. This is left as an exercise for the curious.

Try Exercise 13.7.

Simpson's rule

Simpson's rule is a method of numerical integration which is a good deal more accurate than the Trapezoidal rule, and should always be used before you try anything fancier. It also divides the area under the function to be integrated, $f(x)$, into vertical strips, but instead of joining the points $f(x_i)$ with straight lines, every set of three such successive points is fitted with a parabola. To ensure that there are always an even number of panels, the step-length h is usually chosen so that there are $2n$ panels, i.e. $n = (b - a)/(2h)$.

Using the same notation as we did for the Trapezoidal rule, Simpson's rule estimates the integral as

$$S = \frac{h}{3}\left[f(a) + f(b) + 2\sum_{i=1}^{n-1} f(x_{2i}) + 4\sum_{i=1}^{n} f(x_{2i-1}) \right]. \tag{13.5}$$

Coding Simpson's rule into a new method getIntegralSimpson of Function is left as an exercise (Exercise 13.8).

If you try Simpson's rule on $f(x) = x^3$ between any limits, you will find rather surprisingly, that it gives the same result as the exact mathematical solution. This is a nice extra benefit of the rule (which can be proved mathematically): it integrates cubic polynomials exactly.

13.4 First-order differential equations

The most interesting situations in real life that we may want to model, or represent quantitatively, are usually those in which the variables change in time (e.g. biological, electrical or mechanical systems). If the changes are continuous, the system can often be represented with equations involving the derivatives of the dependent variables. Such equations are called *differential* equations. The main aim of a lot of modelling is to be able to write down a set of differential equations (DEs) that describe the system being studied as accurately as possible. Very few DEs can be solved analytically, so once again, numerical methods are required. We will consider the simplest method of numerical solution in this section: Euler's method (Euler rhymes with 'boiler'). We also consider briefly how to improve it.

Euler's method

In general we want to solve a first-order DE (strictly an ordinary DE—ODE) of the form

$$dy/dx = f(x, y), \quad y(0) \text{ given.}$$

Euler's method for solving this DE numerically consists of replacing dy/dx with its Newton quotient, so that the DE becomes

$$\frac{y(x + h) - y(x)}{h} = f(x, y).$$

After a slight rearrangement of terms, we get

$$y(x + h) = y(x) + hf(x, y). \tag{13.6}$$

Solving a DE numerically is such an important and common problem in science and engineering that it is worth introducing some general notation at this point. Suppose we want to integrate the DE over the interval $x = a$ ($a = 0$ usually) to $x = b$. We break this interval up into m steps of length h, so

$$m = (b - a)/h$$

(this is the same as the notation used in the update process of Chapter 4, except that dt used there has been replaced by the more general h here).

If we define y_i as $y(x_i)$ (the Euler estimate at the *end* of step i), where $x_i = ih$, then $y_{i+1} = y(x + h)$, at the end of step $(i + 1)$. We can then replace Equation (13.6) by the iterative scheme

$$y_{i+1} = y_i + hf(x_i, y_i), \tag{13.7}$$

where $y_0 = y(0)$. Note the striking similarity between Equation (13.7) and Equation (4.3) in Chapter 4 (**Update processes**). This similarity is no coincidence. Update processes can be modelled by DEs, and Euler's method provides an approximate solution for such DEs.

Example: bacteria growth

Suppose a colony of 1000 bacteria is multiplying at the rate of $r = 0.8$ per hour per individual (i.e. an individual produces an average of 0.8 offspring every hour). How many bacteria are there after 10 hours? Assuming that the colony grows continuously and without restriction, we can model this growth with the DE

$$dN/dt = rN, \quad N(0) = 1000, \tag{13.8}$$

where $N(t)$ is the population size at time t. This process is called *exponential growth*. Equation (13.8) may be solved analytically to give the well-known formula for exponential growth:

$$N(t) = N(0)e^{rt}.$$

To solve Equation (13.8) numerically, we apply Euler's algorithm to it to get

$$N_{i+1} = N_i + rhN_i, \tag{13.9}$$

where the initial value $N_0 = 1000$.

It is very easy to implement Euler's method. We use the two-stage process which is hopefully familiar by now:

- an abstract class (ODE) which implements Equation (13.7) in general;
- a class (Bacteria) which defines $f(x, y)$ in an anonymous class and which instantiates an ODE object to integrate itself in true OOP style.

Here is the class ODE:

```java
public abstract class ODE
{

    public abstract double f( double t, double y );

    public void solveEuler( double y0, double a, double b,
                            double h, double opint )
    // integrate from a to b, in steps of h,
    // initial value y0,
    // with results displayed at intervals of opint
    {
        int i;              // loop counter
        int m;              // number of update steps
        double t;           // current value of time

        double y = y0;
        m = (int) Math.floor((b-a)/h);
        t = a;

        if (Math.abs(Math.IEEEremainder(opint,h)) > 1e-6)
            System.out.println
                        ( "Warning: opint not an integer multiple of h!" );

        System.out.println("time    Euler");
        System.out.println(t + "   " + y0);     //initial values

        for (i = 0; i < m; i++)
        {
            y = y + h*f(t,y);
            t = t + h;
            if (Math.abs(Math.IEEEremainder(t, opint)) < 1e-6)
                System.out.println( t + "   " + y);
        }
    }

}
```

Note:

- We have used the general notation $f(x, y)$ in Equation (13.7). However, since the independent variable is more likely to be t than x, ODE uses f(t,x) to represent the right-hand side of the DE. Although t does not appear explicitly on the RHS of the DE we are solving, we nevertheless define a parameter t for the method f to make it as general as possible.
- The method solveEuler implements Euler's method over the period a to b in steps of h, with output printed every opint time units. The initial value of the solution is y0.

We now solve our problem with `Bacteria`, which defines the method `f` to return the RHS of the DE, and integrates the DE over a 10-hour period with a step-length of 0.5 hours:

```
public class Bacteria
{
  public static void main( String args[] )
  {
    ODE germ = new ODE(){
      public double f( double t, double y )
      {
        return 0.8*y;
      }
    };
    germ.solveEuler( 1000.0, 0.0, 10.0, 0.5, 0.5 );
  }
}
```

Results are shown in Table 13.1, and also in Figure 13.4. The Euler solution is not too good. In fact, the error gets worse at each step, and after 10 hours of bacteria time it is about 72%. The numerical solution will improve if we make h smaller, but there will always be some value of t where the error exceeds some acceptable limit.

In some cases, Euler's method performs better than it does here, but there are other numerical methods which always do better than Euler. Two of them are discussed below. More sophisticated methods may be found in most textbooks on numerical analysis. However, Euler's method may always be used as a first approximation as long as you realize that errors may arise.

Try Exercises 13.9 to Exercises 13.11.

A predictor-corrector method

Our first improvement on the numerical solution of the first-order DE

$$dy/dx = f(x, y), \quad y(0) \text{ given,}$$

is as follows. The Euler approximation, which we are going to denote by an asterisk, is given by

$$y_{i+1}^* = y_i + hf(x_i, y_i) \tag{13.10}$$

But this formula favours the old value of y in computing $f(x_i, y_i)$ on the right-hand side. Surely it would be better to say

$$y_{i+1}^* = y_i + h[f(x_{i+1}, y_{i+1}^*) + f(x_i, y_i)]/2, \tag{13.11}$$

Table 13.1 Bacteria growth

Time (hours)	Euler	Predictor-Corrector	Exact
0.0	1000	1000	1000
0.5	1400	1480	1492
1.0	1960	2190	2226
1.5	2744	3242	3320
2.0	3842	4798	4953
...			
5.0	28925	50422	54598
...			
8.0	217795	529892	601845
...			
10.0	836683	2542344	2980958

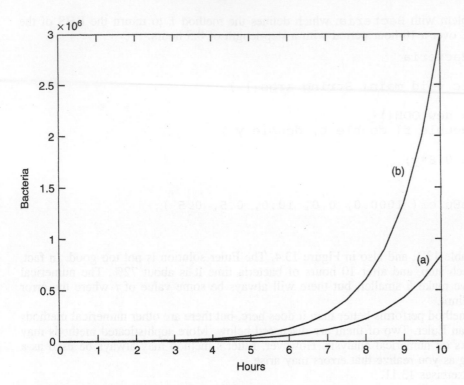

Figure 13.4 Bacteria growth: (a) Euler's method; (b) the exact solution

where $x_{i+1} = x_i + h$, since this also involves the new value y_{i+1}^* in computing f on the right-hand side? The problem of course is that y_{i+1}^* is as yet unknown, so we can't use it on the right-hand side of Equation (13.11). But we could use Euler to estimate (predict) y_{i+1}^* from Equation (13.10) and then use Equation (13.11) to correct the prediction by computing a *better* version of y_{i+1}^*, which we will call y_{i+1}. So the full procedure is:

Repeat as many times as required:
Use Euler to predict: $y_{i+1}^* = y_i + hf(x_i, y_i)$
Then correct y_{i+1}^* to: $y_{i+1} = y_i + h[f(x_{i+1}, y_{i+1}^*) + f(x_i, y_i)]/2$.

This is called a *predictor-corrector* method. We implement it with the method
solvePredictorCorrector, added to the ODE class:

```
public void solvePredictorCorrector( double y0, double a, double b,
                                     double h, double opint )
    // integrate from a to b, in steps of h,
    // initial value y0,
    // with results displayed at intervals of opint
    {
        double yEuler;  // predictor
        double yold;

        double y = y0;
        int m = (int) Math.floor((b-a)/h);  // number of update steps
```

```
    double t = a;  // current value of time

    if (Math.abs(Math.IEEEremainder(opint,h)) > 1e-6)
        System.out.println
                  ( "Warning: opint not an integer multiple of h!" );

    System.out.println("time   Predictor-Corrector");
    System.out.println(t + "   " + y0);   //initial values

    for (int i = 0; i < m; i++)
    {
        yold = y;
        yEuler = y + h*f(t,y);
        t = t + h;
        y = y + h*(f(t,yEuler) + f(t-h,yold))/2;

        if (Math.abs(Math.IEEEremainder(t, opint)) < 1e-6)
            System.out.println( t + "   " + y);
    }
}
```

Once again, the solution is obtained with Bacteria:

```
public class Bacteria
{
  public static void main( String args[] )
  {
    ODE germ = new ODE(){
      public double f( double t, double y )
      {
        return 0.8*y;
      }
    };
    germ.solvePredictorCorrector(1000.0, 0.0, 10.0, 0.5, 0.5);
  }
}
```

The worst error (Table 13.1) is now only 15%. This is much better than the uncorrected Euler solution, although there is still room for improvement.

13.5 Runge–Kutta methods

There are a variety of algorithms, under the general name of Runge–Kutta, which can be used to integrate initial-value ordinary differential equations. The *fourth-order* formulae are given below, for reference. A derivation of these and other Runge–Kutta formulae can be found in most textbooks on numerical analysis.

Runge–Kutta fourth-order formulae

The general first-order differential equation is

$$dy/dx = f(x, y), \quad y(0) \text{ given.} \tag{13.12}$$

The fourth-order Runge-Kutta estimate y^* at $x + h$ is given by

$$y^* = y + (k_1 + 2k_2 + 2k_3 + k_4)/6,$$

where

$$k_1 = hf(x, y)$$
$$k_2 = hf(x + 0.5h, y + 0.5k_1)$$
$$k_3 = hf(x + 0.5h, y + 0.5k_2)$$
$$k_4 = hf(x + h, y + k_3).$$

Systems of differential equations: a predator-prey model

The Runge-Kutta formulae may be adapted to integrate *systems* of first-order differential equations. Here we adapt the fourth-order formulae to integrate the well-known Lotka-Volterra *predator-prey* model:

$$dx/dt = px - qxy \qquad (13.13)$$
$$dy/dt = rxy - sy, \qquad (13.14)$$

where $x(t)$ and $y(t)$ are the prey and predator population sizes at time t, and p, q, r and s are biologically determined parameters. We define $f(x, y)$ and $g(x, y)$ as the right-hand sides of Equations (13.13) and (13.14) respectively. In this case, the Runge-Kutta estimates x^* and y^* at time $(t + h)$ may be found from x and y at time t with the formulae

$$x^* = x + (k_1 + 2k_2 + 2k_3 + k_4)/6$$
$$y^* = y + (m_1 + 2m_2 + 2m_3 + m_4)/6,$$

where

$$k_1 = hf(x, y)$$
$$m_1 = hg(x, y)$$
$$k_2 = hf(x + 0.5k_1, y + 0.5m_1)$$
$$m_2 = hg(x + 0.5k_1, y + 0.5m_1)$$
$$k_3 = hf(x + 0.5k_2, y + 0.5m_2)$$
$$m_3 = hg(x + 0.5k_2, y + 0.5m_2)$$
$$k_4 = hf(x + k_3, y + m_3)$$
$$m_4 = hg(x + k_3, y + m_3)$$

It should be noted that in this example x and y are the dependent variables, and t (which does *not* appear explicitly in the equations) is the independent variable. In Equation (13.12) y is the dependent variable, and x is the independent variable.

Implementation of the numerical solution

It is an interesting exercise to implement the numerical solution of the predator-prey system above, and you should try it. However, it would be more useful to implement a solution which could handle systems of any number of ODEs. In this section we look at such a solution. It is just about as simple as possible, with no 'bells and whistles' attached, in order to concentrate on the basic problem – solving a system of DEs numerically.

In Section 13.6 we present a more versatile and sophisticated version driven by a GUI.

We use our tried and trusted approach of starting with an abstract class ODESystem to implement the basic Runge–Kutta solution. The algorithm used here (Runge–Kutta–Merson) is slightly different to the one quoted in the previous section since it has been adapted to solve a general system of DEs. Here is ODESystem:

```java
import java.text.*;

/* abstract class ODESystem which implements Runge-Kutta
 * integration of a system of ODEs
 */
public abstract class ODESystem
{

    private int numVars;        //number of variables
    protected int order;        //number of DEs

    private double dt;          //step-length
    protected double [] y;      //variable list

    /* Constructor gives variables their values at initial time.
     * The number of variables is deduced from the size of the array
     * passed to the constructor.  The step length is also set
     */
    public ODESystem(double[] vars, double h)
    {
      numVars = vars.length;
      y = new double[numVars];
      for(int i=0; i< numVars; i++) y[i] = vars[i];
      dt = h;  // set the step length
    }

    /* Abstract method.  In the concrete subclass, this method
     * will return an array of the values of RHS's of the
     * differential equations given an array of variable values.
     */
    public abstract double[] diffEquns(double[] y);

    /* Fourth-order Runge-Kutta-Merson for
     *numerical integration of DEs
     */
    private void integrate()
    {
        double a [] = new double[order];
        double b [] = new double[order];
        double c [] = new double[order];
        double d [] = new double[order];
        double x [] = new double[order];
        double f [];   //RHS's of the DEs

        for (int i = 0; i < order; i++)
          x[i]= y[i];
```

```java
      f = diffEquns(y);
      for (int i = 0; i < order; i++)
      {
        a[i]= dt * f[i];
        y[i] = x[i] + a[i]/2;
      }
      f = diffEquns(y);
      for (int i = 0; i < order; i++)
      {
        b[i] = dt * f[i];
        y[i] = x[i] + b[i]/2;
      }
      f = diffEquns(y);
      for (int i = 0; i < order; i++)
      {
        c[i] = dt * f[i];
        y[i] = x[i] + c[i];
      }
      f = diffEquns(y);
      for (int i = 0; i < order; i++)
      {
        d[i] = dt * f[i];
        y[i] = x[i] + (a[i] + 2*b[i] + 2*c[i] + d[i]) / 6;
      }
  }

/* Integrates DEs and displays results on screen
 */
public void solve(double a, double b, double opInt )
{
  order = numVars;              //in general, order <= numVars

  int m = (int) Math.floor((b-a)/dt); //number of integration steps
  double t = a;                       //time

  if (Math.abs(Math.IEEEremainder(opInt,dt)) > 1e-6)
      System.out.println( "Warning: opInt not a multiple of h!" );

  //display heading:
  System.out.println( "time" );

  //display initial values:
  DecimalFormat df = new DecimalFormat( "##.##" );
  System.out.print( df.format(t) + "\t" );
  for (int i = 0; i < numVars; i++)
      System.out.print( "  " + y[i] );
  System.out.println();

  for (int i = 0; i < m; i++)     //integrate over m steps
  {
      integrate();    //perform Runge-Kutta over one step
      t += dt;
      if (Math.abs(Math.IEEEremainder(t,opInt)) < dt/1e6)
                                      // just to be sure!!
```

```
            {
                System.out.print( df.format(t) + "\t" );
                for (int j = 0; j < numVars; j++)
                    System.out.print( "   " + y[j]);
                System.out.println();
            }
        }
    }
}
```

Note:

- As before there is an abstract method, `diffEquns`, to define the DEs. However, the difference now is that the method must return the right-hand sides of a system of DEs, rather than a single DE. This is achieved by returning an *array* of values. We also have to pass an array `y` for the variables of the system.
- The data member `order` is the number of DEs in the system. This is usually the same as `numVars` (the number of dependent variables), but not always. It may, for example, be convenient to define additional variables which do not appear on the left-hand side of the DEs.
- The constructor initializes the variables from values specified in the user class (deducing the number of variables) and sets the step-length `dt`.
- The method `integrate` implements the Runge–Kutta–Merson solution over one time step `dt`. It repeatedly calls `diffEquns` to evaluate and return the right-hand sides `f` for different values of the variables `y`.
- The method `solve` integrates the DEs from time a to b, and prints the solutions every `opInt` time units.

The actual DEs to be solved (Equations 13.13 and 13.14) are defined in `PredPrey`:

```java
public class PredPrey
{
    public static void main( String args[ ] )
    {
        double[] vars = {105,8}; //initial values

        ODESystem model = new ODESystem(vars, 0.1)
        {
            public double[] diffEquns(double[] y)
            {

                //RHS of each DE with parameter values hardcoded
                double[] f = { 0.4*y[0] - 0.04*y[0]*y[1], // Eqn 13.13
                               0.02*y[0]*y[1] - 2*y[1] }; // Eqn 13.14
                return f;
            }
        };

        model.solve(0, 10, 1);
    }
}
```

Note:

- The array `vars` is initialized with the initial values of the variables.
- The array `vars` and the integration step-length are passed to the `ODESystem` constructor.

- Remember to start subscripts at 0! So, for example, y[0] represents the prey x. If your solution is wrong, the error is almost bound to be here.

Here is the output for PredPrey as it stands above, with $x(0) = 105, y(0) = 8, p = 0.4, q = 0.04, r = 0.02$ and $s = 2$:

```
time
0       105.0   8.0
1       110.91273992685059   9.47585179875486
2       108.34882117987631   11.678111115700142
3       98.70276694078372    12.594182228232588
4       90.88963237027195    11.238513732438909
5       90.20163233824925    9.186757812511289
6       95.92760383270371    7.930059573706381
7       104.61647908659504   7.965191885004757
8       110.79799353193195   9.383018234316918
9       108.67027348059051   11.58832800424867
10      99.1694184764759     12.606341988586635
```

To solve any other system of DEs, there is no need to change ODESystem. All you need to do is:

- Write a class similar to PredPrey, which initializes the variables and defines the system of DEs (take care with the subscripts!).

It would, of course, be nice to display solutions graphically: either a selection of variables plotted against time, or any two variables plotted against each other (a phase plane, or trajectory plot). These, and many other helpful features, are implemented in our general ODE solver, Driver, discussed in the next section.

Try Exercises 13.12 and 13.13.

13.6 Driver: a GUI to solve ODEs

Driver is a GUI-driven ODE solver to facilitate the implementation of models based on systems of initial value ODEs. The only coding a user needs to do is when defining the RHS of the system of ODES (see below). The example that is used to demonstrate Driver is the Lotka-Volterra predator-prey model,

$$dx/dt = px - qxy$$
$$dy/dt = rxy - sy,$$

described in Section 13.5.

In Driver terminology, x and y are referred to as 'model variables', and p, q, r and s are called 'model parameters'. Driver has one additional variable, time, and three additional parameters, dt (integration step-length), runTime (the number of step-lengths over which to run the model) and opInt (for 'output interval'—the intervals of time at which results are displayed on the screen). Driver distinguishes between 'model' variables and parameters and the other variable and parameters because of the way they are represented in the program.

Setting up a model to run with Driver

Five files (all available on our website) are required to run a model with Driver:

1. Driver.java
2. DriverGUI.java

3. `ModelDEs.java`
4. a reference file, e.g. `lotka.txt` (see below)
5. `DriverReadme.txt`.

The reference file

You need to set up a *reference file* for your model, using any text editor. The reference file contains information about the variables and parameters, and must be set up in a particular way. The reference file for the predator-prey demonstration is called `lotka.txt`, and looks as follows (explanation below it):

```
2
prey
105
pred
8
0
4
p
0.4
q
0.04
r
0.02
s
2
10
1
1
```

The first line of `lotka.txt` specifies the number of model variables (2). This is followed by the name and initial value (on separate lines) of each of the model variables. The names should be meaningful names, and should also be valid Java identifiers (i.e. start with a letter, underscore or dollar, and contain only these characters and digits). You will be able to use these names when coding the RHS of the system of DEs. The names and initial values here are `prey` (105) and `pred` (8) respectively.

Following the model variable names and initial values you must enter the initial value of `time` (0 in our example) on a separate line.

On the next line enter the number of model parameters (4).

On the following lines enter the names and values of the model parameters. In our example, these are `p` (0.4), `q` (0.04), `r` (0.02) and `s` (2) respectively.

Finally, on separate lines, enter the values of `runTime` (10), `dt` (1) and `opInt` (1).

Generating a customized `ModelDEs.java` file (the system of ODEs)

Compile `Driver.java`, `ModelDEs.java` and `DriverGUI.java` (if you have not done so already).

Run `DriverGUI.class` (`Driver.class` and the prototype `ModelDEs.class` need to be in the same folder as `DriverGUI.class`). When the GUI appears, select the **Reference file** menu and **Load** your reference file. You should see (Figure 13.5) the names and values of the variables and parameters in two drop-down lists, and the names of the variables in a third drop-down list.

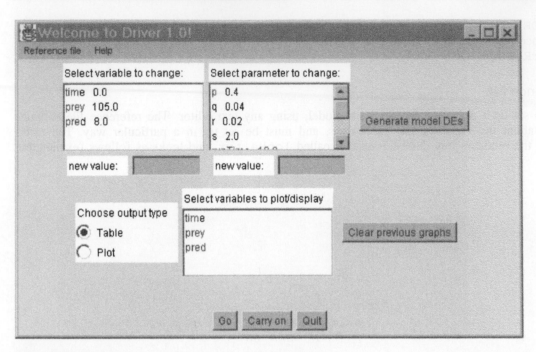

Figure 13.5 Driver running with the `lotka.txt` reference file

At this stage you can't run your model, because you haven't set up the DEs yet. Click the **Generate model DEs** button. You will be asked to enter the number of DEs in the system you wish to model, and then the right hand side of each DE. So, for our example, you would fill in 2 for the number of DEs,

```
p*prey - q*pred*prey
```

for the first DE, and

```
r*pred*prey - s*pred
```

for the second DE.

A file defining the model DEs is generated, and you are asked to save the file. The file which defines the model DEs must always be called `ModelDEs.java`. Since you need one such file for each model, it makes sense to save them all under some other names, and to copy them to `ModelDEs.java` when you want to run them. It is therefore recommended that you save your model DE file with the name `ModelDEs` but with an identifying extension, e.g. `ModelDEs.lotka`.

You now have to quit Driver. The `ModelDEs.lotka` file looks as follows:

```java
//code generated from D:\EJSE\lotka.txt
class ModelDEs extends Driver
{
    public void diffEquns( double[ ] f, double[ ] yyy )
    {
        double prey = yyy[0];
        double pred = yyy[1];
        double p = pars[0].val;
        double q = pars[1].val;
        double r = pars[2].val;
        double s = pars[3].val;
```

```
            f[0] = p*prey - q*pred*prey;
            f[1] = r*pred*prey - s*pred;

      }
   }
```

As you can see, the right hand sides of the system of ODEs has been placed in the file.

Note that the subscripts for the array f start at 0. It follows also that you should not use the name f for a model variable or parameter. If you simply have to use the name f you can change the name of the array to something else (but remember to change its name in the diffEqns argument list as well!).

Note also that this process of generating the template of the ModelDEs file for you enables you to use meaningful variable and parameter names for your DEs. Otherwise you would have to code the DEs as follows, for example:

```
      f[0] = pars[0].val*yyy[0] - pars[1].val*yyy[1]*yyy[0];
      f[1] = pars[2].val*yyy[1]*yyy[0] - pars[3].val*yyy[1];
```

(yyy is used here because y is a natural name for a model variable!)

Finally, copy your ModelDEs.xxx file to ModelDEs.java, and *recompile the new* ModelDEs.java.

You are now ready to use Driver.

Using Driver

Once you have recompiled ModelDEs.java you can run DriverGUI again. Select the reference file as before. You can now run your model. This section serves as a brief user manual for Driver.

Results can either be displayed on the screen, or plotted with Essential Grapher. Use the radio buttons to select either **Plot** or **Table** for the mode of output.

Go runs the model from the initial values of the model variables, for runTime steps of dt, giving the output as selected.

Carry on runs the model, but from the current rather than initial values of the model variables.

You can use the **Select variables to plot/display** list to select which variables you want to see in the output. In **Plot** mode, if you select time as one of the output variables, the other selected variables are plotted against time. If you do not select time, the first two of the selected variables are plotted against each other (i.e. a phase plane plot). In **Table** mode time is always displayed, whether you select it or not.

To change a parameter value or the initial value of a variable, select the item in the appropriate drop-down box and enter its new value in the corresponding textfield.

By the end of a session you may have made several changes to the reference file information. You therefore have the option of saving the changes (**Reference file/Save**).

During the session, if you have made any changes to the variables or parameters, or if any tables have been displayed, the output is echoed to a text file called OP-xxxx, where xxxx is the time of day that the file was created. When you exit the session, you will be asked whether you want to retain or delete this file.

Help/Instructions for use displays the file DriverReadme.txt (which must be in the same folder as all the other Driver files) in a frame. The lines in this file have to be 70 or less columns in length for them to be automatically displayed in the frame (i.e. without having to use the horizontal scrollbar). DriverReadme.txt contains the text in this section up to the end of the previous sentence.

If you run Driver with the predator-prey model as set up here **Table** output should give you output similar to that of PredPreyTester at the end of Section 13.5. **Plot** output is shown in Figure 13.6.

Chaos

The reason that weather prediction is so difficult and forecasts are so erratic is no longer thought to be the complexity of the system but the nature of the DEs modelling it. These DEs belong to a class referred to

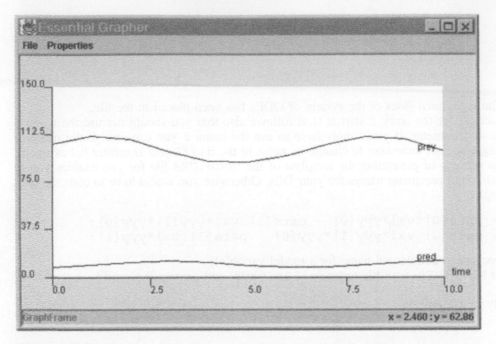

Figure 13.6 Plot output from Driver running with the `lotka.txt` reference file

as *chaotic*. Such equations will produce wildly different results when their initial conditions are changed infinitesimally. In other words, accurate weather prediction depends crucially on the accuracy of the measurements of the initial conditions.

Edward Lorenz, a research meteorologist, discovered this phenomenon in 1961. Although his original equations are far too complex to consider here, the following much simpler system has the same essential chaotic features:

$$dx/dt = 10(y - x), \tag{13.15}$$
$$dy/dt = -xz + 28x - y, \tag{13.16}$$
$$dz/dt = xy - 8z/3. \tag{13.17}$$

This system of DEs may be solved very easily with Driver. The idea is to solve the DEs with certain initial conditions, plot the solution, then change the initial conditions very slightly, and superimpose the new solution over the old one to see how much it has changed. Proceed as follows.

1. Begin by solving the system with the initial conditions $x(0) = -2$, $y(0) = -3.5$ and $z(0) = 21$, over a period of 10 time units, with `dt = 0.01`.

   Set up a reference file, `lorenz.txt`, which should look more-or-less like this:

   ```
   3
   x
   -2.0
   y
   -3.5
   z
   21.0
   0.0
   0
   1000.0
   ```

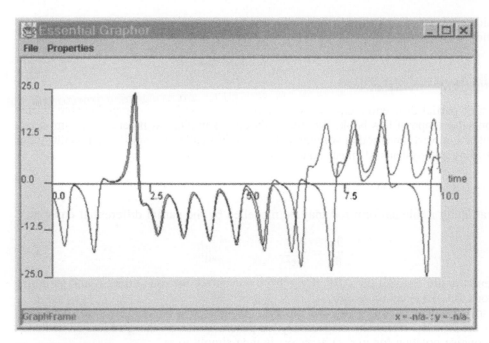

Figure 13.7 Chaos?

```
0.01
1.0
```

Generate the ModelDEs file in the usual way.

Plot y only against time (set the vertical axis limits on the graph to about −25 and 25). You should get one of the plots shown in Figure 13.7.

2. Now we can see the effect of changing the initial values. Let's just change the initial value of $x(0)$, from −2 to −2.04—that's a change of only 2%, and in only one of the three initial values. Plot y against time again for this new initial condition, superimposing the new plot over the old one.

You should see (Figure 13.7) that the two graphs are practically indistinguishable until t is about 1.5. The discrepancy grows quite gradually, until t reaches about 6, when the solutions suddenly and shockingly flip over in opposite directions. As t increases further, the new solution bears no resemblance to the old one.

3. Now clear the graphs and solve the system (13.15)–(13.17) with the original initial values but over 20 time steps (runTime = 2000). Plot y against time as before.

Change dt to 0.005 (and runTime to 4000) and superimpose the graph of y against time again.

This time you will see the two plots deviating after about 15 time units. The initial conditions are the same—the only difference is the size of dt.

The explanation is that the Runge-Kutta formulae have numerical inaccuracies (if one could compare them with the exact solution—which incidentally can't be found). These numerical inaccuraces differ with the size of dt. This difference has the same effect as starting the numerical solution with very slightly different initial values.

How do we ever know when we have the 'right' numerical solution to a chaotic system? Well, we don't—the best we can do is increase the accuracy of the numerical method until no further wild changes occur over the interval of interest.

So beware: 'chaotic' DEs are very tricky to solve!

Incidentally, if you want to see the famous 'butterfly' picture of chaos, just plot x against z as time increases (the resulting graph is called a *phase plane* plot). What you will see is a 2-D projection of the *trajectory*, i.e. the solution developing in time. (You will need to change to change the axis limits so that $-20 \le x \le 20$ and $0 \le z \le 50$.)

13.7 A partial differential equation

The numerical solution of partial differential equations (PDEs) is a vast subject, a comprehensive discussion of which is beyond the scope of this book. We give only one example, but it serves two important purposes. It demonstrates a powerful method of solving a class of PDEs called *parabolic*. It also illustrates a method of solving tridiagonal systems of linear equations.

Heat conduction

The conduction of heat along a thin uniform rod may be modelled by the partial differential equation

$$\frac{\partial u}{\partial t} = \frac{\partial^2 u}{\partial x^2}, \tag{13.18}$$

where $u(x, t)$ is the temperature distribution a distance x from one end of the rod at time t, and assuming that no heat is lost from the rod along its length.

Half the battle in solving PDEs is mastering the notation. We set up a rectangular grid, with steplengths of h and k in the x and t directions respectively. A general point on the grid has co-ordinates $x_i = ih$, $y_j = jk$. A concise notation for $u(x, t)$ at x_i, y_j is then simply $u_{i,j}$.

Truncated Taylor series may then be used to approximate the PDE by a *finite difference scheme*. The left-hand side of Equation (13.18) is usually approximated by a *forward difference*:

$$\frac{\partial u}{\partial t} = \frac{u_{i,j+1} - u_{i,j}}{k}$$

One way of approximating the right-hand side of Equation (13.18) is by the scheme

$$\frac{\partial^2 u}{\partial x^2} = \frac{u_{i+1,j} - 2u_{i,j} + u_{i-1,j}}{h^2}. \tag{13.19}$$

This leads to a scheme, which although easy to compute, is only conditionally stable.

If, however, we replace the right-hand side of the scheme in Equation (13.19) by the mean of the finite difference approximation on the jth and $(j+1)$th time rows, we get (after a certain amount of algebra!) the following scheme for Equation (13.18):

$$-ru_{i-1,j+1} + (2 + 2r)u_{i,j+1} - ru_{i+1,j+1} = ru_{i-1,j} + (2 - 2r)u_{i,j} + ru_{i+1,j}, \tag{13.20}$$

where $r = k/h^2$. This is known as the Crank-Nicolson *implicit* method, since it involves the solution of a system of simultaneous equations, as we shall see.

To illustrate the method numerically, let's suppose that the rod has a length of 1 unit, and that its ends are in contact with blocks of ice, i.e. the *boundary conditions* are

$$u(0, t) = u(1, t) = 0. \tag{13.21}$$

Suppose also that the initial temperature (*initial condition*) is

$$u(x, 0) = \begin{cases} 2x, & 0 \le x \le 1/2, \\ 2(1 - x), & 1/2 \le x \le 1. \end{cases} \tag{13.22}$$

(this situation could come about by heating the centre of the rod for a long time, with the ends kept in contact with the ice, removing the heat source at time $t = 0$.) This particular problem has symmetry about the line $x = 1/2$; we exploit this now in finding the solution.

If we take $h = 0.1$ and $k = 0.01$, we will have $r = 1$, and Equation (13.20) becomes

$$-u_{i-1,j+1} + 4u_{i,j+1} - u_{i+1,j+1} = u_{i-1,j} + u_{i+1,j}. \tag{13.23}$$

Putting $j = 0$ in Equation (13.23) generates the following set of equations for the unknowns $u_{i,1}$ (i.e. after one time step k) up to the midpoint of the rod, which is represented by $l = 5$, i.e. $x = ih = 0.5$. The subscript $j = 1$ has been dropped for clarity:

$$0 + 4u_1 - u_2 = 0 + 0.4$$

$$-u_1 + 4u_2 - u_3 = 0.2 + 0.6$$

$$-u_2 + 4u_3 - u_4 = 0.4 + 0.8$$

$$-u_3 + 4u_4 - u_5 = 0.6 + 1.0$$

$$-u_4 + 4u_5 - u_6 = 0.8 + 0.8.$$

Symmetry then allows us to replace u_6 in the last equation by u_4. These equations can be written in matrix form as

$$\begin{bmatrix} 4 & -1 & 0 & 0 & 0 \\ -1 & 4 & -1 & 0 & 0 \\ 0 & -1 & 4 & -1 & 0 \\ 0 & 0 & -1 & 4 & -1 \\ 0 & 0 & 0 & -2 & 4 \end{bmatrix} \begin{bmatrix} u_1 \\ u_2 \\ u_3 \\ u_4 \\ u_5 \end{bmatrix} = \begin{bmatrix} 0.4 \\ 0.8 \\ 1.2 \\ 1.6 \\ 1.6 \end{bmatrix}. \tag{13.24}$$

The matrix (**A**) on the left of Equations (13.24) is known as a *tridiagonal* matrix. Such a matrix can be represented by three one-dimensional arrays: one for each diagonal. The system can then be solved very efficiently by Gauss *elimination*, which will not be explained here but simply presented in the working program below. Having solved for the $u_{i,1}$ we can then put $j = 1$ in Equation (13.23) and proceed to solve for the $u_{i,2}$, and so on.

Care needs to be taken when constructing the matrix **A**. The following notation is often used:

$$\mathbf{A} = \begin{bmatrix} b_1 & c_1 & & & \\ a_2 & b_2 & c_2 & & \\ & a_3 & b_3 & c_3 & \\ & & & \cdots & \\ & & a_{n-1} & b_{n-1} & c_{n-1} \\ & & & a_n & b_n \end{bmatrix}. \tag{13.25}$$

Take careful note of the subscripts!

The following program (`HeatConductor`) implements the Crank-Nicolson method as a stand-alone solution for this particular problem, over 10 time steps of $k = 0.01$. The step-length h is specified by $h = 1/(2n)$, where **A** is $n \times n$, because of the symmetry. r is therefore not restricted to the value 1, although it takes this value here.

The one-dimensional arrays a, b and c represent the three diagonals of **A**. The program's subscripts are consistent with the subscripts used in Equation (13.25). Consequently, most of the arrays have some unused elements. For example, elements a[0] and a[1] are never used, since the first subscript of a in Equation (13.25) is 2. As a result of this some unnecessary assignments are made in the first `for` loop. The alternative to wasting a few bytes is to get hopelessly tangled up in a forest of subscripts!

```java
import java.text.*;
public class HeatConductor
{

    public void solveCrankNicolson()
```

```
{
    int n = 5;      //size of matrix A
    double [] a = new double[n+1];  //diagonal a
    double [] b = new double[n+1];  //diagonal b
    double [] c = new double[n+1];  //diagonal c
    double [] u = new double[n+2];  //initial conditions
    double [] g = new double[n+1];  //RHS of Eqn 13.20
    double [] ux = new double[n+1]; //solution

    //most elements subscripted 0 are unnecessary
    double k = 0.01;
    double h = 1.0 / (2 * n);          // symmetry assumed
    double r = k / (h * h);

    //some elements at either end of arrays are assigned unnecessarily
    for (int i = 1; i <= n; i++)
    {
        a[i] = -r;
        b[i] = 2 + 2 * r;
        c[i] = -r;
    }

    a[n] = -2 * r;                  // from symmetry

    //print initial conditions
    for (int i = 0; i <= n; i++)
        u[i] = 2 * i * h;

    u[n+1] = u[n-1];
    double t = 0;
    DecimalFormat df = new DecimalFormat( "0.0000" );
    System.out.print( "   x =" );        // headings

    for (int i = 1; i <= n; i++)
        System.out.print( "   " + df.format(i * h) );

    System.out.print( "\nt\n" );
    System.out.print( df.format(t) );

    for (int i = 1; i <= n; i++)          // initial conditions
        System.out.print( "   " + df.format(u[i]) );

    System.out.print( "\n" );

    // solution will be in ux
    for (int j = 1; j <= 10; j++)
    {
        t += 0.01;
```

```
            for (int i = 1; i <= n; i++)
                g[i] = r * (u[i-1] + u[i+1]) + (2 - 2 * r) * u[i];

        ux = solveTriDiag( a, b, c, g, n );
        System.out.print( df.format(t) );

        for (int i = 1; i <= n; i++)
            System.out.print( "   " + df.format(ux[i]) );

        System.out.print( "\n" );

        for (int i = 1; i <= n; i++)  // get ready for next round
            u[i] = ux[i];

        u[n+1] = u[n-1];
    }
}

public static double[] solveTriDiag( double a[ ], double b[ ],
                        double c[ ], double g[ ], int n )
{
    int j;
    double d;
    double [] w = new double[n+1];   // working space
    double [] x = new double[n+1];   // solution

    for (int i = 1; i <= n; i++)
        w[i] = b[i];

    for (int i = 2; i <= n; i++)
    {
        d = a[i] / w[i-1];
        w[i] = w[i] - c[i-1] * d;
        g[i] = g[i] - g[i-1] * d;
    }

    x[n] = g[n] / w[n];     // start back-substitution

    for (int i = 1; i <= n-1; i++)
    {
        j = n-i;
        x[j] = (g[j] - c[j] * x[j+1]) / w[j];
    }

    //solution is in x
    return x;
}

public static void main( String[] args )
```

```
{
    HeatConductor hc = new HeatConductor();
    hc.solveCrankNicolson();
}

}
```

In the following output the first column is time, and subsequent columns are the solutions at intervals h along the rod:

```
x =  0.1000  0.2000  0.3000  0.4000  0.5000
t
0.0000  0.2000  0.4000  0.6000  0.8000  1.0000
0.0100  0.1989  0.3956  0.5834  0.7381  0.7691
0.0200  0.1936  0.3789  0.5397  0.6461  0.6921
0.0300  0.1826  0.3515  0.4902  0.5843  0.6152
0.0400  0.1683  0.3218  0.4461  0.5267  0.5555
0.0500  0.1538  0.2932  0.4047  0.4770  0.5019
0.0600  0.1399  0.2664  0.3672  0.4321  0.4546
0.0700  0.1270  0.2418  0.3330  0.3916  0.4119
0.0800  0.1153  0.2193  0.3019  0.3550  0.3733
0.0900  0.1045  0.1989  0.2738  0.3219  0.3385
0.1000  0.0948  0.1803  0.2482  0.2918  0.3069
```

Note that the method solveTriDiag() can be used to solve any tridiagonal system. It has been made static so that it can be moved to a more general home in a numerical methods package.

Summary

- A numerical method is an approximate computer method for solving a mathematical problem which often has no analytical solution.
- A numerical method is subject to two distinct types of error: rounding error in the computer solution, and *truncation error*, where an infinite mathematical process, like taking a limit, is approximated by a finite process.
- A numerical method can often be implemented perfectly generally as an abstract class. The details of the mathematical functions required to solve a particular problem can then be supplied by means of inheritance, without tampering with the abstract superclass.

Exercises

13.1 Try using Newton's method to solve $x^3 + x - 3 = 0$ for some different initial values of x_0 to see whether the algorithm always converges.

13.2 If you have a sense of history, use Newton's method to find a root of $x^3 - 2x - 5 = 0$. This is the example used when the algorithm was first presented to the French Academy.

13.3 Try to find a *non-zero* root of $2x = \tan(x)$, using Newton's method. You might have some trouble with this one. If you do, you will have discovered the one serious problem with Newton's method: it converges to a root only if the starting guess is 'close enough'. Since 'close enough' depends on the nature of $f(x)$ and on the root, one can obviously get into difficulties here. The only remedy is some intelligent trial-and-error work on the initial guess—this

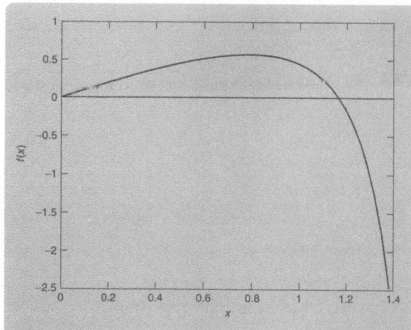

Figure 13.8 $f(x) = 2x - \tan(x)$

is made considerably easier by plotting $f(x)$ (see Figure 13.8). (The derivative of $\tan(x)$ is $\sec^2(x)$. See Section 13.2 on how to estimate a derivative numerically.)

13.4 Write programs which use the class `Function` to solve the following with Newton's method (you may have to experiment a bit with the starting values).

   Hint: It may help to use Essential Grapher to get an idea of where the roots are.

   (a) $x^4 - x = 10$ (two real roots and two complex roots)
   (b) $e^{-x} = \sin x$ (infinitely many roots)
   (c) $x^3 - 8x^2 + 17x - 10 = 0$ (three real roots)
   (d) $\log x = \cos x$
   (e) $x^4 - 5x^3 - 12x^2 + 76x - 79 = 0$ (four real roots)

13.5 Use the Bisection method to find the square root of 2, taking 1 and 2 as initial values of x_L and x_R. Continue bisecting until the maximum error is less than 0.05 (use Inequality (13.2) of Section 13.1 to determine how many bisections are needed).

13.6 Add a new method `getRootBisection` to the `Function` class of Section 13.1 to implement the Bisection method.
   Test it on $x^3 + x - 3 = 0$.

13.7 Use the Trapezoidal rule to evaluate $\int_0^4 x^2 dx$, using a step length of $h = 1$.

13.8 The luminous efficiency (ratio of the energy in the visible spectrum to the total energy) of a black body radiator may be expressed as a percentage by the formula

$$E = 64.77 T^{-4} \int_{4 \times 10^{-5}}^{7 \times 10^{-5}} x^{-5} (e^{1.432/Tx} - 1)^{-1} dx,$$

where T is the absolute temperature in degrees Kelvin, x is the wavelength in cm, and the range of integration is over the visible spectrum.
   Write a new method `getIntegralSimpson` of the `Function` class to implement Simpson's rule as given in Equation (13.5).

Taking $T = 3500°$K, use simp to compute E, firstly with 10 intervals ($n = 5$), and then with 20 intervals ($n = 10$), and compare your results.
(Answers: 14.512725% for $n = 5$; 14.512667% for $n = 10$)

13.9 Use Euler's method to solve the bacteria growth DE (13.8), comparing the Euler solutions for $dt = 0.5$ and 0.05 with the exact solution. You should get results like this (after a bit of cut-and-paste):

time	dt = 0.5	dt = 0.05	exact
0	1000.00	1000.00	1000.00
0.50	1400.00	1480.24	1491.82
1.00	1960.00	2191.12	2225.54
...			
5.00	28925.47	50504.95	54598.15

13.10 A human population of 1000 at time $t = 0$ grows at a rate given by

$$dN/dt = aN,$$

where $a = 0.025$ per person per year. Use Euler's method to project the population over the next 30 years, working in steps of (a) $h = 2$ years, (b) $h = 1$ year and (c) $h = 0.5$ years. Compare your answers with the exact mathematical solution.

13.11 The springbok (a species of small buck, not rugby players!) population $x(t)$ in the Kruger National Park in South Africa may be modelled by the equation

$$dx/dt = (r - bx \sin at)x,$$

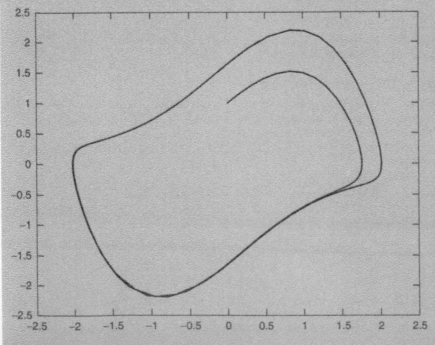

Figure 13.9 A trajectory of Van der Pol's equation

where r, b, and a are constants. Write a program which reads values for r, b, and a, and initial values for x and t, and which uses Euler's method to compute the impala population at monthly intervals over a period of two years.

13.12 The basic equation for modelling radio-active decay is

$$dx/dt = -rx,$$

where x is the amount of the radio-active substance at time t, and r is the decay rate.

Some radio-active substances decay into other radio-active substances, which in turn also decay. For example, Strontium 92 ($r_1 = 0.256$ per hr) decays into Yttrium 92 ($r_2 = 0.127$ per hr), which in turn decays into Zirconium. Write down a pair of differential equations for Strontium and Yttrium to describe what is happening.

Starting at $t = 0$ with 5×10^{26} atoms of Strontium 92 and none of Yttrium, use the Runge-Kutta formulae to solve the equations up to $t = 8$ hours in steps of $1/3$ hr. Also use Euler's method for the same problem, and compare your results.

13.13 Van der Pol's equation is a second-order non-linear differential equation which may be expressed as two first-order equations as follows:

$$dx_1/dt = x_2$$
$$dx_2/dt = \epsilon(1 - x_1^2)x_2 - b^2 x_1.$$

The solution of this system has a stable limit cycle, which means that if you plot the phase trajectory of the solution (the plot of x_1 against x_2) starting at any point in the positive $x_1 - x_2$ plane, it always moves continuously into the same closed loop. Use the Runge-Kutta formulae (or Driver) to solve this system numerically, for $x_1(0) = 0$, and $x_2(0) = 1$. Draw some phase trajectories for $b = 1$ and ϵ ranging between 0.01 and 1.0. Figure 13.9 shows you what to expect.

Appendix A
Keywords

The following keywords in Java are reserved and may not be used as names.

abstract	do	implements	private	throw
boolean	double	import	protected	throws
break	else	instanceof	public	transient
byte	extends	int	return	true
case	false	interface	short	try
catch	final	long	static	void
char	finally	native	super	volatile
class	float	new	switch	while
continue	for	null	synchronized	
default	if	package	this	

Appendix B
Operators

Operator precedence and evaluation order are set out in the following table.

Level	Operators	Evaluation order
1.	( ) [ ] . (member selection)	left to right
2.	++ -- + - ! (NOT) (*type*)	right to left
3.	* / % (modulus)	left to right
4.	+ -	left to right
5.	< <= > >=	left to right
6.	== (equals) != (not equals)	left to right
7.	^ (logical exclusive OR)	left to right
8.	&& (logical AND)	left to right
9.	|| (logical OR)	left to right
10.	= += -= *= /= ...	right to left

Note:

- The operators + and - at level 2 are unary, while at level 4 they are binary.
- Parentheses always have the highest precedence.

Appendix C
Syntax quick reference

The following sections give examples of code segments to serve as a quick reference for Java syntax.

Angle brackets indicate something which is not to be coded literally but which represents a statement, an expression, or a condition, e.g. `<statement1>`.

C.1 Primitive type declarations

```
char c;                 //character

final float g = 9.8;    //can't be changed

double y;               //+-4.9e-324 to +-1.8e308; 18 figures

double x = 1e-6;        //initialize

float x;                //+-1.4e-45 to +-3.4e38; 9 figures

float y = 23.45f;       //initialize and cast from double

int i;                  //-2147483648 to 2147483647

long k;          //-9223372036854775808 to 9223372036854775807
```

C.2 Methods

```
/* methodName : takes an int and a double as arguments and
 * returns a double
 */
public double methodName( int i, double x ) { ... }

public double [ ] methodName( ... )
                                //returns an array of doubles
```

```
public static void main( String[ ] args )
                                    //called when program runs

private boolean methodName( double[ ] list )
    //takes an array of doubles as argument and returns a boolean

public void methodName()              //no arguments or return type
```

C.3   Classes

```
import essential.*;        //if necessary
public class MyClass {     //save file as MyClass.java
    private double x;
    private int m;

    //default constructor (note: no return type)
    public MyClass()
    {
        x = 0; m = -23;
    }

    //parameterized constructor (note: no return type)
    public MyClass( double x, int m )
    {
        this.x = x; this.m = m;
    }

    public double getX()
    {
        return x;
    }

    public void setX( double x )
    {
        this.x = x;
    }

    public static void main(String[ ] args)
    {
        MyClass myObj = new MyClass( -1.5, 13 );
        System.out.println( myObj.getX() );
    }
}
```

C.4   Decisions

```
if (i == 1)                //equals
    <statement>;
```

```
if (i != 2)                    //not equals
  <statement>;

if ((i < 2) && (j > 3))        //AND
{
  <statement1>;
  <statement2>;
}

if ((i < 1) || (x == 3))       //OR
  <statement>;

if (x >= 0)
  doThis();                    //semi-colon please
else
  doThat();

if (!finished)                 //finished is boolean
  <statement>;

if (<condition1>) {            //if-else-if ladder
  <statement1>;
  <statement2>;
}
else if (<condition2>) {
  <statement3>;
  <statement4>;
}
...
else {
  <statementi>;
  <statementj>;
}

switch (<expression>)   //expression must be int or char
{
  case 'a':
    doThis();
    break;
  case 'b':
  case 'c':
    doTheOther();
    break;
  default:
    doNothing();
}
```

C.5 Loops

```
while (<condition>)
{
  <statement1>;
```

```
    <statement2>;
    ...
}

do {
    <statement1>;
    <statement2>;

    ...
} while ( <condition> )

for (int i = 1; i <= n; i++) //absolutely no semi-colon here!
{
    <statement1>;
    <statement2>;
    ...;
}
```

Appendix D
Solutions to selected exercises

Chapter 1

1.1
```java
public class Stars
{
   public static void main(String[] args)
   {
     System.out.println("Stars");
     System.out.println("*****");
     System.out.println("The End");
   }
}
```

1.3
```java
import essential.*;

public class RequestName
{
   public static void main(String[] args)
   {
     System.out.print("Please enter your surname: ");
     String surname = Keyboard.readLine();
     System.out.print("Please enter your first name: ");
     String firstName = Keyboard.readLine();
     System.out.println(firstName + " " + surname);
   }
}
```

1.5
```java
import essential.*;

public class MultiplyWholeNumbers
{
   public static void main(String[] args)
   {
     System.out.print("Please enter first whole number: ");
     int firstNum = Keyboard.readInt();
     System.out.print("Please enter second whole number: ");
     int secondNum = Keyboard.readInt();
     System.out.println(firstNum*secondNum);
   }
}
```

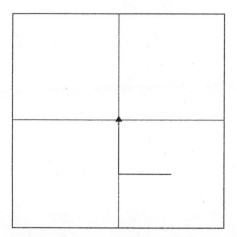

Figure D.1 Output from running `TurtleEx1.java`

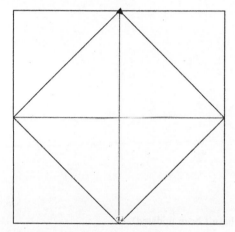

Figure D.2 Output from running `TurtleEx3.java`

1.7   The output is shown in Figure D.1.

1.9   The output is shown in Figure D.2.

1.11
```java
import essential.*;

public class Graph1
{
  public static void main(String[] args)
  {
    Graph g = new Graph();
    g.addPoint(0, 0);
    g.addPoint(0.5, 3);
    g.addPoint(1, 4);
    g.addPoint(2, 4.5);
    g.addPoint(5, 4.8);

    g.setAxes(0, 6, 0, 5);
  }
}
```

1.12
```
import essential.*;

public class Graph2
{
    public static void main(String[] args)
    {
     /* calculated 2 points by substituting
      * 5 and -5 as x values into the equation
      */

        Graph g = new Graph();
        g.addPoint(-5, -13);
        g.addPoint(5, 7);

        g.setAxes(-10, 10, -15, 15);
    }

}
```

Chapter 2

2.1   (a) Prints out

```
New balance: 1090.0
```

(b) Prints out

```
New balance: 2180.0
```

Interest has been calculated on the new balance of 2000.

(c) Prints out

```
New balance: 2000.0
```

The original balance has not had the interest added to it (i.e. it hasn't been updated).

(d)
```
public class CompInt
{
    public static void main(String[] args)
    {
        double original_balance, new_balance, interest, rate;
        /* have 2 variables to hold the original balance
           and the new balance, instead of 1 variable for balance*/
        original_balance = 2000;
        rate = 0.09;
        interest = rate * original_balance;
        new_balance = original_balance + interest;
        System.out.println("Original balance: " + original_balance +
                            " and New balance: " + new_balance);
    }
}
```

2.2   In scientific notation: `1.234e5`, `-8.765e-4`, `1e-15`, `-1e12`

2.3   Constants not acceptable in Java:
(a) `9,87`: a decimal point is represented by a dot and not a comma.
(e) `3.57*E2`: Java does not accept scientific notation with * before the E.
(f) `3.57E2.1`: the exponent must be a whole number.
(h) `3,57E-2`: the same reasoning as for (a).

2.4   Identifiers not acceptable in Java:
  (b) a.2: dot is not acceptable as part of an identifier.
  (c) 2a: an identifier cannot begin with a digit.
  (d) 'a'one: apostrophe is not acceptable as part of an identifier.
  (h) pay day: identifiers must be single words.
  (i) U.S.S.R: same reason as (b).
  (k) min*2: * cannot be used in an identifier.
  (l) native: is a keyword in Java, and therefore cannot be an identifier.

2.5   7, 3, 4, 2, 1, 64.0, 0, 2, 5.0

2.6
```
float a = 1f/(2*3);
double b = Math.pow(2, 2*3);
double c = 1.5e-4 + 2.5e-2;
double d = Math.sqrt(2);
float e = (3f+4)/(5+6);
float f = (5+3)/(5f*3);
double g = Math.pow(2, Math.pow(3,2));
double h = Math.pow(2*Math.PI, 2);
double i = 2*Math.pow(Math.PI, 2);
double j = 1/(Math.sqrt(2*Math.PI));
double k = 1/(2*Math.sqrt(Math.PI));
double l = Math.pow(2.3*4.5, 1/3f);
double m = (1-(2f/(3+2)))/(1+(2f/(3-2)));
double n = 1000*Math.pow(1+(0.15/12), 60);
double o = (1.23e-5 + 5.678e-3)*0.4567e-4;
```

  (a) 0.16666667
  (b) 64.0
  (c) 0.025150000000000002
  (d) 1.4142135623730951
  (e) 0.6363636
  (f) 0.53333336
  (g) 512.0
  (h) 39.47841760435743
  (i) 19.739208802178716
  (j) 0.3989422804014327
  (k) 0.28209479177387814
  (l) 2.179282141726763
  (m) 0.20000000298023224
  (n) 2107.1813469512354
  (o) 2.59876001E-7

2.7   11.0, 16.0, 1.2, 0.3, 0.33333334, 0.0, 3.0, 0.0, division by zero, 0.0

2.8
  (a) p + (w/u)
  (b) p + (w/(u+v))
  (c) (p+(w/(u+v)))/(p+(w/(u-v)))
  (d) Math.sqrt(x)
  (e) Math.pow(y, y+z)
  (f) Math.pow(x, Math.pow(y, z))
  (g) Math.pow(Math.pow(x, y), z)
  (h) x - (Math.pow(x, 3)/(3*2*1)) + (Math.pow(x, 5)/(5*4*3*2*1))

2.9
```
public class CelsiusToFahrenheit
{
    public static void main(String[] args)
    {
        float C = 37;        //normal human temperature in Celsius
```

```
                float F = (9*C)/5 + 32;
                System.out.println("Normal human temperature in Fahrenheit: "
                                    + F + " degrees");
            }
        }
```

2.10 (a) 20.1168 metres, (b) 165.195 pounds, (c) 72.62 pounds, (d) 176.4 km/hr, (e) 275.716 kPa, (f) 1493.786 calories. Code for (a):

```
public class YardsToMetres
{
    public static void main(String[] args)
    {
        int x = 22;                 //yards
        double m = 0.9144 * x;   //metres
        /*
            one yard = 36 inches = (36 x 2.54) cm
            but one metre = 0.01cm
            so 2.54cm = 0.0254 metres
            so one yard = (36 x 0.0254) metres
                        = 0.9144 metres
        */

        System.out.println(x + " yards = " + m + " metres");
    }
}
```

2.11 (a) i += 1;
     (b) i = i*i*i + j;
     (c) x = (a + b)/(c * d);

2.12 (a) The left hand side of an expression statement should have a single variable—this one has two operands and an operator.
     (b) The variable on the left hand side should be one word. Alternatively, the variable on the left hand side should be of type `double`, not `Fahrenheit`.
     (c) Variable should be on left hand side.

2.13 ...
     ```
     int a = 2, b = -10, c = 12;
     double x = (-b + Math.sqrt(b*b - 4*a*c))/(2*a);
     ```

2.14 ...
     ```
     double E = 2;
     double R = 5;
     double C = 10;
     double L = 4;
     double omega = 2;
     double intermediate_expr = (2*Math.PI*omega*L -
                                 (1/(2*Math.PI*omega*C)));
     double I = E/(Math.sqrt(R*R +
                 intermediate_expr*intermediate_expr));
     ```

2.15 ...
     ```
     double gallons = 2.5;  //2 gallons and 4 pints
     double litres = (gallons * 8)/1.76;
                     //times 8 for pints, divide 1.76 for litres
     ```

2.16   ...
```
System.out.println("Please enter distance in kilometres (e.g. 100)");
double distance = Keyboard.readDouble();
System.out.println("Please enter petrol used in litres (e.g. 10.34)");
double petrol = Keyboard.readDouble();

double km_per_litre = distance/petrol;
double litres_per_100km = petrol/(distance/100);

System.out.println("Distance \t\tLitres used \t\tkm/L \t\tL/100km");
System.out.print(distance + "\t\t\t" + petrol + "\t\t\t");
System.out.print((double)Math.round(100*km_per_litre)/100 + "\t\t");
System.out.println((double)Math.round(100*litres_per_100km)/100);
    //use Math.round in this way to print out 2 decimal points
```

2.17
```
int a = 1;
int b = 2;

int t;                  //temporary variable

t = a;                  //store a in temp
a = b;                  //make a equal to be
b = t;                  //make b equal to t (which contains a)
```

2.18
```
int a = 3;
int b = 4;

a = a - b;
b = b + a;
a = b - a;
```

2.19
```
double r = 0.15;
double L = 50000;
double N = 20;

double intermediate_expr = Math.pow(1 + r/12, 12*N);

double P = (r*L*intermediate_expr)/(12*(intermediate_expr - 1));

System.out.println("P: $" + (double)Math.round(100*P)/100);
```

2.20
```
double P = 800;
double r = 0.15;
double L = 50000;

double numerator = Math.log(P/(P - (r*L)/12));
double denominator = 12*Math.log(1 + r/12);

double N = numerator/denominator;
```

2.21   x = 2.08333...
       a = 4.

2.22
```
int i = 1;
double a = 0, x = 0;
```

```
        for (int iter = 1; iter <= 4; iter++)
        {
            a = a + i;
            x = x + i/a;
        }
```

2.23   Output is 2.9226. Limit is π.

2.26
```
        double sum = 0;
        int num_students = 10;

        FileIO f1 = new FileIO("marks.txt", FileIO.READING);

        for (int i = 1; i <= num_students; i++)
        {
            double mark = f1.readDouble();
            sum += mark;
        }

        double average = sum/num_students;
```

2.27
```
        double x;
        x = Math.random();

        if (x < 0.67)        //this will occur 2 thirds of the time
            System.out.println( "Heads" );
        else                 //this will occur 1 third of the time
            System.out.println( "Tails" );
```

2.32
```
        DecimalFormat df = new DecimalFormat("#.00");

        double balance = 100000;

        double interest_rate = 0;

        double deposit = 1000;

        System.out.println("Month\t\tInterest Rate\tInterest\tBalance");
        System.out.println();

        for (int i = 1; i <= 12; i++)
        {
          if (balance <= 110000)
          {
              interest_rate = 0.01;
          }
          else if (balance <= 125000)
          {
              interest_rate = 0.015;
          }
          else if (balance > 125000)
          {
              interest_rate = 0.02;
          }

          double interest = balance*interest_rate;   //calculate interest
          balance += interest;             //add interest to balance
          balance += deposit;              //deposit made at end of month
```

```
        System.out.print(i + "\t\t" + interest_rate);
        System.out.println("\t\t$ " + df.format(interest) + "\t$ " +
                        df.format(balance));
    }
```

2.33
```
    int k = 30;      // number of terms
    double a = 10;
    double x = 1;

    for (int n = 1; n <= k; n++)
    {
        x = a * x / n;

        if (n%10 == 0)   //n%10 is n modulus 10 i.e. remainder of n/10
        {   //if n/10 has no remainder, n is divisible by 10
            System.out.println( n + "   " + x );
        }
    }//end for
```

2.34   true, false, true, false, true (false || true gives true)

2.36   (b)
```
    for (char c = 'z'; c >= 'a'; c--)
    {
        System.out.println(c);
    }
```

2.37
```
    for (int line = 1; line <= 20; line++)
    {
        for (int letter = 1; letter <= 60; letter++)
        {
            char c = (char)(97 + (Math.random() * 26));
            System.out.print(c);
        }//end inner for

        System.out.println();
    }//end outer for
```

2.38   (a) `double first = Math.log(x + x*x + a*a);`
       (b) `double second = (Math.exp(3*t) + t*t*Math.sin(4*t))`
                        `* (Math.pow(Math.cos(3*t), 2));`
       (c) `double third = 4*(Math.atan(1));`
       (d) `double fourth = 1/(Math.pow(Math.cos(x), 2)) + 1/(Math.tan(y));`
       (e) `double fifth = Math.atan(Math.abs(a/x));`

2.39
```
    System.out.print("Please enter a length in metres: ");
    double metres = Keyboard.readDouble();
    double num_inches = metres*39.37;
    int yards = (int)Math.floor(num_inches/36);
      //12 inches in a foot and 3 feet in a yard, so 36 inches in a yard
    double remaining_inches = num_inches%36;  //gives remainder of division
    int feet = (int)Math.floor(remaining_inches/12);  //12 inches in a foot
    double inches = remaining_inches%12;      //gives remainder of division

    System.out.print(metres + " metres converts to " + yards + " yds ");
    System.out.println(feet + " ft " + Math.round(100*inches)/100f + " in.");
```

```
2.40   double minutes = Keyboard.readDouble();

       int hours = (int)Math.floor(minutes/60);
       double remaining_minutes = minutes%60;

       System.out.print(minutes + " minutes = " + hours + " hrs ");
       System.out.println("and " + remaining_minutes + " mins");

       double total_seconds = Keyboard.readDouble();

       int hours = (int)Math.floor(total_seconds/3600);
       double remaining_seconds = total_seconds%3600;

       int minutes = (int)Math.floor(remaining_seconds/60);
       double seconds = remaining_seconds%60;

       System.out.print(total_seconds + " seconds = " + hours + " hrs ");
       System.out.print(minutes + " mins ");
       System.out.println("and " + seconds + " seconds.");
```

Chapter 3

```
3.1    public class UseSquare
       {
         public static void main (String[] args)
         {
           Square s1 = new Square();
           s1.size = 10;
           s1.pattern = 'x';
           s1.draw();
         } // main method
       }

3.3    class Square
       {
         int size = 2;
         char pattern = '*';
         boolean fill = true;

         void draw()
         {
           // draw the first line of chars:
           for(int i = 1; i <= size; i++)
               System.out.print(pattern);
           System.out.println();
           // draw the inner rows
           for(int row = 2; row <= size-1; row++)
           {
             System.out.print(pattern);  // first char
             for(int col = 2; col <= size-1; col++)
               if (fill)
                 System.out.print(pattern);
               else
                 System.out.print(' ');  // draw space
             System.out.println(pattern);  // draw last char
           }

           // draw the last line of chars:
           for(int i = 1; i <= size; i++)
```

```
              System.out.print(pattern);

          System.out.println();
      }   // draw method
   }   // Square class
```

3.5   The program does not compile. There are two errors indicating that variables t1 and t2 have not been initialized. The program should be modified as follows:

```
      ...
      public static void main (String[] args)
      {
        Turtle t1 = new Turtle();
        Turtle t2 = new Turtle();
        ...
```

3.7
```
      import essential.*;

      public class TestStrings
      {
        public static void main(String[] args)
        {
          System.out.println("Enter first string:");
          String s1 = Keyboard.readLine();
          System.out.println("Enter second string:");
          String s2 = Keyboard.readLine();
          if (s1.equals(s2))
            System.out.println("The strings are the same");
          else
            System.out.println("The strings are different");
        }
      }
```

3.9   (a) Name: readLine
           Arguments: none
           Return value: a String (whatever the user types in)
           Side effect: keystrokes are read in from the keyboard.
      (b) Name: home
           Arguments: none
           Return value: none
           Side effect: The state of t changes and consequently the output on the screen changes.
      (c) Name: setAxes
           Arguments: four ints
           Return value: none
           Side effect: The minimum and maximum values of the graph axes change.
      (d) Name: Turtle
           Arguments: a colour
           Return value: a Turtle object handle
           Side effect: space is allocated for a Turtle object in memory.

3.11
```
      public class UseRabbitColony
      {
        public static void main(String[] args)
        {
          RabbitColony rc = new RabbitColony();
          for(int year = 1; year <= 15; year++)
          {
            rc.grow();   // grow rabbit colony for 1 month
```

```
            int num = rc.getNumRabbits();
            System.out.println("Number of rabbits in year " + year + ": " + num);
        }
    }
}
```

3.12 Change the grow() method as follows:

```
void grow()
{
    adults += young;   // all the young become adults
    young = babies;    // all the current babies become young
    babies = adults;   // all adult pairs produce a baby pair
    int die = babies/4;  // 1 out of 4 babies die
    babies -= die;
}
```

3.15 Default constructor for Tree class:

```
/* Default constructor sets height to 0.1 and growth
 * rate to 10cm/year
 */
public Tree()
{
    height = 0.1f;
    rate = 10;
}
```

main method that uses the constructor defined above:

```
public class UseTree
{
    public static void main(String args[])
    {
        Tree defaultTree = new Tree();
        System.out.println("Default Tree height: "
                    + defaultTree.getHeight() + "m");
    }
}
```

3.17 It does not compile because variable local2 is referenced outside its scope in method1. The output would be:

```
150
200
```

3.21
```
import essential.*;
public class Weight
{
    public static void main(String[] args)
    {
        System.out.print("Enter weight in kg: ");
        String s = Keyboard.readLine();
        if (s.endsWith("kg"))
            s = s.substring(0, s.length() - 2);
        System.out.println(s);
    }
}
```

Chapter 4

4.2
```
int sum = 0;

for (int i = 2; i <= 200; i+=2)
{
    sum += i;
}
```

4.4
```
DecimalFormat df = new DecimalFormat("00.00");
System.out.println("Degree\tSine\tCosine\tTangent");
System.out.println();
double degree2Radian = Math.PI/180;

for (int degree = 0; degree <= 360; degree+=30)
{
    System.out.print(degree + "\t");
    System.out.print(df.format(Math.sin(degree2Radian*degree)) + "\t");
    System.out.print(df.format(Math.cos(degree2Radian*degree)) + "\t");
    System.out.print(df.format(Math.tan(degree2Radian*degree)));
    System.out.println();
}
```

4.5
```
System.out.println("Integer\tSquare root");
System.out.println();

for (int i = 10; i <=20; i++)
{
    System.out.println(i + "\t" +
                       Math.round(Math.sqrt(i)*1000)/1000f);
}
```

4.6
```
DecimalFormat df = new DecimalFormat("00.00");

for (int C = 20; C <= 30; C++)
{
    double F = 9*C/5f + 32;
        // put f in otherwise decimals lost in division
    System.out.println("  " + df.format(C) + "\t  " + df.format(F));
}
```

4.7
```
for (int t = 1790; t <= 2000; t+=10)
{
    double x = -0.03134*(t - 1913.25);
    double P = 197273000/(1 + Math.exp(x));

    System.out.println(t + "\t\t" + Math.round(100*P)/100f);
}
```

4.10
```
double balance = 1000;
DecimalFormat df = new DecimalFormat("0000.00");
System.out.println("\nYear\tBalance\n");

for (int y = 1; y <= 10; y++)      //outer for loop for years
{
    for (int m = 1; m <=12; m++)
    {
        balance = balance + balance*0.01;
    }
```

```
            System.out.println(y + "\t$" + df.format(balance));
    }

4.11  (a)  double p = 0;
           int terms = 100;
           double sign = 1;

           for (int n = 1; n <= terms; n++)
           {
               p = p + sign / (2*n-1);
               sign = -sign;
           }

           double approx_PI = p*4;

4.14  double E = 0;
      DecimalFormat df = new DecimalFormat("0.0000000");

      System.out.println("\n x\t\t  E");

      for (int i = 1; i <= 1000; i+=100)
      {
          double x = 1f/(i*100);   //as i grows, x gets closer to 0
          E = Math.pow((1 + x), 1/x);
          System.out.println(df.format(x) + "\t" + df.format(E));
      }

4.16  DecimalFormat df = new DecimalFormat("000.00");

      int A = 1000;             //amount invested
      double r = 0.04;          //nominal annual interest rate
      int k = 10;               //number of years

      int n = 1;                //number of compounding periods per year

      System.out.println("  n" + "\t  V \n");

      for (int i = 1; i < 15; i++)
      {
          double V = A*(Math.pow((1 + r/n), n*k));

          System.out.println(n + "\t" + df.format(V));

          n *= 2;               //double n, after calculation and printing
      }

      double formula = A*Math.exp(r*k);
      System.out.println("\nValue of formula: " + df.format(formula));

4.17  Graph one = new Graph();

      double a = 0.1;

      for (int i = 1; i <= 360; i++)
      {
          double theta = i*0.1;
          double r = a*theta;
```

```
        double x = r*Math.cos(theta);
        double y = r*Math.sin(theta);
        one.addPoint(x,y);
    }
```

4.23
```
    /* This class has been adapted from the Dice class given in the chapter;
     * the throwUntil method now returns the number of throws taken, and the
     * print statements have been removed.
     */

    public class Dice
    {
        public int thro()
        {
            int numberOnDice = (int) Math.floor(6*Math.random())+1;
            return numberOnDice;
        }

        //this method now RETURNS the number of throws taken
        public int throwUntil( int n )
        {
            int numberOfThrows = 1;
            int numberOnDice = thro();

            while (numberOnDice != n)
            {
                numberOnDice = thro();
                numberOfThrows++;
            }

            return numberOfThrows;
        }

    }

    import essential.*;

    public class AveThrowsTillSix
    {
        public static void main(String[] args)
        {
            System.out.print
                ("Please enter the number of times to throw until a 6: ");
            int n = Keyboard.readInt();
            System.out.println();

            Dice d = new Dice();
            int tot_num_throws = 0;

            for (int i = 1; i <= n; i++)
            {
                int num_throws = d.throwUntil(6);
                System.out.println("Number of throws: " + num_throws);
                tot_num_throws += num_throws;
            }

            double average_throws = (double)tot_num_throws/n;
            System.out.println("Total number of throws: " + tot_num_throws);
```

```
                    System.out.println("Average number of throws: " + average_throws);
            }
    }


4.27    double x = 1;
        int k = 1;          //term counter
        double error = 1e-4;
        double term = 1;        //first term in series
        int maxTerms = 20;
        double approx_cos = term;       //sum of series

        while (Math.abs(term) > error && k <= maxTerms)
        {
            term = -term *x*x/((2*k-1)*(2*k));
                //form next term from previous one!
            k++;
            approx_cos += term;
        } //end while

        System.out.println( "My cos: " + approx_cos +
                            "   Java cos: " + Math.cos(x) );

4.32    import essential.*;
        public class GuessingGame
        {
            //generate random integer between 1 and 10:
            private int javaNum = (int) Math.floor(10*Math.random())+1;

            public void play()
            {
                int userGuess = 0;

                do
                {
                    System.out.print( "Your guess please: " );
                    userGuess = Keyboard.readInt();

                    if (userGuess > javaNum)
                    {
                        System.out.println( "Too high" );
                    }
                    else if (userGuess < javaNum)
                    {
                        System.out.println( "Too low" );
                    }
                } while (userGuess != javaNum);

                System.out.println( "At last!" );
            }

            public static void main(String[ ] args)
            {
                GuessingGame g = new GuessingGame();
                g.play();
            }
        }
```

Chapter 5

5.2

```java
import essential.*;

public class NumberTriangle
{
  public static void main(String[] args)
  {
    System.out.print("Enter size of number triangle:");
    int size = Keyboard.readInt(); for(int row=size;
    row>0; row--) {
      for(int num = row; num>0; num--)
        System.out.print(num);
      System.out.println();
    }
  }
}
```

5.3

```java
public class NewtonQuotient
{
    private double h;

    public double f (double x)
    {
        return x*x;
    }
    public double df (double x)
    {
        double nQ = (f(x+h)-f(x))/h;
        return nQ;
    }

    public void getNewtonQuotient()
    {
        h = 1;

        for (int i = 1; i <= 20; i++)
        {
            System.out.println( h + "   " + df(2) );
            h = h/10;
        }

    }

    public static void main( String[] args)
    {
        NewtonQuotient n = new NewtonQuotient();
        n.getNewtonQuotient();
    }

}
```

Chapter 6

6.1   (a)

```java
int[] num = new int[100];
for (int i = 0; i < 100; i++)
{
    num[i] = i + 1;          //so num[0] = 1 ... num[99] = 100
}
```

```
(b)    int[] num = new int[50];

       for (int i = 0; i < 50; i++)
       {
           num[i] = (i + 1) * 2;    //so num[0] = (0+1)*2 = 2 ...
                                    //  num[49] = (49+1)*2 = 100
       }


(c)    int[] num = new int[100];

       for (int i = 0; i < 100; i++)
       {
           num[i] = 100 - i;              //so num[0] = 100-0 = 100 ...
                                          //  num[99] = 100-99 = 1
       }
```

```
6.3    int[] f = new int[30];

       f[0] = f[1] = 1;     //the first two terms in the sequence

       //loop to put the numbers into an array
       for (int i = 2; i < 30; i++) //start at 2 (i.e. the third term) because
       {                            //the first 2 terms have already been assigned
           f[i] = f[i-1] + f[i-2];
       }

       //loop to print out the first 29 numbers in the array, each followed
       //by a comma
       for (int i = 0; i < 29; i++)
       {
           System.out.print(f[i] + ", ");
       }
       //print out the thirtieth number (i.e. in position 29 of the array)
       System.out.println(f[29]);
```

```
6.7    //Note: this class adds only the two new methods - see chapter 3 for
       //the other methods to be found in this class

       public class EssentialMath
       {
           public static double mean(double[] data)
           {
               double sum = 0;
               int num_items = data.length;

               for (int i = 0; i < num_items; i++)
               {
                   sum = sum + data[i];
               }

               double mean = sum/num_items;

               return mean;
           }

           public static double std(double[] data)
           {
               double mean = mean(data);
               double sum = 0;
```

```
            int num_items = data.length;

            for (int i = 0; i < num_items; i++)
            {
                sum = sum + Math.pow(data[i] - mean, 2);
            }

            double standard_variation = (1f/(num_items - 1))*sum;
            double standard_deviation = Math.sqrt(standard_variation);

            return standard_deviation;
        }
    }

    public class TestEssentialMath
    {
        public static void main(String[] args)
        {
            double[] x = {5.1, 6.2, 5.7, 3.5, 9.9, 1.2, 7.6, 5.3, 8.7, 4.4};

            System.out.println("Mean: " + EssentialMath.mean(x));
            System.out.println("Std Dev: " + EssentialMath.std(x));
        }
    }
```

6.8
```
    public class EssentialMath
    {
        ...
        public static double furthestFromMean(double[] data)
        {
          double mean = mean(data);
        int num_items = data.length;
          double greatest_gap = -1;
          int index_of_greatest_gap = -1;

          for (int i = 0; i < num_items; i++)
          {
            double gap = Math.abs(mean - data[i]);
            if (gap > greatest_gap)
            {
              greatest_gap = gap;
              index_of_greatest_gap = i;
            }
          }

          return data[index_of_greatest_gap];
        }
        ...
    }
```

6.9
```
    public class Ant
    {
        ...

        //The first and second parameters indicate range to
        print; the third //parameter indicates the number of
        steps that were generated public void
        printBarChart(int start, int end, int num_steps) {
```

```
            int scale = 1;              //default increment; used
            for scaling if (num_steps > 500)    //set scale
            value to 2 if number of steps scale = 2;
               //is greater than 500; so bar chart height
                                   //is half the length of the
                                       original
        System.out.println("\nBar chart with scale 1/" +
        scale);

        for (int i = start; i <= end; i++)
        {
          System.out.print(i + ": ");
          int scaled_frequency =
          (int)Math.floor(f[i]/(float)scale);

          for (int j = 0; j < scaled_frequency; j++)
            System.out.print("*");
          System.out.println();
        }
      }
      ...
    }
```

Chapter 7

7.1 (a) House subpart: room
          House superpart: neighbourhood
          House subclass: semi-detached house
          House superclass: building

     (b) CD subpart: track
          CD superpart: CD collection
          CD subclass: CD-ROM
          CD superclass: Storage medium

7.4   import essential.*;

```
      public class CleverTurtle extends Turtle
      {
        public void square(int size)
        {
          penUp();
          forward(size/2);
          right(90);
          backward(size/2);
          penDown();
          for(int i=1; i<=4; i++)
          {
            forward(size);
            right(90);
          }
          penUp();
          forward(size/2);
          left(90);
          backward(size/2);
          penDown();
        }
      }
```

7.5
```
public class UseCleverTurtle
{
  public static void main(String[] args)
  {
    CleverTurtle t = new CleverTurtle();
    int size = 5;
    for(int i=1; i<15; i++)
    {
      t.square(size);
      size+=10;
    }
  }
}
```

7.7   The two classes below must be stored in separate files:

```
import essential.*;
public class MyKeyboard extends Keyboard
{
  public static Complex readComplex()
  {
    Complex c = Complex.read();
    return c;
  }
}
```

```
import essential.*;
public class TryMyKeyboard
{
  public static void main(String[] args)
  {
    System.out.println("Enter a complex number: ");
    Complex c = MyKeyboard.readComplex();
    System.out.println(c);
    System.out.println("Enter a real number: ");
    double d = MyKeyboard.readDouble();
    System.out.println(d);
  }
}
```

7.11
```
  ...
  public CleverTurtle()
  {
  }

  public CleverTurtle(Color c)
  {
    super(c);
  }
  ...
```

7.13   FertilisedTree class including main method:

```
public class FertilisedTree extends Tree
{
  public void grow()
  {
    if ((height > 1) && (height<3))
      rate *= 0.95;
```

```
            else if (height > 3)
              rate *= 0.9;
            float add = rate/100; // convert rate to metres per year
            height += add;        // then increment height
          }

          public FertilisedTree(float h, float GR)
          {
            super(h, GR);
          }

          public static void main(String args[])
          {
            Tree t1 = new Tree(0.1f, 20f);
            FertilisedTree t2 = new FertilisedTree(0.1f, 20f);
            for (int i =1; i <= 30; i++)
            {
              t1.grow();
              t2.grow();
            }
            System.out.println("Normal Tree: " + t1.getHeight());
            System.out.println("Fertilised Tree: " + t2.getHeight());
          }
        }
```

7.14 (a) Class `MyObject` inherits from the class `Object` by default. The method `getClass` is defined in the class
           `Object`, so is inherited by all classes.
      (b) The output is:

```
            class MyObject
            class java.lang.Object
```

Chapter 8

8.1
```
        import javax.swing.*;
        public class FirstGUI
        {
          public static void main(String[] args)
          {
            JFrame f = new JFrame();
            f.setDefaultCloseOperation(JFrame.EXIT_ON_CLOSE);
            f.setTitle("My first GUI application");
            f.setVisible(true);
          }
        }
```

8.3
```
        import javax.swing.*;
        public class SimpleFrame extends JFrame
        {
          private JButton button = new JButton("Press me!");
          private JLabel label = new JLabel("Go on, press the button");
          private JTextField text = new JTextField("this is a text field");
          private JPanel background = new JPanel();

          public SimpleFrame()
          {
            background.add(button);  // add button to background
            background.add(label);   // add label to background
            background.add(text);    // add text field to background
```

```
                getContentPane().add(background); // add background to frame
                setDefaultCloseOperation(JFrame.EXIT_ON_CLOSE);
                pack();
            }
        }
```

8.4
```
        import javax.swing.*;
        public class SimpleFrame extends JFrame
        {
            ...
            private String[] choices = {"red","green","blue"};
            private JComboBox cb = new JComboBox(choices);

            public SimpleFrame()
            {
                ...
                background.add(cb);        // add combo box to background
                ...
            }
        }
```

8.6   Here is code for FirstWindow:

```
        import javax.swing.*;
        import java.awt.event.*;

        public class FirstWindow extends JFrame
        {
            private JButton button = new JButton("Open");

            public FirstWindow()
            {
                button.addActionListener( new ActionListener()
                {
                    public void actionPerformed(ActionEvent e)
                    {
                        SecondWindow s = new SecondWindow();
                        s.setVisible(true);
                    }
                });
                getContentPane().add(button); // add button to frame
                setDefaultCloseOperation(JFrame.EXIT_ON_CLOSE);
                pack();
            }
        }
```

Here is code for SecondWindow, which contains a label simply to display something:

```
        import javax.swing.*;
        public class SecondWindow extends JFrame
        {
            private JLabel test = new JLabel("This is the 2nd window");

            public SecondWindow()
            {
                getContentPane().add(test); // add label to frame
                setDefaultCloseOperation(JFrame.EXIT_ON_CLOSE);
```

```
            pack();
        }
    }
```

Finally, here is a main method class for opening FirstWindow:

```
    public class OpenFirst
    {
        public static void main(String[] args)
        {
            FirstWindow f = new FirstWindow();
            f.setVisible(true);
        }
    }
```

8.8   (a) The default layout manager for the content pane of a frame is the border layout. When the label is added to the frame, the default position is assumed (i.e. the CENTER position). After that, when the button is added, it is also placed in the CENTER position, thereby 'overwriting' the label.

      (b) One of the ways of ensuring that both components display is to specify positions when they are added to the content pane, e.g.:

```
            back.add(label,BorderLayout.NORTH);
            back.add(button,BorderLayout.SOUTH);
```

8.10   ...

```
    public class ColourChooser extends JFrame
    {
        ...
        JButton reset = new JButton("Reset");
        ...
        public ColourChooser()
        {
            ...
            reset.addActionListener(new ActionListener()
            {
                public void actionPerformed(ActionEvent e)
                {
                    redSlider.setValue(0);
                    greenSlider.setValue(0);
                    blueSlider.setValue(0);
                }
            });
            ...
            bottomPanel.add(reset);
            bottomPanel.add(exit);
            ...
        }
        ...
    }
```

Chapter 9

9.1   The error generated: array index out of bounds.
Reason: No arguments are given, so the array args is empty. Accessing args[0] inside the program therefore generates an error.

9.2   The output is:

Reason: the arguments are stored as strings, so the + operator performs string concatenation, rather than addition.
Solution:

```
public class CommandLine
{
  public static void main(String args[])
  {
    int num1 = Integer.parseInt(args[0]);
    int num2 = Integer.parseInt(args[1]);
    int num3 = Integer.parseInt(args[2]);
    System.out.println("The sum of the arguments is: " + (num1 + num2 +
    num3));
  }
}
```

9.6
```
import java.io.*;
public class InputChar
{
  public static void main(String args[]) throws IOException
  {
    BufferedReader din = new BufferedReader(
                         new InputStreamReader(System.in));
    System.out.print("Enter a character: ");
    int c = din.read();
    System.out.println("unicode value of " + (char)c + " = " + c);
  }
}
```

9.8
```
import java.io.*;
public class DirJava
{
  public static void main(String[] args)
  {
    File dir;
    if(args.length != 0)
      dir = new File(args[0]);
    else
      dir = new File(".");
    if (dir.exists())
    {
      if (dir.isDirectory())
      {
        String[] list = dir.list();
        for(int i=0; i<list.length; i++)
        {
          if (list[i].endsWith(".java"))
            System.out.println(list[i]);
        }
      }
      else System.out.println("Folder not valid");
    }
    else System.out.println("Folder does not exist");
  }
}
```

9.10
```
import java.io.*;
public class TimesTables
{
  public static void main(String args[]) throws IOException
```

```
        {
          PrintWriter pout = new PrintWriter(new FileWriter("tables.txt"));
          for(int i = 2; i <= 12; i++)
          {
            for(int j = 1; j <= 12; j++)
              pout.println(i + " X " + j + " = " + i*j);
              pout.println("--------------------");
          }
          pout.close();
        }
      }
```

9.11
```
      import java.io.*;
      import java.util.*;

      public class PrintDown
      {
        public static void main(String[] args) throws IOException
        {
          String fileInStr = args[0];
          String fileOutStr = args[1];
          BufferedReader fileIn = new BufferedReader(
                                  new FileReader(fileInStr));
          PrintWriter fileOut = new PrintWriter(
                                  new FileWriter(fileOutStr));

          String line = fileIn.readLine();   // read in numbers on same line
          StringTokenizer st = new StringTokenizer(line);
          while(st.hasMoreTokens())
            fileOut.println(st.nextToken());
          fileIn.close();
          fileOut.close();
        }
      }
```

Chapter 10

10.1 (a) FileNotFoundException
      (b) IndexOutOfBoundsException
      (c) NullPointerException
      (d) MalformedURLException
      (e) IOException

10.2 The exception is thrown if a matrix is constructed with an invalid number of rows or columns (i.e. a number less than 1).

10.3 A NullPointerException is generated. NullPointerException is a subclass of RuntimeException, so it does not have to be caught or specified, unlike checked exceptions.

10.4 The program does not compile.
      Error message: unreported exception java.net.MalformedURLException ...
      Solution: change the main method header as follows:

```
      public static void main(String[] args) throws MalformedURLException
```

10.7 import java.io.*;

      public class ReadBinary

```
  {
    public static void main(String[] args) throws IOException
    {
      boolean finished = false;
      int numWords = 0;
      DataInputStream in;
      try
      {
        in = new DataInputStream(
                    new FileInputStream("trc_v1.data"));
        while(!finished)
        {
          try {
            String s = in.readUTF();
            numWords++;
          } catch(EOFException e) {
            finished = true;
            System.out.println("Total number of words: " + numWords);
          }
        } // while
        in.close();
      }catch(FileNotFoundException e) {
        System.out.println("Could not find file trc_v1.data");
        System.exit(0);
      } // end of try

    } // end of main
  }
```

Chapter 11

11.3
```
double numberOfHeads = 0;
int numberOfSpins = 1000;
double randomNumber;

for (int i = 1; i <= numberOfSpins; i++)
{
    randomNumber = Math.random();
    if (randomNumber < 0.5)
        numberOfHeads++;
}

double probabilityOfHeads =
    (double) numberOfHeads/numberOfSpins*100;
    //express as a percentage

System.out.println( "Probability of getting heads: "
    + probabilityOfHeads + "%" );
```

11.6
```
/* This codes "shuffles" the numbers 1 to 99 by
 * starting with a sorted array of the numbers 1 to 99
 * and swopping them at random
 */

int [ ] bingo = new int[99];
int n, temp;

for (int i = 0; i <= 98; i++)
    bingo[i] = i+1;
```

```
    for (int i = 0; i <= 98; i++)
    {
        n = (int) (99*Math.random());
        temp = bingo[n];      // swop elements n and i
        bingo[n] = bingo[i];
        bingo[i] = temp;
    }

    for (int i = 0; i <= 98; i++)
    {
        if (i%10 == 0)
            System.out.println();
        System.out.print( bingo[i] + "   " );
    }
```

11.7
```
    int numberOfPoints = 10000;
    int numberInsideCircle = 0;
    double x, y;

    for (int i = 1; i <= numberOfPoints; i++)
    {
        x = Math.random();
        y = Math.random();
        if (x*x + y*y < 1)
            numberInsideCircle++;
    }

    System.out.println( "MonteCarloPi: "
        + 4.0*numberInsideCircle/numberOfPoints );
        //numberInsideCircle only counts points inside the
        //first quadrant so we multiply by 4
```

11.8   Theoretically (from the binomial distribution), the probability of a DFII crashing is 1/4, while that of a DFIV crashing is 5/16; more can go wrong with it since it has more engines!

11.10 On average, A wins 12 of the possible 32 plays of the game, while B wins 20, as can be seen from drawing the game tree. Your simulation should come up with these proportions. (However, it can be shown from the tree that B can always force a win, if she plays intelligently.)

Chapter 13

13.4   (a) Real roots at 1.856 and −1.697, complex roots at −0.0791 ± 1.780i.
       (b) 0.589, 3.096, 6.285, ... (roots get closer to multiples of π).
       (c) 1, 2, 5.
       (d) 1.303
       (e) −3.997, 4.988, 2.241, 1.768.

13.5   Successive bisections are: 1.5, 1.25, 1.375, 1.4375 and 1.40625. The exact answer is 1.414214..., so the last bisection is within the required error.

13.7   22 (exact answer is 21.3333...)

13.8   With 10 intervals ($n = 5$), the luminous efficiency is 14.512725%. With 20 intervals it is 14.512667%. These results justify the use of 10 intervals in any further computations involving this problem. This is a standard way of testing the accuracy of a numerical method: halve the step-length and see how much the solution changes.

13.10 The exact answer, after 30 years, is 2 117 ($1000\,e^{at}$).

13.12 The differential equations to be solved are

$$dS/dt = -r_1 S,$$
$$dY/dt = r_1 S - r_2 Y.$$

The exact solution after 8 hours is $S = 6.450 \times 10^{25}$ and $Y = 2.312 \times 10^{26}$.

Index

break, 45
buffer, 201
BufferedReader class, 201, 205
bug, 114
byte, 23
bytecode, 4, 7

call-by-reference, 76
call-by-value, 76
camel caps, 25
Card class, 140
case sensitivity, 6, 25
catch or specify requirement, 213
catch statement, 216
ChangeListener interface, 173
chaos, 112, 287, 288
    butterfly, 289
    trajectory, 290
char, 45
character, 45
checked exception, 214
class, 12, 22, 56
    abstract, 154
    anonymous, 167
    nested, 166
.class file, 7
class hierarchy, 143
class provider, 56
class user, 56
CleverTurtle class, 146, 157, 158
code reuse, 146
coercion of type, 24
Color class, 170
colour chooser application, 170
ColourChooser class, 171, 196
command line parameters, 198
comment, 11
common delimited, 204
Comparable interface, 156
compareTo method, 156
compilation errors, 114
compiler, 3
compiling
    explained, 7
    Java, 6
Complex class, 157, 267
complex numbers, 267
complex roots of an equation, 267
component, 162
    border around, 169
    button, 162
    combo box, 195
    frame, 161
    hierarchy, 170
    label, 164
    layout, 167
    list, 195
    panel, 164

    slider, 170, 172
    text field, 195
composition, 143
concrete example, 130
concrete method, 155
constant, 81
constructor, 13, 64, 72
    default, 65, 73, 151
    inheritance, 151
    parameterised, 65
container, 162
content pane, 163
Convert class, 82
Crank-Nicolson method, 290
current directory, 207

data member, 58
data type, 23
Debugger, 119
debugging, 114
decimal places, restricting, 23
DecimalFormat, 96
decrement operator, 28
default constructor, 65, 73, 151
delete method, 202
delimiter, 204
derived class, 144
determinant, 259
determinate repetition, 33, 89
dice, rolling, 41
differential equation, 274
    Driver, 284
    systems, 280
directed network, 245
disk storage, 59
division operator, 27
do-while, 104
double, 11
Double.parseDouble, 201
drawLine, 189
Driver, 284

editor, 4
eigenvalue, 251
eigenvector, 252
ellipse, equation of, 112
encapsulation, 55
end user, 56
endsWith method, 207
EOFException, 218
equals method, 63
error
    compilation, 114
    logical, 119
    rounding, 119
    runtime, 117
    syntax, 114
escape sequence, 45
Essential Grapher, 15, 91

Printed and bound by CPI Group (UK) Ltd, Croydon, CR0 4YY

03/10/2024

01040331-0011